JOURNEY
THROUGH THE
BIBLE LANDS

by Luis Alonso Schökel, S.J.

Translated by John Drury

The Bruce Publishing Company
Milwaukee

NIHIL OBSTAT:

JOHN A. SCHULIEN, S.T.D.
Censor librorum

IMPRIMATUR:

✠ WILLIAM E. COUSINS
Archbishop of Milwaukee
April 28, 1964

Library of Congress Catalog Card Number: 64-22617

© 1964 THE BRUCE PUBLISHING COMPANY
MADE IN THE UNITED STATES OF AMERICA

PROLOGUE TO THE ENGLISH TRANSLATION

IT WILL soon be ten years since I took the trip which is the subject of this journal. In our day ten years are quite a long time, enough to dull the edge of once vivid memories and emotions. But for me this journey is still a living reality, shrouded perhaps in a thin veil of nostalgia. Time has not dulled its vividness. It was a journey filled with enthusiam and excitement.

How much we derive from a journey usually depends upon our previous knowledge of the area visited. I set out on this trip just after finishing three years of specialized study. My mind was packed with biblical, archeological, and geographical data. Now I was going to unpack it all in its original setting, filling the present scene with the events of the past.

However, I chose to approach this journey with a pre-critical attitude: neither for nor against modern scholarship, but in an intellectual stage which does not yet raise critical questions. My views on biblical criticism have been made sufficiently clear in my book, *Understanding Biblical Research*. And archaeological data do crop up in this book when they have some bearing on the historicity of certain places and events But the general treatment is orientated in a different direction.

Suppose I were to take a trip through La Mancha and relive the exploits of Don Quixote. Such an excursion would not summon up an historical reality but a fictional, though very intense, adventure. By reliving in my fantasy and sensitivity the old *hidalgo*, I do not make him historical; I leave him in a state of purely literary consistency. But I bring him close to me, I understand him better; he enters my life and influences it.

Or I might follow the footsteps of St. Teresa over the paths of Avila. By so doing, I do not deny or diminish her historical reality;

[iii]

only, this reality reaches me in a literary condition, and so enters into my spirit; I understand her, she enriches me.

This is what I have done in my journey through Palestine. As I traveled down from Jerusalem to Jericho, the surrounding landscape evoked the parable of the good samaritan. I did not picture it as an historical event, but I did let the story, as a literary reality, work its full effect on me. And as I stood by Lake Gennesareth I tried to summon up the figure of St. Peter as he is presented to us in the pages of the Gospel.

The events of salvation-history come down to us in the form of a literary work. And we have every right to attempt to relive these events in their original setting. In doing this we are not touching on the historical or fictional character of the various biblical narratives: we leave to them their own consistency. But, by reliving them, we open ourselves to these stories, that they may influence our own lives.

The sights and scenes which I experienced in the land of the Old Testament are presented in well-defined units. I have correlated biblical events and scholarly data with the experiences of the journey itself. Past and present are woven together so that the reader can share my experiences and fall under the spell of the biblical narrative at the same time. If, after accompanying me on this journey, the reader feels closer to the Old Testament, then both of us will have profited from the trip.

Rome, December, 1963

PROLOGUE TO THE ORIGINAL
SPANISH EDITION

THIS book is a mixture of three ingredients. The first, and most important, is the Old Testament. After a lengthy preparation I set out in search of ancient history. The themes and the pathways of the gospel story are well known to everyone, but there are relatively few popular books which deal with the Old Testament. This lack and my own special interests determined the theme of this book. By restricting the subject matter I hope to provide the reader with a greater quantity of new and informative material.

The second ingredient is the technical material which has been discussed in scholarly books and periodicals. The Old Testament poses many specialized problems which have been investigated by the various branches of biblical research — philology, history, archaeology, geography, ethnography, etc. I have tried to integrate a fair amount of this material into my presentation without, however, getting bogged down in technical discussions which might bore the reader. The material is accurate and up to date, but the pages are not cluttered with footnotes. The book is a solidly based popularization of the many themes running through the Bible.

The third ingredient is the journey itself. Some trips are made purely for pleasure; and the accompanying narrative relies mainly on the curious anecdote and the unusual experience. Some trips are made by people who have not prepared themselves by specialized study; their accounts are made up of diverting ramblings. But some trips are meaningful only in terms of their purpose and their destination. On such trips information is the most important item, anecdotes are of secondary importance. That is why I have included relatively few anecdotes (although many different ones could be told) and arranged the book according to biblical chronology rather than the chronology of the journey itself.

[v]

Prologue

I have tried to integrate these three ingredients into sections which form distinct units. The divisions are not arbitrary and can be easily justified. The sober data of modern research enable us to construct a fairly accurate historical perspective; thanks to these data we can make a precise and accurate leap backward to the events of the past. And the journey itself brings these cold data to life. So our leap into the past is not only accurate but also filled with emotion.

All during the journey I wanted to relive to the fullest the events of Old Testament history. I would like the reader to do the same, either through my evocation of the past or through his own ability to immerse himself in it.

The reader will pass from today's facts to yesterday's events, from a biblical story to its historical setting. And in passing from one to the other he will see again and again how history repeats itself in different ways and how the land's geography can easily explain events which seem so strange.

Today groups of Bedouins pass through the region traversed by Abraham. Just as a conflict arose long ago between Isaac, the forefather of the Jews, and Ishmael, the forefather of the Arabs, so today there is a conflict of international proportions between Arabs and Jews. The Jews have returned to conquer the Promised Land, as they did thirty-two centuries ago. Gideon's stratagem has succeeded again — in its original setting. History has taken delight in repeating the battles of Megiddo because of their strategic value. In short, today's events make it easy to relive the past, especially when one takes a journey steeped in ancient history.

If we can grasp this underlying unity between past and present, it will be easy to see biblical events as present-day realities, and to immerse ourselves in the happenings of long ago. And we can do this most easily if the biblical events are presented in sharply defined sections which do not try to say too much. So I have taken liberties in my account of the journey; and I have not hesitated to include observations which might clarify historical events or give us an insight into the mentality of the characters.

A WORD ON SPELLINGS AND
CITATIONS FROM SCRIPTURE

THE spelling of proper names, both personal and local, poses a difficulty in any book dealing with the Bible. Many times the spellings given in the Douay, Knox, and Confraternity versions differ from the spellings found in the King James. Thus, for example, the Douay, Knox, and Confraternity have Achab and Josaphat whereas the King James has Ahab and Jehosaphat; the Douay and Knox have Isaias and the Confraternity has Isaia, while the King James has Isaiah. In conformity with the practice of a growing number of Catholic writers, we have adopted the spellings of the King James version, inasmuch as these are those commonly used by English-speaking people. A glossary at the end of the volume lists the variant spellings found in the Douay, Knox, and Confraternity Bibles, and the reader should find this glossary of some help in keeping the names straight.

Another problem has to do with the names of the biblical books. In the Douay, Knox, and Confraternity Bibles one finds four books of Kings, two books of Paralipomenon, and two books of Esdras, whereas the King James lists two books of Samuel, two books of Kings, two books of Chronicles, one book of Ezra and one book of Nehemiah. The two books of Samuel correspond to the first two books of Kings in the Douay, Knox, and Confraternity, while the two books of Kings correspond to the third and fourth books of Kings in these volumes. The two books of Paralipomenon are called Chronicles in the King James, while 1 Esdras is called Ezra and 2 Esdras, Nehemiah. In this volume we have followed the numbering and names of the King James. Thus a reference to 1 and 2 Samuel would be found in 1 and 2 Kings in Catholic Bibles, while references to 1 and 2 Kings would be found in 3 and 4 Kings in Catholic Bibles.

The Psalms also present a problem. The numbering of the Psalms,

[vii]

A Word on Spellings and Citations from Scripture

from 9 to 147, differs by one in the Douay and Knox Bibles from the numbering found in the King James and other Protestant Bibles. This difference goes back to the Greek and Latin Bibles for the first group and to the Hebrew Bible for the other group. Here, with the Confraternity Old Testament, we follow the practice of giving two numbers for the Psalms, the first indicating its number in the Douay, the second its number in the King James: thus Psalm 104 (105).

Direct citations from Scripture are taken from the following versions: All books of the Old Testament, with the exception of 1 and 2 Samuel, 1 and 2 Kings, 1 and 2 Chronicles, Ezra, Nehemiah, and 1 and 2 Maccabees, are from the Confraternity version (Copyright by the Confraternity of Christian Doctrine) ; citations from the books excepted are taken from *The Complete Bible: An American Translation* (Copyright by the University of Chicago Press). All citations from the New Testament are taken from the Kleist-Lilly translation (Copyright by The Bruce Publishing Company) . In direct citations from the Confraternity, the spellings of the Confraternity have naturally been retained. Otherwise the spellings, as already noted, follow those in the King James.

CONTENTS

Contents

[x]

Contents

[xi]

Contents

JOURNEY THROUGH THE BIBLE LANDS

THE START . . .

ON OUR WAY

THE *Esperia* weighs anchor at noon. We spend the afternoon getting acquainted with the ship and its passengers as the coast of Italy slips by on our right. The approach of evening invites us to meditation — in solitude or in small groups.

We just finished final exams and already we are cutting our ties with Rome, with Italy, with Europe. A big step — and serious in its own way.

Traveling seems to be a custom peculiar to this era of the twentieth century. The historian of culture will have to devote his attention to this interesting postwar phenomenon. It might prove to be an important chapter in man's social history. Travel agencies and transportation companies are doing a thriving business. When the old tourist attractions wear thin, new ones are invented; and Baedeker's guidebook no longer stands alone. Little excuse is needed to take a trip. And something which is commonplace at home takes on new luster in a foreign land.

Among the passengers is a group of young Americans who are going to film some documentaries in the Sudan, which in July is hardly the most enticing spot in the world. But, then, neither is the climate we are going to encounter in the Sinai desert and in the arid wastes of the Middle East. But we are willing to endure the heat because Palestine is unique among the tourist attractions of the world. The natural landscape has less to offer than many parts of Europe; and it is hardly a treasure-house of art and architecture. But Palestine is the land of promise.

THE CLOCK MOVES AHEAD

The next day the coast of Italy falls away behind us and the coast of Greece looms up on our left. We pass by with a tinge of sadness. But Greece is too close to us in time; our journey is to take us farther back.

Near Crete the ship set its course directly for Alexandria. To-night we would set the clock ahead one hour. So much time gained, so much sleep lost. While we are asleep, the clock will jump forward. But we feel the opposite sensation. We are moving backward through days, years, centuries. . . .

Hezekiah, the faithful servant of Yahweh, had fallen ill (2 Kgs 20). The prophet Isaiah came to tell him that death was near: "Set your house in order, for you shall die." Hezekiah turned his face to the wall and prayed to Yahweh saying: "Remember now, O Lord, I pray thee, how I have walked before thee in truth and sincerity of heart, and have done that which was good in thy sight. . . ." And Hezekiah wept mournfully.

Yahweh listened to the tearful prayer of the king. And through Isaiah He told him that he would get well and live for another fifteen years. Hezekiah asked Isaiah: "What will be the sign that the Lord will heal me?" Isaiah replied: "This will be the sign . . . shall the shadow go forward ten steps, or back ten steps?" Hezekiah said: "It is easy for the shadow to go forward ten steps; rather let the shadow turn back ten steps." So Isaiah called on Yahweh and He made the shadow go back ten steps on the sundial.

So it is with us. Modern man can easily look into the future through the science fiction of Verne, Wells, Orwell, and many others. But we want to go back in time, to return to the days of long ago and make ourselves at home in them. Standing at the ship's stern, it seems that the sea is really the vast ocean of time and that we are sailing into the distant past.

SCRUTINIZING THE PAST

Homer called these waters the "barren sea"; a poetic view — and very superficial. For these waters are rich in algae, fish, minerals, and plankton. But to discover this fertility, one must plunge into the depths.

Palestine is "the land of promise." But if we restrict our view to the superficial features of this disputed land, we shall gain little. It will not compensate for the summer heat and the hardships involved. In Palestine we must plunge into the past. We must summon up the spirits of the dead and make them our companions. Only by immersing ourselves in the past can we savor the sweetness of Palestine. We must focus our attention on the days of long ago, until they fall into place and reveal the pattern of history lying beneath the surface of the land.

SPIRITS OF THE CAVE

From his encampment on the heights of Gilboa, Saul looked down on the camp of the Philistines and "he was afraid" (1 Sam 28). He decided to consult a sorceress because Yahweh had not answered his prayers. He and his companions disguised themselves and came to her by night. Saul said: "Divine now for me by the talisman, and bring up for me the one whom I shall indicate to you." The woman replied: "Surely you know what Saul has done, how he has cut off the mediums and the wizards from the land. Why then are you laying a snare for my life, to bring about my death?" Saul swore by the name of Yahweh: "As the Lord lives, no guilt shall come upon you." Then the woman said: "Whom shall I bring up to you?" And Saul answered: "Bring Samuel up for me." Then the old woman saw an old man appear, wrapped in a long mantle. And the figure said to Saul: "Why have you disturbed me by bringing me up? . . . Tomorrow you and your sons with you will fall; the Lord will also deliver the camp of Israel into the hands of the Philistines."

If we were to enter the cave of Endor, we would find it empty and quite like any other cave. Without the spirit of Samuel it holds no interest for us. We must conjure up his spirit, the spirit of the soothsayer, and the spirit of Saul who trembled as he heard the evil tidings. When peopled by the spirits of old, any nook or cave has special significance. But who is going to conjure up these spirits for us, if history has driven out the seers and magicians?

GOD'S MEMOIRS

One day God decided to write His memoirs. He did not dictate them to a secretary; nor did He write them with His own hand.

[3]

Instead He came to certain men on the wings of inspiration; and these men wrote God's memoirs. We possess this precious book of memoirs. It gives a vivid account of those days when God took a special hand in the events of history. Sometimes He intervened in person; at other times He used messengers. War and peace, victory and defeat, tribes and nations — all these became divine messengers. The Bible is a living account because God wrote it. And in its pages the men whom God directed through the course of history come to life. With the help of this book it will be easy to populate the scenes of ancient history with living figures. We shall not need a conjurer because God Himself will unfold the story for us. With Bible in hand we shall find our journey informative and profitable.

And so we shall satisfy the growing interest in the Book of books. The New Testament has always held the attention of Christians. But the Old Testament has had a checkered career. Protestant exaggerations in the sixteenth century made it suspect in the eyes of Catholics. And we have not yet overcome this reaction. So I would invite the reader to follow my narrative with the Bible in hand. If these pages help him to read the Bible with greater interest and understanding, I shall have accomplished my purpose.

INVOCATION TO THE PILGRIMS

Another day has dawned at sea. We are approaching the coast of Africa. But before the moment for disembarking arrives, I want to invoke my muses.

It is customary for one who writes such a journal to recall the names of the illustrious pilgrims who have preceded him. A Spaniard thinks immediately of Etheria, the Galician nun of the fifth century, who wrote such a charming account of her pilgrimage. It is almost certain that she was a nun, and fairly probable that she was a Galician (although the French say that she came from southern France).

I have more than one good reason for recalling another Spanish pilgrim who came to the Holy Land without a cent in his pocket. In his autobiography he refers to himself as "the pilgrim"; and he gave parts of his writing-case to the guards so that he might get a look at the places hallowed by the presence of Jesus Christ. His name, of course, was Ignatius Loyola.

But I am not even going to invoke his name, although I have good reasons for doing so. Ignatius visited a few spots which have some historical or traditional connection with Jesus Christ, his King. I am going to visit these sites and many others besides. But the object of my study demands that I concentrate on the sites of Old Testament history and bypass those of devotional interest.

INVOCATION TO THE ARCHAEOLOGISTS

I may be criticized for a lack of devotion. But nevertheless I must recall the names of some other travelers. Flinders Petrie, the bearded patriarch who collected pieces of pottery and deciphered them; Clermont-Ganneau, who was so good at showing up frauds and pinpointing the authentic; Macalister, the fine English writer; Starkey, who was murdered on a lonely byroad; and P. Vincent, O.P., who was respected for his high degree of learning and his wide range of interests. These men will be my guiding muses.

I am going to visit the land of the Old Testament, and this is found primarily in the Bible. But it is not easy to travel through the pages of the Bible; one must engage in several years of specialized study before he can really start. Many scenes of Old Testament history can be readily pinpointed by the traveler: and he has no trouble in re-creating these events. But the most important points of the Old Testament are embedded deeply in the land and cannot be seen at first glance. The pilgrims of bygone days did not see them and apparently were not interested in them. Even pilgrims of rather recent times unwittingly passed them by. To discover these scenes, one must dig up the topsoil, bore through the hillsides, and sift the earth. Then one must interpret his findings and re-create the scenes of long ago. All this has been done by three generations of archaeologists. A few individuals carry on this work in spite of the difficulties involved.

And so, with Bible in hand, I call upon the help of these indefatigable workers.

ARCHAEOLOGY AND THE BIBLE

The reader, however, should not get the wrong impression. The

[5]

archaeologists did not come to prove that the Bible is true. An overanxious desire to prove the accuracy of the Bible could seriously impede their work and prejudice their interpretations. The archaeologists came to unearth ancient civilizations; they came simply to find the truth buried in the earth. And it is only natural that the truths recorded in the Bible should coincide with the truth buried in the earth. Archaeology did not purport to prove the accuracy of the Bible; but in many cases it could prove that the Bible was trustworthy, that its accounts fitted into our reconstructed picture of ancient history.

This was enough to change the attitude of scholars toward the Bible, which for a time during the nineteenth century had been regarded with a certain distrust. Strangely enough this distrust originated in Protestant circles where the Bible was viewed as the sole norm of faith. The patriarchs were regarded as legendary beings; the cities mentioned were thought to have been invented; and detailed accounts were regarded as glosses added in a later age. The best way to prove the accuracy of the biblical narrative would be to discover the authentic sites of the events narrated. But archaeology up to the early twentieth century had made no such discoveries.

TWO EXAMPLES

The fourteenth chapter of Genesis puzzled commentators for a long time; in fact, it still contains unsolved problems. In it we read about the military expedition of four kings through the Dead Sea region. The four kings were named Amraphel, Arioch, Chedorlahomer, and Tidal. They were battling against five rebel kings, the kings of Sodom, Gomorrah, Admah, Zeboiim, and Bela. "Four kings against five," remarks the sacred writer. The four kings won victory in the valley "which had many bitumen pits." After the victory they sacked the citadels of their enemy, as was the custom in those days. In this pillage Lot and his whole household were taken prisoners. A survivor reached Mamre where Abraham, Lot's uncle, was living. The patriarch gathered a force of 318 men, pursued and scattered the coalition of the four kings, and rescued Lot and his household.

Some critics regarded this chapter as "pure fiction"; some said that the events were outside the realm of possibility and proved the ridiculousness of the story; some conjectured that the invasion of Sennacherib against Hezekiah, which took place almost a thousand years later, had been transposed to this chapter; some said that the narrative was a fictitious piece written around the fifth century before Christ; and later on, some demanded that the archaeologists dig up concrete proof for the historicity of this expedition.

Well, archaeology has not pinpointed the exact location of the bitumen pits. It has not found the personal seals of the kings mentioned, nor has it found stelae commemorating their victory. But it has been able to prove that the names of kings mentioned are completely accurate and fit in which our knowledge of that era and that region. A fifth-century writer could never have dreamed up such an accurate set of names.

*   *   *

Here is another example of the Bible's accuracy in detail. The Book of Chronicles relates that Manasseh revolted against the Assyrians, was defeated and carried off to Babylon as a prisoner. Babylon! The historians were appalled. If Manasseh revolted against Assyria and was taken prisoner, he would have been brought to Nineveh, the capital of Assyria, where Assurbanipal resided. In short, it seemed that the author of Chronicles had erred or had been misinformed.

Then new historical material was uncovered. Assurbanipal had appointed his brother Samasumukin as king of Babylon. The latter managed to form a coalition against his brother. And Manasseh was a member of the coalition. But Assurbanipal descended on Babylon and routed his brother. The remaining rebels, including Manasseh, were then brought down to Babylon. The author of Chronicles is accurate.

THE BIBLE AND ITS SETTING

Today scholars have more confidence in the Bible and know how to suspend judgment on moot questions. But archaeology has done us another service. Until recent times the Bible seemed to be a theodolite, a closed world of the divine existing outside human

[7]

history and geography. Now, however, we can fit it into the vast panorama of ancient history and culture. We know that Palestine is a narrow stretch of land with the sea on one side and mountains on the other, separating it from the desert. Through this land passed the great empires of antiquity to trade or do battle. We now look back on the chosen people and see them quite open to outside cultural influences but clinging tenaciously to their monotheism. This small nation, dwelling in the midst of great empires, survived to fulfill its unique religious mission. We know all about the grandeur of Babylon, Assyria, Elam, and Phoenicia; we have come to appreciate the achievements of the Hittites and Mitanni. But in the midst of these fleeting glories we discover a new dimension, a higher dimension marked by the active presence of God.

That is why I have invoked the names of the great archaeologists who discovered these buried cities. Perhaps they will allow me to dwell in the authentic land of the Old Testament for a few months.

My invocation has covered much ground. The Promised Land looms up ahead and opens wide to receive me.

This ship is a piece of Italian territory in the twentieth century. When my feet touch shore, I shall begin to live in another world, a world of long ago.

I. THE WORLD OF THE PATRIARCHS

He, the Lord, is our God;
    throughout the earth his judgments prevail.
He remembers forever his covenant
    which he made binding for a thousand
      generations —
Which he entered into with Abraham
    and by his oath to Isaac;
Which he established for Jacob by statute,
    for Israel as an everlasting covenant,
Saying, "To you will I give the land of
      Chanaan
    as your allotted inheritance."

When they were few in number,
    a handful, and strangers there,
Wandering from nation to nation
    and from one kingdom to another people,
He let no man oppress them,
    and for their sake he rebuked kings:
"Touch not my anointed,
    and to my prophets do no harm."
                 (Psalm 104[105])

Abraham, father of many peoples, kept his glory without stain: He observed the precepts of the Most High, and entered into an agreement with him; in his own flesh he incised the ordinance, and when tested he was found loyal. For this reason God promised him with an oath that in his descendants the nations would be blessed, that he would make him numerous as the grains of dust, and exalt his posterity like the stars; that he would give them an inheritance from sea to sea, and from the River to the ends of the earth.

                 (Sirach 44)

    Thare was the father of Abram, Nabor and Aran. . . . Thare took his son Abram and his . . . daughter-in-law Sarai, the wife of his son Abram, and led them from Ur of the Chaldees toward the land of Chanaan; but when they reached Hăran, they settled there. . . .

(Genesis 11)

. . . Thus says the Lord, the God of Israel: In times past your fathers, down to Thare, father of Abraham and Nahor, dwelt beyond the River and served other gods. But I brought your father Abraham from the region beyond the River and led him through the entire land of Chanaan. I made his descendants numerous. . . .

(Joshua 24)

Abram took Sarai his wife, Lot his brother's son, all the property they had acquired and the persons they had got in Haran; and they departed for the land of Chanaan.

(Genesis 12)

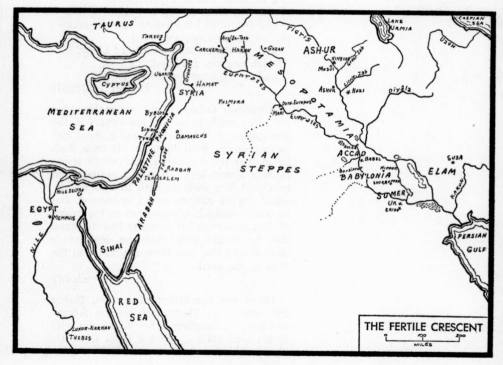

THE FERTILE CRESCENT

1. THE HOMELAND OF ABRAHAM

UNFORTUNATELY our journey begins with a disappointment. For technical reasons we cannot start out in Iraq, the homeland of Abraham. The idea for starting there had come to me during the voyage. It was a whimsical illusion entertained during our free moments, a piece of fantasy conjured up in the heat of the day.

It led to a vain effort to obtain the necessary permits. Finally we had to resign ourselves to failure. Thus we are spared the hot climate and the expense involved, but this cannot compensate for our frustrated desire to visit Abraham's first home, the place where the history of the chosen people begins.

To make up for this disappointment, I spend the free time thumbing through the photographs and the books which describe the great excavations in "Ur of the Chaldees."

THE FLOOD AND THE TOWER OF BABEL

The first eleven chapters of Genesis present us with a religious message which is quite clear and precise. But their exact historical import is still quite problematic. It is generally accepted that these chapters are dependent on Accadian and Sumerian sources. But we are not so certain that Abraham brought a collection of these sources with him — in written or oral form — when he emigrated.

If Abraham himself did transmit these ancient traditions in some way, certain points can be explained more easily. But any attempt to provide a clear-cut simple explanation for everything seems doomed to failure.

Ur, Abraham's homeland, is situated west of the Euphrates, not far from the Persian Gulf. In Abraham's time, the river did not deposit much sediment and the sea came up near Ur. In earlier times, however, the sea came up higher, and river waters emptying

[11]

into it at one point deposited so much sand that eventually "dry land appeared." This area was well irrigated by the branches of the river, and soon "sprouted grass, grains and fruits." As time went on, people settled in this area and learned herding and agriculture. Cities began to spring up and a more urbane culture developed. Some men "played musical instruments" and others made metal tools. But these city dwellers began to sin shamelessly and God sent the flood.

SIX FEET OF CLAY

The vestiges of the flood! What a feat it would be to find certain proof of this catastrophe recorded by different peoples in different regions. Sir Leonard Woolley directed excavations in Babylon from 1922 to 1934, and in a slim but delightful book he has told us about his most interesting discoveries. One of these was the trace of a flood.

The excavators were digging deep into the earth, uncovering the various layers of pottery and detritus. Suddenly they came to a homogeneous stratum of clay undoubtedly deposited by water. The excavators announced that they had reached the bottommost level, the earliest alluvial substrate. The director examined the stratum and the layout of the surrounding region. And he was able to prove that this stratum of clay was too near the surface to be the lowest. He ordered the digging to continue. The clay surface was dense; and the only extraneous matter found was a bone fossil carried along by the waters. About eight feet deeper, the clay stratum suddenly stopped and a new stratum appeared, containing pottery and flint tools. Another dig was started 330 feet to the north; the results were the same. The data were clear enough. A clay sediment deposited by water lay between two cultural strata, the lower containing hand-worked pottery and flint tools, the upper containing machine-produced pottery and metal tools.

The excavators drew their conclusion: a prolonged period of flooding occurred between the two cultural periods. And certain things came to mind: the lists of the Sumerian kings divided into two series — "before the deluge . . . after the deluge"; the legend of Gilgamesh and Utnapistim, and the biblical story of Noah.

Woolley's conclusion caused a sensation. "Considering all the data, there can be no doubt that the flood, whose only possible traces we have uncovered, is the flood recorded in history and in the Sumerian legend, and is the one on which the story of Noah is based."

Unfortunately it is necessary to revise Woolley's views in the light of new evidence and deeper analysis. In this case new evidence came to light. Further excavation showed that the clay bed did not extend over the whole hill. Thus it was not a question of a general flood but rather of a canal or river which coursed through one section of the city for many years.

THE ZIGGURAT OF UR

Perhaps we shall have better luck with the "tower of Babel." The object in question is a tall mound which dominates the ruins of an ancient Babylonian city. Just about a century ago, excavators found cylinders with inscriptions in the corners of this mound. The inscriptions indicated that the work had been started by Ur-Nammu and his son Dungi and had been finished many centuries later in the time of Nabonido. It identified the site as Ur, Abraham's homeland. However, this excavation work was not continued because at that time scholars and the general public were more interested in the astonishing finds at Nineveh. It was left to Sir Leonard Woolley to complete a systematic excavation of the structure.

The mound is a kind of pyramid, 196 feet by 147 feet and 65 feet high. The interior is a solid block of adobe; the outside is made of bricks cemented with pitch. "And they used bricks for stone and bitumen for mortar" (Gn 11:3). The bottom section of the pyramid is 50 feet high. Then comes a series of terraces gradually diminishing in size and connected by stairs. On the uppermost terrace one finds the altar or sanctuary of the deity. The three main stairways are located on the northeast side. Two of them run parallel to the wall while the third cuts up at a right angle. All three converge at a great doorway and there one finds several side staircases. The lines of the building are not straight but slightly curved; the architect used a device which the Greeks would call "entasis" many centuries later. Apparently some of the upper terraces had trees and gardens; and the bricks covering the outside were multicolored and arranged in geometrical patterns.

The whole edifice conveys an impression of harmony and variety, and reminds one not so much of the pyramids as of a sculptured mountain where the moon goddess resided. In front of this "tower" runs an esplanade, dotted with buildings which probably housed the sanctuary personnel and served as administrative offices. This was the religious, political, and economic center of the kingdom; "a tower with its top in the heavens" to bolster their prestige "lest [they] be scattered all over the earth" (Gn 11:4).

Among the different scenes depicted in relief, three deal with the construction of the ziggurat. In the first, the king is making an offering to the deity who extends to him the measuring rod and the coiled rope, symbols of architecture. In the second, the king stands before the deity holding the architect's tools — compasses, baskets of mortar, mortarboard, and trowel. In the third, the workers are carrying hods of mortar up the stairways and cementing bricks on the tower. The edifice was constructed around the beginning of the second millennium B.C. and remained intact for 1750 years. On these stairways Abraham's ancestors ascended to worship the local gods; and here, perhaps, Abraham took part in solemn religious functions before receiving God's message. For us, this is a venerable monument.

But it is not the tower of Babel. That tower would have to be in Babel, and this one is in Ur. However, this tower in Ur is the best preserved ziggurat in Mesopotamia and it gives us a good idea of what the "tower of Babel" was meant to be.

THE CITY OF ABRAHAM

The flood and the tower are two historical realities of stupendous proportions. But we would learn just as much if we could find some common relics revealing the cultural setting in which Abraham was born and nurtured. The two most instructive items in this area are the royal tombs and some of the houses.

The royal tombs go back to the ancient dynasties, and most of them have been pillaged. But those which have survived intact give us an idea of the wealth and the technical skill of their builders. Along with the king was buried his whole retinue — court ladies and the court soldiers, the king's coach with its two donkeys and the queen's coach with its three oxen, the four musicians with their various kinds of harps, the wooden drums inlaid with jewels. The slaves keep watch over their precious bowls and pitchers; the ladies wear precious stones and gold diadems; the soldiers still have their copper daggers. There are game boards and various tools imitated in gold. One is struck by the high combs on the women and by the engraving which depicts different animals playing the part of men. And there are also a silver boat and other precious items. In another tomb there is an illustrious character with a magnificent gold helmet and two copper plates depicting various scenes of war and peace. It was probably the standard of the people which they used to carry on a banner.

All these things belong to another race which antedated Abraham and his tribe. Perhaps successive waves of invading peoples caused a cultural decline. But we have every reason to picture Abraham's home city as a flourishing cultural center. Its citizens knew mathematics — even quadratic and cubic roots. Writing was obligatory in commercial transactions. The priests studied the Sumerian language in bilingual dictionaries and wrote their hymns, legends, and myths on tablets of baked clay. And they worshiped various deities whose number tended to increase.

The houses are spacious, containing a courtyard in the center, an upper floor, an inside staircase, a wooden balcony supported by pillars, and a small shrine. The walls are made of brick and adobe coated with chalk and lime.

ABRAHAM'S VOCATION

God summoned Abraham from this urbane and sophisticated environment and launched him on a seminomadic way of life. Abraham heeded the call and exchanged his two-story house for a tent made of camel skin, the hustle and bustle of city life for the lonely life of a shepherd, his stable and comfortable existence for a life of frequent shifts in search of fertile lands.

In return Abraham received something of greater value: a call from God and a promise:

The Lord said to Abram: "Leave your country, your kinsfolk and your father's house, for the land which I will show you; I will make a great nation of you. I will bless you, and make your name great, so that you shall be a blessing. I will bless them that bless you, and curse them that curse you. In you shall all the nations of the earth be blessed" (Gn 12:1–3).

For all practical purposes, revealed religion begins at that moment. The whole Old Testament stems from this divine promise. And through his descendant Jesus Christ, Abraham continues and extends his universal fatherhood in the true religion.

St. Paul, explaining Abraham's faith to the Romans, says that he received the sign of circumcision "that he might be the father of all who believe, even though uncircumcised, and thus have their faith credited to them as holiness. He will also be the father of the circumcised, provided they are not merely circumcised, but direct their steps in the path of that faith which was our father Abraham's before he was circumcised" (Rom 4:11–12).

2. *IN SEARCH OF SODOM AND GOMORRAH*

. . . Now Abram was very rich in cattle, silver and gold. He journeyed by stages from the Negeb to Bethel. . . . Lot, who went with Abram, also had flocks, herds and tents, so that the land would not support them dwelling together. . . . Then Abram said to Lot, ". . . Withdraw from me. . . ." Then Lot looked about and saw that the whole region of the Jordan toward Segor was well-watered. . . . So Lot chose for himself the whole region of the Jordan and journeyed eastward . . . pitching his tent near Sodom. Now the men of Sodom were wicked, and sinned exceedingly against the Lord.

(Genesis 13)

Then the Lord said: ". . . the outcry against Sodom and Gomorra is great, and their sin is very grave. . . ." Abraham drew near and said: "Will you destroy the good with the wicked? . . ." The Lord said: "I will not destroy it for the sake of ten just men."

(Genesis 18)

Now the two angels came to Sodom . . . and entered his house. . . . Then they said to Lot: ". . . we are about to destroy this place, because the outcry against them has become so great before the Lord. . . ." When morning came . . . the visitors took him, his wife and his two daughters . . . and set him outside the city. . . . And the Lord poured down on Sodom and Gomorra sulphur and fire. . . .

(Genesis 19)

[17]

The World of the Patriarchs

IF YOU should go to Jerusalem and visit the Pontifical Biblical Institute's quarters there, you will be shown a huge picture hanging in one of the parlors. Actually it is not a canvas painting but a fresco of enormous proportions. It is not in its original setting but still bears the marks of the wall on which it was painted. It simply depicts a huge star with long sharp points and multi-colored geometrical patterns.

This star — for better or for worse — is the souvenir of a diligent search and a heated dispute. And it is no accident that it hangs in a place of honor in this house.

A LONG LINE OF SEARCHERS

In 1927 the Pontifical Biblical Institute in Rome established a daughter house in Jerusalem. In this house, with its magnificent terraces and gallery, its choice library, and its valuable museum, our party enjoyed several days of rest and comfort.

During the early days of this establishment, interest in archaeology reached a new peak and threatened to displace the other aspects of biblical study. No biblical institute deserved the consideration of serious scholars unless it undertook archaeological investigations. Today, for various reasons, the wave of enthusiasm for archaeology has subsided. There are fewer excavations and the findings are pretty routine. (This is not meant to imply that archaeology is unimportant. Far from it!) Present work at Hayor, Masada, Gebeon and elsewhere has renewed the interest of Palestine for the arch-aeologist.

Father Mallon and his successor, Father Köppel, both Jesuits, undertook the necessary work of excavation. And they chose "Teleilat Ghassul" (hill of judgment or lye) as the area of study.

Sodom, Gomorrah, Zeboiim, Admah and Bela (Zoar) . Perhaps only the first two names have a familiar ring to the reader. They evoke in our imagination a terrible scene of smoke and fire. These were the flourishing cities which Lot chose as a home, the wicked cities which gave their name to a particular sin, the cities which were cursed by God's wrath.

Don't think that the Jesuits were the first to take up the suggestion to hunt for these cities. The itineraries of the pilgrims of old included a visit to these sites where God taught men an object lesson. But, as in so many other cases, the traditional sources do not agree on the exact location of these cities. Some locate them to the south of the Dead Sea, others to the north; later pilgrims pinpointed them in a more accessible area, in the region around Hebron. In 1909 Father Abel, O.P., scouted the region around the Dead Sea, and settled on the southern area. But in 1924, an American expedition excavated this area and could not find the cities. In 1930 archaeological finds gave Father Mallon reason to think that he had discovered the five cities.

ASHES!

Formerly it was very difficult to make a trip directly to this region. We contemplated it from different vantage points — Mount Nebo, the mouth of the Jordan river, or the Amman-Jerusalem highway. The most important archaeological finds are housed in the Biblical Institute at Jerusalem. The hillsides (like every *tell* conscious of its duty) yielded a large quantity of pottery, some original pieces, and various implements of stone and bone. But there were two items of special importance: frescoes dating from an unbelievably remote age, and a thick layer of ashes. The most spectacular and eye-catching finds were the frescoes — the star, the bird, and the official reception. But the excavators were more interested in the ashes. These ashes were not completely homogeneous. It would have been easier if they had been clearly arranged in distinct horizontal layers. Unfortunately they were mixed together, and even chemical analysis could not separate them into clearly distinct groups. Even so, they were very valuable to the excavator. A great conflagration ravaging several cities around the Dead Sea sometime before 2000 B.C. — what further evidence was needed to pinpoint the location of the five cities?

The age of the pottery was the crowning piece of evidence. It pointed to a date around the end of the third millennium, the time of Abraham. But this date was to scatter the ashes to the wind.

NORTH OR SOUTH?

One afternoon in March, 1931, Father Köppel set out alone in his canoe. Around 8 p.m. a big storm arose. The lone traveler headed for shore, and, oblivious to the possible danger from hyenas and leopards, he waited there fourteen hours for the storm to subside. It was the second time he had to return on foot from this trip; he headed back to his starting point, dragging the canoe behind him a part of the way and paddling it the rest of the time. His mind was now made up. He would make the next trip on foot.

This was not a pleasure trip nor a romantic adventure. He had set out in the afternoon to escape the intense heat of the day. And his purpose was to examine the southern shore of the Dead Sea. The next time he would travel on land. He would not be in danger from storms and wild animals but rather from the bandits who prey on travelers and their police escorts. But his interest in the project far outweighed the potential danger.

He reasoned as follows. If the cities could not be found to the south of the Dead Sea, then either they were submerged in the southern part of the sea or else they were actually located in the north. The excavators had tried to glean an answer from the land but without success. So Father Köppel tried the sea. If a cataclysm took place along the southern coast in recent times (4000 years is a short time span in geology), then it would have left its traces along the seashore. The sea gave its answer to Father Köppel — No! So the cities must have been situated to the north.

The same conclusion was reached shortly before by Father Power, S.J., who had consulted the biblical texts and the ancient traditions. It seemed that the ashes of Teleilat Ghassul were a valuable piece of historical testimony.

WE ARE LEFT WITH THE STAR

But this line of reasoning failed to convince everyone, and a heated debate ensued. Abel attacked this opinion vigorously, and others joined in the discussion. There was still much unexplored territory to the south; and the traditions favoring the north were weak and rather suspect. The biblical testimony was questionable to say the least, and, most important of all, so were the dates involved.

Albright claimed that the ashes antedated Abraham by more than a thousand years. The Pentapolis had not yet been discovered.

In Search of Sodom and Gomorrah

And what about the famous layer of ashes? Abel said that they were the shavings left over from the manufacture or use of lye and soap which the natives extracted from a certain plant called *Salicorna fruticosa;* hence the hill's name — *ghassul* (lye).

At the end of the debate the view favoring the north fell into disrepute. Had the search been a complete failure?

Well, here is the moral of the story. Mallon and Köppel at one point believed that they had found the accursed cities. But they actually returned home as the discoverers of a culture technically labeled "ghassulian," which still was being written up in 1949 and 1951. The symbol of this important find is the precious star, with its eight points and its geometrical patterns, hanging in the Biblical Institute at Jerusalem.

THE REGION OF SODOM

Today the controversy has subsided. And the Israelis have organized a rather tiring tour to this region. You start out from Tel Aviv in comfortable automobiles, and cross the infamous region around the Dead Sea, the vast desert which extends as far as Beer-sheba. Only the last few miles make the trip worthwhile. It is a quick descent through a desolate countryside. When you get near the sea, you can see Mount Usdum honed out of a layer of salt 164 feet thick. You gaze in wonder at the imposing dimensions of this salt mountain, at the irregular peaks which jut up between clay ridges, at the glistening pillars of salt. Then you enter the salt cavern. You feel the constant air current running through it and you see the stalactites decorating the ceiling. Next you examine the shallow sea which raised its level not long ago. Then you start back because the tour has no more to offer and because the Jordan frontier prevents you from going any farther. The highway continues as far as Engadi, now a national park and the place of many excavations. During the octave of Easter in 1964 some fifteen thousand persons visited this zone.

It is a real pity because this is only the beginning of the accursed region. A little farther on we would be able to see the steppe composed of sulphur, the sulphurous waters, the bushes bearing ash-colored fruits, the stone blocks piled in masses of asphalt, the

[21]

chalk ridges shining a sulphurous yellow, the awesome and imposing desolation of this region.

And a little farther still, we would have been shown the spot where the city of Zoar (or Segor) stood — even into the Middle Ages. Zoar was the city of palm trees for the crusaders, the fifth city of the Pentapolis which was preserved fresh and green as a perpetual witness against her four sinful sister cities.

But the sites we have seen are enough to make us meditate on the cities which will ever serve as an example of God's wrath. "A field of nettles and a salt pit and a waste forever" (So 2:9); "all its soil being nothing but sulphur and salt, a burnt-out waste, unsown and unfruitful, without a blade of grass" (Dt 29:23).

And the Book of Wisdom reminds us of Lot, who was saved from God's punishing hand, and his wife, who was turned into a pillar of salt: "She saved the just man from among the wicked who were being destroyed, when he fled as fire descended upon Pentapolis — where as a testimony to its wickedness, there yet remains a smoking desert, plants bearing fruit that never ripens, and the tomb of a disbelieving soul, a standing pillar of salt. For those who forsook Wisdom first were bereft of knowledge of the right, and then they left mankind a memorial of their folly — so that they could not even be hidden in their fall" (Wis 10:6–9).

Here we might well read the prophecy against Edom, which lay to the south of this region, found in the book of Isaiah. His words apply to the land of Sodom just as well:

> Edom's streams shall be changed into pitch
>   and her earth into sulphur,
>   and her land shall become burning pitch;
> Night and day it shall not be quenched,
>   its smoke shall rise forever.
> From generation to generation she shall lie waste,
>   never again shall anyone pass through her.
> But the desert owl and hoot owl shall possess her,
>   the screech owl and raven shall dwell in her.
> The Lord will measure her with line and plummet
>   to be an empty waste
>   for satyrs to dwell in.
> Her nobles shall be no more,

nor shall kings be proclaimed there;
    all her princes are gone.
Her castles shall be overgrown with thorns,
    her fortress with thistles and briers.
She shall become an abode for jackals
    and a haunt for ostriches.
Wildcats shall meet with desert beasts,
    satyrs shall call to one another;
There shall the lilith repose,
    and find for herself a place to rest.
There the hoot owl shall nest and lay eggs,
    hatch them out and gather them in her shadow;
There shall the kites assemble,
    none shall be missing its mate.

(Is 34:9–15)

3. THE CITY OF WELLS: BEER-SHEBA

> Sarai, Abram's wife, had borne him no
> children. She had an Egyptian maid named
> Agar. . . . Sarai his wife took Agar, her
> Egyptian maid, and gave her to Abram,
> her husband, to be his wife. . . .
>
> (Genesis 16)

> Sarai conceived and born Abraham a son
> in his old age at the time which God had
> promised. . . . When his son was eight days
> old Abraham circumcised him as God had
> commanded him. . . . The child grew and
> was weaned; and Abraham gave a great
> feast on the day of his weaning.
>
> (Genesis 21)

> Then Abraham took sheep and cattle and
> gave them to Abimelech; and the two men
> made a covenant. . . . Therefore, that place
> was called Bersabee, because both of them
> took an oath there.
>
> (Genesis 21)

IF YOU take a train trip from Salamanca to Astorga at the end of
August, the scenery will give you a vivid impression of the importance of water. An arid plain stretches into the distance; the fields
have already lost their verdure and the wheat stalks lie scorched in
the sun. You try to scan the countryside but your eyes are dazzled
by the sun. Suddenly, the scene changes. There is green everywhere,
as far as the eye can see. You feel a cool freshness running through
your pores and your eyes relax in the softened sunlight. Soon you
can make out the many irrigation ditches running through the fields
like so many veins of freshness. The lifeless plain has become an
orchard, and you see countless trees. You experience the fresh sweetness of a countryside which is not at the mercy of fickle rain clouds
because it is blessed with springs (of fresh waters) and wells.

The City of Wells: Beer-sheba

The thirst of a wounded man or a traveler can arouse our compassion. But the thirst of a parched land, which brings famine to its inhabitants, is an awesome thing. The psalmist cries out: "Lord, my soul thirsts after you; my flesh longs for you, as the parched earth longs for water."

The people of Spain know the terrible meaning of drought; we can appreciate the significance of Palestine's arid wastes, and the importance attached to those regions which do not lack water. Our appreciation of water is reflected in the names of villages and towns: Fuentes de Oñoro, Fuente-lareina, Fontiveros, Fuensaldaña, Fuentesauco, Fuentes de San Esteban, etc. (akin to such names as Cold Springs, Hot Springs, Silver Springs). The Hebrew word 'ain (often written En) means "fountain" and "eye"; and on the map of Palestine we shall come across many towns bearing this name 'Ain Fashka, 'Ain Karem (gracious spring), En-dor (fountain of habitation), En-gedi (fountain of the ram), En-gannim (fountain of gardens), En-shemesh (fountain of the sun), En-hattanim (fountain of the dragon), En-eglaim (spring of the calves), En-haddah (bubbling fountain), etc.

No site could become a permanent settlement, a city, unless it could provide sufficient water. When the springs did not gush to the surface of their own accord, the people dug into the earth to provide an outlet. A well was regarded as a rare treasure. Springs and wells were landmarks along the traveling routes, strategic points of great importance. They helped to guarantee a measure of security to an ordered way of life. In Spain I can point to the name Ciempozuelos (100 wells). In the United States one finds Hot Springs. In Italy one recalls the name of the town where St. Paul disembarked — Puteoli (well town). In Palestine we find places named Bera (well) — Beer-elim (well of terebinths), Beer-sheba (well of oaths), etc.

BEER-SHEBA

The town of Beer-sheba still bears its ancient biblical name. Since the days of Abraham this name evokes memories of his presence. "From Dan to Beer-sheba" is an expression used to describe the limits of the Promised Land from north to south. It is a quaint confining city without borders, walls, or defenses. For the desert itself is its best defense. An army coming from the south could not sustain a prolonged march without water; and below Beer-sheba there are few sources of water. Situated in the middle of a desert, Beer-sheba is impregnable. But it is still sought eagerly by Bedouin nomads who wander freely through the spacious desert wastes.

About 3600 years ago one of these nomads, or rather seminomads, was Abraham. A seminomad sets up his tent near a well and tills a small stretch of the surrounding land until he gives up or it gives out. Then he sets out in search of another spot. A given site may prove to be fertile, and his offspring may settle in this spot permanently. If the well is abandoned for some time, Bedouins or nomads may pass by and camp there for several days. But they never till the land.

Abraham had found a well or had dug it himself. But the servants of a neighboring king, Abimelech, forbade him to use it. Abraham went to complain to the king. The king replied: "I do not know who did this; you did not tell me, nor did I hear of it till today."

Abraham made a pact with Abimelech and gave him sheep and cattle to seal the alliance. He picked out seven ewes and gave them as a token of his oath of alliance. So the place was called Beer-sheba (well of oath, or seven wells).

"And Abraham planted a tamarisk tree at Beer-sheba where he called on the name of the Lord, the everlasting God" (Gn 21:33).

BEER-SHEBA TODAY

What a fine start for this town! In the days of old the patriarch dug a well and planted a tree. Today the Israelis use every known technique to dig wells and plant trees. The highway from Jerusalem must cut through many miles of desert and arid country before it reaches this city. A water pipe stretches along one side of the highway, and on both sides of the road grow several rows of eucalyptus trees, a variety of tree which grows quickly but absorbs a great deal of water.

In this region archaeology has offered its services to the department of irrigation. An Israeli described the recent excavations to us and showed us the city's small museum. However, he was not an archaeologist but a civil engineer. He and his colleagues are looking for human relics dating from the remote past, especially Chalcolithic pottery; such traces of human life indicate that water is nearby. On any given day they might hit upon a hidden vein of water or a stopped-up well.

One of the most cruel forms of vengeance in the olden days was stopping up a well. The inhabitants of this region did this to some of the wells which Abraham had excavated. Isaac had to turn around and reopen them for his fields and livestock.

The modern city of Beer-sheba stretches over a large area. Strangely enough, this sunny southern city reminded me of a district bordering the North Sea which is heavy with a gray dampness. The district of Fedderwardengroden, north of Wilhelmshaven, was built to accommodate those who worked in the naval shipyards. The houses are arranged in the same way, the streets are of the same width, and there are gardens in the front or the back of the apartments. Only the color scheme is different. There it is a dull gray: here it is a brilliant white. Only afterward was I informed that this city was planned by a German engineer. Now the city has grown out of proportion and new streets curve around to give a little flair to the monotonous ground plan.

THE NEW SIGNIFICANCE OF MODERN BEER-SHEBA

In the time of Solomon, the golden age of the Hebrew kingdom, Israel stretched from Dan to Beer-sheba, in theory at least. The consecrated formula continued to be used: "In Solomon's time Judah and Israel dwelt in harmony, each under its grapevine and its fig tree, from Dan to Beer-sheba."

But undoubtedly this city acquired a new function when Solomon extended his dominion to the gulf of 'Aqaba where he operated mines and chartered ships. The new state of Israel also needs Beer-sheba as a communications center on the road to the gulf, even though the Israeli fleet lies in the Mediterranean.

But the new state does not regard this site as a mere stopover point. If you examine the geographical layout of modern Israel, you will see a roughly shaped handle at the top and a triangular dagger with its point (Elath) fixed in the sea. This gilded blade of sand must be put to good use. The government has proclaimed its objective: the conquest of this triangle, the desert of the Negeb, for agriculture and human habitation. And Beer-sheba has a new mission as the vital center of this conquest.

All the houses of the city have storage tanks on the roof to catch the little rain which falls. It is not enough. They are hunting for all the abandoned wells and subterranean currents. This too is not enough. They are storing the surplus water in the north around Nazareth and sending it to Beer-sheba; but still it is not enough. However, it is all that can be done for the present. In time they will utilize the waters of the Jordan for the final conquest of the desert. In Jerusalem there is a permanent display which is nicely set up. It depicts the accomplishments so far and the plans for the future. The planning will be done in Beer-sheba; the waters will be distributed from Beer-sheba and the new roads will intersect in this city. The Jews of today have sworn a new oath in the "city of oaths," where Abraham made a peaceful alliance with Abimelech.

THE PAST RECALLED

In keeping with our promise to populate these regions with biblical figures, we are going to cast our gaze over this desert region. We leave Beer-sheba around 2:00 p.m. The sun is warm and bright on this tropical afternoon. Some distance from the highway we see groups of tents belonging to Arab nomads. They have roamed around this region for centuries. Are they plotting to expel the Israelis from this region, to seize all the water-holes?

Many centuries ago a quarrel broke out over Isaac, the forefather of the Jews, and Ishmael, the forefather of the Arabs. This desert we are now crossing was the backdrop for the tragic conflict.

Abraham had married Sarah (called Sarai before the birth of Isaac), but she was not bearing him any sons. So she made use of one of the contemporary laws known to us through Hammurabi, the great Mesopotamian legislator. Sarah had an Egyptian slave named Hagar, and she gave her to Abraham as a second wife. According to law any child of Hagar would belong to Sarah, the first wife. But laws are one thing, and female jealousy quite another, especially in the case of motherhood. When Hagar felt the child stirring in her womb, she began to look down on her barren mis-

[28]

The City of Wells: Beer-sheba

tress. "Then Sarai said to Abram: 'The injury done me is your fault! I gave my maid to your embrace and when she was aware that she had conceived she looked on me with disdain. The Lord judge between you and me!' Abram answered Sarai: 'Your maid is in your power; do to her what seems good to you.' Then Sarai humiliated her, and she fled from her" (Gn 16:5–6).

An angel of the Lord consoled Hagar and induced her to return to Sarah's house. The issue was settled temporarily, but Sarah did not forget Hagar's disdainful glances. Hagar gave birth to Ishmael, and Sarah watched him grow. Thirteen years later God made a promise to Abraham: "Sara your wife shall bear you a son, and you shall call him Isaac. I will establish my covenant with him as a perpetual covenant for his descendants after him" (Gn 17:19).

Sarah gave birth to the promised child, Isaac, and he grew up in the same house with Ishmael. Sarah watched the two children at play, and her old bitterness returned. Emboldened by her new status and by God's promise, she spoke to her husband once again: "Cast out this slave-girl with her son; for the son of this slave-girl shall not be heir with my son Isaac." What intensity of emotion lay underneath this antithesis! But the slave's child was also Abraham's son, and the patriarch had to make a difficult decision.

"God said to Abraham: 'Be not distressed on account of the boy and your slave-girl; heed all that Sara says to you; for through Isaac shall your descendants be called. But I will also make the son of the slave-girl a great nation because he is your offspring.' Abraham rose early in the morning, took bread and a bottle of water, and gave them to Agar, placing them on her shoulder. Then he dismissed her with the child. She departed, and wandered about in the desert of Bersabee. When the water in the bottle was gone, she left the child under a bush. Then she went and sat opposite the place at about the distance of a bowshot; for she said: 'Let me not see the child die.' As she sat opposite the spot, the child cried aloud. God heard the boy's cry, and the angel of God called to Agar from heaven, and said to her: 'What is the matter, Agar? Fear not, for God has heard the boy's cry in this plight of his. Rise up, take the boy, be assured in his regard; for I will make him a great nation.' Then God opened her eyes, and

[29]

she saw a well. She went and filled the bottle with water and gave the boy a drink . . ." (Gn 21:10–19).

The empty gourd, the hidden well, the despairing mother, and the weeping child — these are the ingredients of the drama. It is resolved by the intervention of God's angel. We certainly cannot object to this extraordinary intervention, because a tragedy is averted. As Abraham's son and the father of a great people, this child enjoyed special privileges.

According to Arab tradition recorded in the Koran, Ishmael is the father of the Arab people. It is very difficult, perhaps impossible, for the historian to check the accuracy of this patriarchal lineage. But if it were shown to be accurate, it would be an interesting back-drop for the events of the present day. Once again in these lands, in the deserts and fields of Palestine, the two brothers have met. Once again countless sons of Hagar have been driven out by the sons of Sarah who regard this land as their patrimony. Once again thousands of Ishmael's sons, driven out of their traditional home-land, have fainted from hunger and thirst in the wilderness. But the basic premises have changed radically. Do the Jews still have a divine right to the Promised Land, or does the historical right of the Arabs take preeminence? It is a complicated problem, and it would take an angel to solve it. The Arabs and the Jews are blood sons of Abraham. But the true sons of Abraham, the promised line of descendants, are the Christians. And Christians do not look for a promised temporal kingdom but for a supernatural kingdom. And from our kingdom we implore God, the one God of Arabs, Jews, and Christians, to intervene in the conflict.

4. *HEBRON*

Sara lived one hundred and twenty-seven years. She died in Cariath-arbe, that is, Hebron, in the land of Chanaan. Abraham prepared to mourn for Sara and weep over her.

(Genesis 23:1–2)

THE bus is traveling southward. Suddenly it comes to an unexpected stop — at a police station. Our guide gets off, a telephone call is made, and then he returns to the bus accompanied by a Jordanian policeman. We get an official escort. During the short ride which follows, the guide gives us some words of caution about our visit. We are going to visit a treasure which is zealously guarded by the Moslems in one of their holy villages. It is of central importance to the Moslem religion.

One would hardly realize it as the bus goes through the village. The houses are white and all the windows have a pointed arch and a structure dating from the Crusades. Little children are coming out of school carrying their notebooks and aprons. We can see Arabs seated around tables in a cafe. To all appearances our bus is like the many others which ply the highways of Jordan. Only the cargo inside distinguishes it from all the others. When one of the children notices this cargo, he passes the word quickly and in a moment we are surrounded by a flock of children.

We get off the bus in a compact group. The policeman takes up the rear to protect us from the mob of children. Perhaps that is why the children do not think of throwing stones; they are content to play a game of advance and retreat with the police.

Meanwhile we have gone up a narrow lane and stand on the top of the sunlit steps leading to the great treasure. From there we look down the shady street up which the noisy gang of children is coming, more playful than anything else.

[31]

NEGOTIATIONS BEGIN

We must wait a little because the Moslems are at prayer. Then the guard tells us that each person must pay fifty cents. This, of course, leads to a friendly argument. We have a permit from the governor of Jerusalem. But there is no mention of the word "free." The discussion becomes more heated, but nothing is settled. We must pay a visit to the mufti.

Our guide does not dare to leave us alone on the steps of the lofty sanctuary; so we are herded into the bus once again. Then he goes off to see the mufti. From the bus the flock of children seems to dance around like flies over a jar of marmalade. Their movements are orderly and unobtrusive. Now and then one of them does something unexpected and attracts our attention once again. One of the more courageous approaches to ask for a *baksis*. Another is brave enough to put his foot up on the running board and I have to close the door.

Meanwhile our guide has reached the mufti's house and is received most courteously. He thinks about his passengers shut up in the bus and tries to speed up the proceedings. But in an oriental country this is impossible. The mufti is wearing a friendly smile because he was present when our guide first asked for the permit. He offers personally to show us the treasure which he guards. But first they must leisurely drink a cup of oriental coffee. Everything must take place in an atmosphere of calm friendliness.

AN ANCIENT BUSINESS DEAL

A half hour has gone by and we are still in the bus. Rather than sulk impatiently I prefer to open a book and read about a business deal which took place here more than thirty-six centuries ago.

A band of Hittites had settled in this city. Apparently they had been there for a long time and had adopted the language and customs of the area. An old woman, who lived in this region, had just died. Her husband sought an audience with the elders to make a proposition.

They assembled at the city gates, as was the custom. The old man wanted to buy the cave of Machpelah as a burial place. But he had to broach the subject tactfully, because he was not a citizen.

Hebron

So Abraham began to speak: "I am a stranger resident among you; give me burial ground among you that I may bury my dead." Once he acquired this land, he would have citizenship rights.

The Hittites answered: "Hear us, my lord, you are a mighty prince among us. Choose any of our tombs to bury your dead. None of us will refuse you a tomb for your dead." In short, he could have a tomb but not his own plot of land.

But the old man wanted ownership rights. He loved his wife too much to bury her in a rented tomb. So he rose and bowed to the assembly: "If it is acceptable to you that I bury my dead then hear me; ask Ephron, the son of Sohar, in my behalf to give me the cave of Machpela which he has at the end of his field. Let him sell it to me in your presence for its full value, as a burial ground." In buying a portion of Ephron's land he would acquire citizenship rights but would not have to pay tithes to the city's ruler.

Ephron heard Abraham's words and rose to give his answer. "No, my lord! hear me: I give you the field and the cave that is in it. In the presence of my people do I give it; bury your dead."

It was a very generous offer but Abraham was insistent. He rose and bowed before the assembly. "If you are really willing, hear me. I will give you money for the field; accept it from me that I may bury my dead there."

Ephron replied: "Hear me, my lord! A piece of land worth four hundred shekels of silver, what is that between you and me? Bury your dead in it."

"Abraham came to terms with Ephron and weighed out for him the sum he had mentioned in the hearing of the Hethites, four hundred shekels of silver of commercial standard. Thus Ephron's field in Machpela, facing Mamre, that is, the field, the cave and all the trees in the entire field, became the property of Abraham in the presence of all the Hethites, his fellow citizens. After this Abraham buried his wife Sara in the cave of the field at Machphela, facing Mamre, that is, Hebron, in the land of Chanaan" (Gn 23:4–19).

IN THE SANCTUARY

The bargaining was finished. The mufti — impeccably dressed in a European suit and wearing an Egyptian hat with a tassel — returns with our guide. Once again we get off the bus, ascend the street, cross the arch, and reach the flight of steps. The prayers and a picturesque procession leaves the temple. A group of Moslem elders descend solemnly. There is an air of curiosity and reverence on both sides, the latter perhaps stemming from the presence of the mufti. A winding ramp leads to the door, where we take off our shoes in ritual fashion. Groups of Moslems in a squatting position watch us pass. Our first impression of the overall scene is one of melancholy. The outside walls are constructed in Herodian style, but the vaulted roofs show clear evidence of crusader influence. Does this sanctuary belong to Moslems, Jews, or Christians? Herod built a sanctuary for the Jews here; Byzantine Christians built a basilica; the Arabs constructed a series of cenotaphs. The crusaders built a huge church, and the Arabs transformed it into a mosque. Today the Jews have hopes of regaining this ancestral shrine, while the Arabs are determined to prevent any such thing.

This enclosure, so revered by the three most important religions, contains the venerable relics of the patriarchs: Abraham and Sarah, Isaac and Rebekah, Jacob and Leah. In the mosque we gaze on the cenotaphs covered with precious cloths. Through a small grating on the floor we can see the cave below, which we cannot enter. That is the final resting place of the sacred remains. But an historical tradition prohibits our entrance.

THE SACRED CAVERN

Until the British arrived on the scene it was almost impossible for non-Moslems to enter this mosque. But during the British Mandate, non-Moslems were able to obtain permits. Formerly Jews and Christians were only allowed to climb to the sixth step, where a crack in the wall allowed one to take a guess at the exact location of the cavern. Today no Jew would dare to come to Hebron; by contrast Christians have gained some measure of toleration from the Moslems.

However tolerance is not involved where the cavern is concerned. Not even Moslems are admitted into it. More than twenty years ago the mufti took over the administration of the cavern. We ask

him if he ever felt a desire to go into it. "Once upon a time" —
he replies — "I felt the temptation to do this. But I did not succumb because it would show a lack of faith. I firmly believe that
Abraham is buried here, just as I believe that Mahomet is buried
in Mecca; I do not need to have visual proof." Other Moslems tell
of the punishments reserved for anyone who enters the mysterious
cavern.

In 1523 a well-disguised Jew, David the Rubenite, was admitted
into the mosque, but not into the cavern. The guards told him the
story (i.e., the legend) connected with the cave. The second successor of Mahomet opened the cavern and ordered four men to
enter it. When they came out, three died on the spot. The fourth
was struck dumb for three days, but then was able to tell what
he had seen.

INSIDE THE CAVE

It is useless to dream of obtaining such a wondrous privilege.
All we can do, after visiting the mosque, is to sit down in the
shade of the courtyard, form a quiet group like the Moslems, and
call upon someone who has descended into the cavern so that he
may tell us what he saw.

The first to appear is a traveler from the eighth century named
Abu Bekr el Esqafy. He speaks slowly, his voice seems to come
from afar, and his words resound with mysterious harmonies. . . .
"I was a noted benefactor of this sanctuary; so the guard agreed
to let me into the grotto. He chose a day when it was snowing
heavily and the cold kept the pilgrims away. We stole into the
sanctuary — myself, the guardian, and several workers. The latter
lifted a flagstone which covered the entrance. The guardian, lamp
in hand, led me down a staircase with seventy-two steps. There I
beheld a huge black slab on which lay the body of Isaac, face
upward. A full green cloth covered the body, and his long white
beard was spread over the cloth. On two other slabs lay the bodies
of Abraham and Jacob, their hair and beards spread out on top
of the cloths. The guardian approached a wall in the cavern; I too
drew near to look over his shoulder. Just at that moment a voice
cried out: Get out of the harem! We fell down in a faint, and when

we recovered, we were able to ascend to the sanctuary."

The old Arab's story is a delightful tale. And since our interest is a mixture of devotion and scientific curiosity, we are delighted to listen to another raconteur. He is an Augustinian canon from the twelfth century who got the story from the lips of the discoverers themselves.

THE CANON'S STORY

"It was the twenty-first year of the Frank's reign (1119). A certain Ranier, of pious memory, was the prior in Hebron. Among those who came to serve God under his tutelage were Odon and Arnulf from whom I heard the story I now relate. These three men had begged God to grant them a favor which He had refused to many others. And at long last God heard their plea.

"One afternoon in June, while the Canons Regular were taking their customary siesta, a monk who had been working in the scriptorium took refuge from the heat inside the church. He lay down against the pavement alongside one of the cenotaphs. Through a crevice in the flagstones came a gentle current of fresh air. The monk began to throw pebbles through the opening; on hearing them fall, he concluded that there was a cavern or cistern below. He took a stick, fastened a rope to it, and attached a lead weight at the bottom. Then he lowered it to the floor of the cavern: 11 elbow lengths. At the time the prior was in Jerusalem on business.

"When the monks had arisen and chanted Nones, this monk told them of his discovery. They at once suspected that he had found the double cave (Machpelah). Two or three days were spent praying to God and preparing the cutting tools. For the rocks were solid and posed a problem to any iron tool. When everything was ready, the monks voted unanimously to begin work, and the governor, Balduin, gave his approval. And so they set to work in the name of the Blessed Trinity, not without some feeling of trepidation.

"After three days of hard work they finished drilling through the rocks and were able to lift them. They found themselves at the entrance of a cavern. All the monks were anxious to go inside, but there was only room for one. So they picked out the oldest monk, who had been in the monastery for the longest time. Since he was, as it were, the father of all those present, he would be most likely to discover the patriarchs of so many nations. The elderly monk consented readily and was let down into the cavern, but he was unable to find another exit and asked to be hoisted up. The next day Arnulf was let down into the cavern, armed with a candle. He looked around with curious wonder, trying to figure out the situation. The walls of the cavern fitted together so well that they seemed to be cut from a single slab of stone; and the layout was similar to that of the basilica above. He was at a loss and felt very annoyed at not being able to discover another passageway. But he was a practical man; so, taking heart, he grabbed an iron hammer and began to tap the wall, looking for hollow spaces. At last he found what he was looking for.

"With renewed hope he ordered others to come down and help him open the passageway. It took four days to remove the rock. Behind it they found a large canal, now dried up, eleven feet high, seventeen feet long, and a foot wide. All were struck by the fact that the walls of the narrow passageway were composed of square blocks carefully cut like the walls of the basilica above. Arnulf resolved to find the relics and began to sound for hollow spaces. When he found another spot, he ordered the others to open up a passageway. After four days of hard work they were able to remove the stone; behind it they found a round basilica capable of holding thirty people, its entrance blocked by a single slab of rock. The monks began to weep for joy and gave thanks to God; but they did not dare to enter because they thought the relics were inside. So they waited for the prior to return. When he came, they told him everything. He was delighted with the news and his only regret was that he had not been there from the start.

"The community assembled that day and decided to enter the basilica after their siesta and the recitation of Nones. Once inside they would investigate the area and make further plans. So, at the appointed hour they descended into the cavern, drew back the rock, and entered the rotunda. But they could not find what they were looking for. They examined the shrine with a feeling of awe because one does not expect to find such rooms underground. While the other monks were examining the walls, looking for an exit,

Arnulf returned to examine the entrance. After careful scrutiny of the bright rock, he found a wedge-shaped stone. He ordered it removed, and there was the entrance to the second cavern! With tears of joy they gave thanks to God.

"On June 25 the prior ordered Arnulf, out of obedience and penance, to enter the second cavern, because he had done the most work in this endeavor. Thus he would bring the project to its final conclusion. Arnulf did not delay for a moment. Taking a candle, he blessed himself, chanted the *Kyrie* in a loud voice, and entered the cavern with some trepidation. Thinking that Balduin, the protector of the monastery, might suspect that there was a treasure of gold or silver hidden there, he asked the prior to invite him inside. The prior extended the invitation and Balduin accepted. He entered the cavern, but, overcome by fear, withdrew immediately.

"Arnulf wandered through the cave, searching for bones, but he found nothing except earth dyed the color of blood. He left the cavern and reported his findings. Everyone was disappointed as the monks ascended to the surface. The next day the prior begged Arnulf to examine the cavern once again and to dig around very carefully. Arnulf obediently took a staff, entered the cave once again, and began to dig up the earth. Finally he came upon the bones of holy Jacob (although he did not know this at the time), and gathered them together. Then he noticed the entrance to another cave near the skull of Jacob. He cleared a passageway and went inside. There he found the sealed remains of Abraham and, at his feet, the bones of Isaac. Thus, all the remains were not in the same cave, as some think. Rather, the remains of Abraham and Isaac were found in an inner cave, while the remains of Jacob were found in an outer cave.

"Arnulf had discovered a wondrous and priceless treasure. He hurried from the grotto and informed the prior and the monks that he had found the remains of the venerable patriarchs. They all glorified God. Arnulf washed the sacred remains with water and wine, placed them on separate wooden slabs prepared for the occasion, and then withdrew. When everyone had withdrawn, the prior sealed the entrance so that no one could get in without his permission.

"On the following day, a few monks came down to pray and

found several inscriptions on a rock to the right; but no one could read them. They drew back the stone, but found nothing except earth. Assuming that the stone had been placed in this spot for a very good reason, they dug to the left and found fifteen earthen jugs filled with bones. But they could not learn anything about these relics. Presumably they were the remains of some Israelite leaders.

"After all these events had taken place, the prior went to Jerusalem to inform the patriarch Garmund of the discoveries and to invite him to Hebron so that he might venerate the relics. The patriarch promised to come, but failed to keep his word. When the prior realized that he was not coming, he prepared a celebration on his own. A huge crowd of pilgrims from Jerusalem and the neighboring cities came to this celebration held on October 6. The clergy sang the *Te Deum* and the prior, in solemn procession, brought the relics out for public veneration."

DEPARTURE FROM HEBRON

The reader can well imagine how interested archaeologists would be to examine the cavern once again. Toward the end of 1919, Captain Mackay and Father Vincent, O.P., were granted extraordinary permission to study the upper floor of the mosque for one week. But they were not allowed into the cavern.

In a short farewell speech the mufti emphasized America's obligation to safeguard the freedom of other nations, and he stressed the need for unity between Christians and Moslems to prevent these shrines from falling into the hands of the Israelis.

But will the day ever come when the Moslems will allow scholars to make a thorough study of this site — one of the most sacred in the entire world?

And so we leave Hebron, knowing that we have visited sites hallowed by the memory of Abraham and the remains of the patriarchs.

"Abraham's life span was one hundred and seventy-five years when he expired. He died at a good old age, an old man after a full life, and was gathered to his kinsmen. His sons Isaac and Ismael buried him in the cave of Machphela, facing Mamre, in the field of Ephron, the Hethite, the son of Sohar. Abraham was buried with his wife Sara in the field which he had brought from the Hethites" (Gn 25:7–10).

"Jacob went to his father Isaac at Mamre in Cariath-arbe, that is, Hebron, where Abraham and Isaac had sojourned. The lifetime of Isaac was one hundred and eighty years. Isaac breathed his last and died, and was gathered to his kin, an old man who had lived a full life. His sons Esau and Jacob buried him" (Gn 35:27–29).

"Then Jacob summoned his sons and said: '. . . I am about to be gathered to my people. Bury me with my fathers in the cave which is in the field of Ephron, the Hethite, the cave in the field of Machphela, facing Mamre in the land of Chanaan. . . . There Abraham and his wife Sara are buried; there Isaac and his wife Rebecca are buried; and it was there I buried Lia.'

"When Jacob had finished giving directions to his sons, he drew up his feet into the bed and expired. And he was gathered to his people. . . . They carried him into the land of Chanaan, and buried him in the cave in the field of Machphela, facing Mamre" (Gn 49:1, 29–33; 50:13).

5. BETHEL: CITY OF CONTRASTS

Abraham was the father of Isaac. Isaac
. . . married Rebecca. . . . Rebecca conceived. . . . When the time of her delivery
came, there were indeed twins in her womb.
The first to come forth was red. His whole
body was like a hairy garment, so they
named him Esau. Afterwards, his brother
came forth, with his hand gripping Esau's
heel; so he was called Jacob. . . . When
the boys grew up, Esau became a skillful
hunter, a man of the open country, while
Jacob was a settled man who stayed among
the tents. Isaac preferred Esau because he
was fond of game, but Rebecca preferred
Jacob.

. . . So Esau swore to Jacob, and sold
him his birthright. Then Jacob gave Esau
some bread and lentils. He ate and drank
and went his way. Thus lightly did Esau
value his birthright.

(Genesis 25)

When Isaac was old and his eyesight had
failed . . . he blessed him [Jacob] and said:
". . . Let nations serve you, peoples bow
down to you. Be master of your brothers;
may your mother's sons bow down to you.
Cursed be those who curse you, blessed be
those who bless you."

. . . his brother Esau returned from hunting . . . saying, "Sit up father . . . that you
may bless me." His father Isaac said to him,
"Who are you?" He answered, "I am Esau,
your first-born son." . . . He answered,
"Your brother came deceitfully and received
your blessing." Then he said, "Must he,

[41]

true to his name Jacob, supplant me now a second time? He took my birthright and now he has taken my blessing." . . .

Esau bore Jacob a grudge because of the blessing his father had given him. He said to himself, "The time of mourning for my father is coming; then I will kill my brother Jacob." . . . She [Rebecca] summoned . . . Jacob and said to him, "Your brother Esau intends to revenge himself on you by killing you. Listen to me, therefore, my son; flee to my brother Laban in Haran. Stay with him awhile until your brother's fury subsides."

(Genesis 27)

Meanwhile, Jacob left Bersabee and journeyed toward Haran. He came to a place where he spent the night because the sun had set.

(Genesis 28)

WE TRAVEL from one place to another in a bus quite like any other belonging to the transportation company. It seems to be a typical group of tourists; but this is only a surface impression. No other bus traveling over the highways of Jordan carries a similar group of passengers. In the Holy Land itself it would be difficult to find a group of pilgrims with similar interests. For all of us come with a very specific and distinctive religious background.

After studying the history and the religion of Israel we have formed an overall mental picture. Certain details stand out in our minds while others have receded into the general backdrop. And in journeying through the Holy Land, it is interesting to compare the sights observed with our own mental picture.

In this framework our visit to Bethel proves to be one of contrast — between the place we see and the preconceptions and prejudices we bring with us.

THE CITY AND HISTORY

Historically, Bethel crops up throughout the Bible — in the days of the patriarchs, in the time of Joshua and the Judges, during the period of the united kingdom, the divided kingdom, the return from Babylon, and the battles fought by the Maccabees.

In our tour it seems to be one of the most commonplace and least important towns we have visited — an impression conveyed by the heat, the dust, and the plain houses.

But if I were to review the history of Bethel, I would have to write a great deal. So I shall merely mention a few names which the reader will recognize at once. In this town Abraham pitched his tent. Here Jacob had his nocturnal vision and buried Rachel's nurse. Here Joshua set up camp; here Deborah the prophetess (the great poetess of the heroic age) settled disputes. Samuel roamed around here, and Saul passed through the village after being secretly anointed. Jeroboam converted this town into a religious center after setting up a separate kingdom, and thus introduced idolatry into Israel. On Bethel's altar Josiah sprinkled the ashes of the idols burned in the valley of Kidron.

We could read many pertinent biblical paragraphs as we stand in this town. But present-day tours allow little time for reading. In a very short time we are back on the bus, feeling somewhat disillusioned. Our hasty visit is strangely similar to that of the prophet who came to reprimand Jeroboam. The king had come to offer sacrifice to the golden calf. Standing by the altar he heard someone cry out: "O altar, altar . . . behold a son shall be born to the house of David, Josiah by name, and upon you he shall sacrifice the priests of the high places who burn incense upon you, and he shall burn men's bones on you.

"Now when the king heard . . . [he] put forth his hand . . . saying: 'Arrest him.' But his hand . . . withered up, so that he could not draw it back to himself. . . . Then the king . . . said to the man of God: 'Entreat now the favor of the Lord your God . . . that my hand may be restored to me.' So the man of God entreated . . . and the king's hand was restored. . . . Thereupon the king spoke. . . . 'Come home with me and take refreshment and I will give you a reward.' But the man of God said . . . 'If you were to give me half your house, I would not go with you, nor would I eat bread or drink water in this place. For so it was charged me by the word of the Lord . . ." (1 Kgs 13:2–9).

The World of the Patriarchs

The religious contrast is even more striking.

At the consecration of a church, or on the anniversary of this consecration, the liturgy recalls this place to which we have paid such a brief visit. For Bethel is one of the most sacred cities in biblical history. Its very name proclaims this fact. Once upon a time it was called Luz (which some interpret as "refuge" and others as "village of almonds"). But with the coming of the patriarchs and God's appearances, it became a sacred city and was renamed *Beth-el* (i.e., "House of God"). In other words, the city itself is a temple, a sacred site, a dwelling place for God. That is why the liturgy links its memory to God's presence in our Christian churches.

It is curious how the presence of Jesus Christ, the Virgin Mary, and the Apostles in the Holy Land has been commemorated by the erection of churches and basilicas, while nothing stands as a memorial to the great deeds and heroic figures of the Old Testament. This lack of memorials would be understandable in many places which were the scene of historical events with minor religious import; but Bethel does not fit into this category. Most of the historical events which I mentioned above had explicit and profound religious import. Among them the vision of Jacob stands out.

The banal atmosphere of the whole place led me to conclude that if one wished to have a dream such as Jacob's, he would have to go to the same spot and fall asleep with a prayer to the angel of pleasant dreams.

Jacob was coming from the south, from Beer-sheba. Night overtook him as he approached the town of Luz. He lay down to sleep, using a rock as a headrest. Even summer nights are cool in these mountain regions (2900 feet above sea level). The heat faded with the setting sun, and the night air was free of bad dreams.

"He dreamed that a ladder was set up on the ground with its top reaching to heaven: angels of God were ascending and descending on it. The Lord stood beside him and said: 'I am the Lord, the God of Abraham your father, and the God of Isaac. I will give you and your descendants the land on which you lie. They shall be as the dust of the earth. You shall spread abroad to the west,

[44]

to the east, to the north, and to the south; in you and in your descendants, all the nations of the earth shall be blessed. I will be with you and protect you wherever you go. I will bring you back to this land; indeed I will not forsake you till I fulfill my promise.'

"When Jacob woke from his sleep he said: 'Truly the Lord is in this place and I did not know it.' Reverently he continued: 'How awesome is this place! This is none other than the house of God: this is the gate of heaven.' Jacob arose in the morning, took the stone which he had placed under his head, set it up as a memorial pillar and poured oil over it. He called the place Bethel; formerly the name of the city was Luz" (Gn 28:12–19).

A FLEETING RECOLLECTION

Artists have depicted Jacob's ladder descending miraculously from the sky. Some have painted it as a ship's ladder made of rope and wood; others have imagined a glowing transparent one. I think Jacob's ladder was really a staircase, wide and awesome as the steps of a Babylonian temple, something akin to a temple or the great gate of heaven.

That is why I am reminded of the vision on Mount Tabor, another wondrous happening in the night. Instead of angels there are Moses and Elijah, the splendor of Jesus' divinity radiating from His body, the sweet air of contemplation, and the Father's thunderous voice giving testimony to His Son.

In memory of this vision Christians have erected the most beautiful basilica in Palestine on Tabor. It is a masterpiece of glistening gold and quiet simplicity — the finest work of the architect Barluzzi.

But there is nothing at all at Bethel to commemorate Jacob's heavenly vision. So we must console ourselves with the thought that the vision which took place 35 centuries ago and the accompanying blessing found their fulfillment in the blessing voiced on Tabor: "This is my beloved Son."

6. *SHECHEM (BALATAH):*
BLOODY NUPTIALS

Then Jacob continued his journey . . . and stayed with him [Laban]. . . . He [Laban] brought Lia, his daughter to Jacob. . . . Then Laban gave him his daughter Rachel in marriage. Lia conceived and bore . . . Ruben . . . Simeon . . . Levi . . . Juda. . . . Bala, Lia's maid conceived and bore . . . Dan . . . and Nephthali. . . . Zelpha, Lia's maid, bore . . . Gad . . . and . . . Aser . . . Lia . . . conceived and bore . . . Issachar . . . and Zabulon. Afterwards she bore a daughter whom she named Dina. But God remembered Rachel. . . . She conceived and bore a son. . . . She named him Joseph.

(Genesis 29–30)

Thus [Jacob] . . . became exceedingly rich and had large flocks. . . . Jacob began by mounting his children and wives on camels. Then he took away all his herds, all the property he had acquired . . . to go to his father Isaac in the land of Chanaan.

(Genesis 30–31)

They journeyed from Bethel, and when they were still a distance from Ephratha, Rachel gave birth to a child amid great pain. . . . As her soul was departing her — for she was at the point of death — she named him Benoni, but his father called him Benjamin. Rachel died and was buried on the way to Ephratha, that is, Bethlehem. Jacob erected a memorial over her grave . . . Jacob went to his father Isaac at Mamre in Cariath-arbe, that is Hebron.

(Genesis 35)

[46]

Shechem (Balatah): Bloody Nuptials

ON THIS trip we take enough provisions for a couple of days. Other times we would leave Jerusalem in the morning and return in the evening. But Shechem is too important in biblical history for just a cursory visit.

We have seen it from the highway as we traveled back and forth to different places; we looked down on it from Mount Gerizim; and we paid a quick visit to it one hot day around noon. Each new view revealed another aspect of this city, linked of course to some biblical story.

CURIOSITY AND FEAR

From the highway we could make out two distinct settlements: one more stable and made up of brick and adobe houses and dotted with fig and olive trees; the other, a newer settlement composed of barrack houses and tents. This scene is repeated in different parts of the country. As the Israeli forces advanced, Arab families fled from the war, hoping to return some day to recover their belongings. But they lost everything, and today they live like refugees. I do not know whether this refugee colony gets along well with the permanent residents, but from a distance it seems that the two groups live alongside each other without intermingling. The refugees do not participate in the normal life of the town because they cannot own their own plot of land, and there are no factories in which they can work. Perhaps intermarriage might serve to unite these two groups. But it is not my place to propose solutions.

In ancient times this town had much the same appearance — but on a much smaller scale. A few houses surrounded by a wall lay sequestered at the foot of Ebal, guarding the caravan route through the narrow gorge. A short distance away, a small encampment of tents had been set up on the plain by some nomads from the north. The nomad chief, a man named Jacob, met with the king of the city, Hamor, and bought ground for an encampment. The deal was made, and they — Canaanites and a band of men who are not yet a nation but who cherish a promise and a blessing — began to discuss their common way of life in the peaceful central valley of Palestine. Perhaps an intertribal marriage would bring these two peoples together? Is this God's plan or will the promise be kept

[47]

unshared in the bosom of the small band? For a short time it appears that the two groups will unite.

When we get off the bus to visit the excavated city, the inhabitants eye us with curiosity. There is no fear in their eyes, but it must be a novel experience for them to see a group of strangers, all dressed in white cassocks and wearing tropical helmets. Their curiosity is greater than ours.

Fear appears on their faces when we try to take photographs. Even in the most picturesque places, where the inhabitants could be justly proud of the natural scenery, the people are afraid of photographers. Perhaps some foreign photographers have insulted the people in some way; perhaps they have instilled this attitude in the people. At any rate, as long as we just look at each other, everything is all right.

THE SPARK OF LOVE

It all started with a stroll taken out of curiosity (Gen 34). A young girl, wide-eyed and innocent, leaves her father's (Jacob) encampment, separates from her girl friends, and walks toward the nearby town to take a look at the girls of that region. She might have been attracted by their clothes — the Canaanites knew how to dye wool — or by the gold jewels and stones which they fashioned after Egyptian models and in native style.

The girl does not realize that she too is watched by eyes which are less innocent. The fires of passion lurk behind this gaze. In a moment the daughter of Leah had been ravished by Shechem, Hamor's son.

"Sichem said to his father Hemor: 'Get me this girl as my wife.' Now Jacob heard that Sichem had defiled his daughter; but his sons were out in the fields with his stock, so he held his peace until their return."

Even today courtship is not the customary procedure in these regions. When the time comes, the father must try to obtain a wife for his son. The son makes known his preference, and may complain about his father's slackness, but the actual negotiations are out of his hands.

[48]

Shechem (Balatah): Bloody Nuptials

A PROMISING DEAL

"Hemor, the father of Sichem, came out to Jacob to speak with him. Now Jacob's sons came in from the field as soon as they heard the news. They were aroused and very angry because Sichem had committed a crime against Israel by lying with Jacob's daughter — an intolerable crime. Hemor said to them: 'My son Sichem has set his heart on your daughter; give her to him as wife. Intermarry with us; give us your daughters in marriage and marry ours. Live with us, and the land will be yours; dwell and trade and settle here.' Sichem, too, said to her father and brothers: 'Let me find favor with you; I will pay whatever you demand of me. Increase the marriage price and gifts as you will. I will give whatever you demand of me; only give me the girl as wife.'

"The sons of Jacob answered Sichem, who had defiled their sister Dina, and his father Hemor; and they spoke deceitfully. They said to them: 'We cannot do this: give our sister to a man who is uncircumcised; for to us that would be a disgrace. We will agree to you only on condition that you become like us, by having every male among you circumcised. Then we will give you our daughters and take yours; we will live among you and become one people. But if you refuse to be circumcised, we will take our daughter and depart.'" (Gn 34:1–20).

Those final words are very significant: "We shall be one people." For a moment it seems that a marriage will solidify the two peoples, because the Canaanites are disposed to accept the terms. The small group chosen by God will unite with another tribe to form a new nation. Palestine will become their home and they will increase rapidly in accordance with God's blessing.

But this is not Yahweh's plan. He has chosen only the children of Abraham, not the Canaanites. His blessing will be realized within the line of Abraham, and from him alone will sprout a great nation. It may take time, but God has centuries at His disposal. His people will grow steadily in the fertile delta of the Nile. It is not yet time to settle in the land promised to Jacob.

The peaceful settlement contains an undercurrent of treachery. It will be broken in a bloodbath of vengeance. And through this bloodbath God's plans will be fulfilled.

[49]

The World of the Patriarchs

AT THE CITY GATES

Few tourists bother to scrutinize the dust and the ruins of the ancient city. Excavation went on at this site intermittently. Sellin began the work in 1913. His first excavations produced interesting finds, but World War I interrupted this work. He had to wait thirteen years before he could continue. In 1926 he started a second series of excavations and, with the help of a large number of workers, had excellent results. But he was taken off the project and did not return until 1933. In 1939 he decided to complete the work and publish the final results and conclusions. Again war intervened. This time Sellin did not survive.

In his very first excavations Sellin discovered the famous triple gate which was of such great interest to scholars. We had seen a rough sketch of it and an architect's reconstruction. So our disappointment was keener when we came to view it firsthand. Even before the second series of excavations, the Arab villagers began to use it as a quarry. The ready-made stones became their building materials. When Sellin returned, he found only the despoilers; we can barely make out the place where the gate stood.

But we are still interested in this gate because of its place in the ancient history of the city. However, a second gate discovered in a later investigation might be a more likely candidate. It faces the plain to the east rather than the mountain to the north. And it opens to a spacious courtyard where the town's population could congregate as they were wont to do in the days of antiquity.

"So Hemor and his son Sichem went to the gate of their city and spoke to their fellow citizens. 'These men,' they said, 'are friendly; let them dwell with us and trade in the land, since there is ample room for them. Let us marry their daughters and give them our daughters to marry. Only on this condition will the men agree to live with us and form one people: all the males among us must be circumcised as they are. Will not their stock, their property, and all their beasts be to our advantage? Let us agree with them, so that they may dwell with us.' All their fellow citizens were persuaded by Hemor and his son Sichem, and all the males were circumcised" (Gn 34:20–24).

[50]

Shechem (Balatah): Bloody Nuptials

REVENGE

The city area is small, but it is surrounded by a strong sloping wall. In certain places one can get a better view of the shape of the wall. Until recently this particular type of defense arrangement had always been attributed to the Hyksos, the conquerors of Egypt. But a couple of years ago some proposed to revise this theory. However, they did not reject the approximate chronological date assigned to these fortifications, the epoch of the patriarchs. We cannot say for certain that this is the wall which Jacob's sons saw from their tents; but it is not a rash supposition. The well-built wall would discourage any frontal assault. So the plan for revenge was thought out carefully. Dinah's two brothers, who felt themselves wronged the most, count the hours and wait, one day, two days . . .

"On the third day, when they were in pain, the two sons of Jacob, Simeon and Levi, Dina's brothers, took their swords, advanced boldly against the city and slew all the males. They put Hemor and his son Sichem to the sword, and took Dina from Sichem's house. Then the sons of Jacob went out, attacked the sick men, and sacked the city, because their sister had been defiled. They took its flocks, herds and asses, whatever was in the city and in the fields. All its wealth, its women and its children they carried off; and they looted whatever was in the houses. Jacob said to Simeon and Levi: 'You have brought trouble on me, making me loathsome to the inhabitants of the land. . . . I have but few men; if they unite against me . . . my family will be destroyed.' They answered: 'Should our sister have been treated as a harlot'" (Gn 34:25-31).

Jacob and his family had to head southward; the moment for occupying the Promised Land had not yet arrived. Shechem still endures for the archaeologist; the palace and the temple, excavated by Sellin in successive excavations, remain standing. But Shechem disappears from biblical history for five centuries, to reappear in the story of Abimelech.

A RECENT EPISODE

The ancient story begins peacefully: the family of Jacob (or

[51]

Israel) buys some land in Palestine. But it ends tragically: the
Canaanites murdered and Jacob a fugitive. It brings to mind the
course of recent events. Again the Arabs were living in Palestine;
again the Jews, descendants of Jacob, come in peace to buy some
land, ready to pay the Arabs' highest price. The small legal deal was
part of a much larger operation: the Jews planned to occupy the
land peacefully by means of such deals. Finally, the Arabs caught
on to the plan. Moslem dealers warned of the danger and the British
magistrates prohibited such sales. But neither action was effective.
Neighboring Nablus was one of the first places where the Arabs
rebelled against the British policy of admitting Jewish immigrants.
The bloody result of the peaceful sales was war. There were many
betrayals and intrigues; and in the end the Arab inhabitants had
to flee before the Jewish newcomers.

And who is the woman in the modern version of the story? The
bride-to-be is not a woman of flesh and blood, but the land itself.
The Jews have plowed and watered and cultivated the earth to
make it fertile. The new inhabitants of Palestine have a deep love
for their land and an amazing ability to make it productive, even
where it was once sterile. With manly vigor they have mated with
their betrothed, the land of Palestine.

7. THE PLAIN OF DOTHAN

> When Joseph was seventeen years old,
> still a mere youth, he was pasturing the
> flock with his brothers . . . and he brought
> a bad report to his father concerning them.
> Israel loved Joseph the best of all his
> sons because he was born in his old age.
> He made him a long tunic. When his
> brothers saw that their father loved him
> best of all his sons, they hated him and
> could not even greet him.
> Now Joseph had a dream, and when he
> told it to his brothers, they hated him the
> more. . . . So his brothers envied him,
> while his father pondered the matter.
>
> (Genesis 37)

OUR visit to Dothan did not hold any unexpected surprises. The trip is easy to make because Dothan lies quite close to the highway between Jerusalem and Nazareth. But its appearance in the Bible is connected with important events. Here Joseph was sold and taken into Egypt; and thus the history of the chosen people took on a new and decisive aspect.

Strangely enough, it was only in 1953 that excavations were begun on the hill overlooking the plain itself, although it was very enticing to the archaeologist. An abundant water supply made it an ideal spot for setting up operations; there were even houses which could be rented.

But one basic problem remained: renting the land so that the excavations could proceed freely. The proprietors were wont to be exacting in their demands. And when there are many different proprietors to deal with, negotiations become very complicated.

But Doctor Free took a hand in the business and eventually was completely successful. He brought groups of American pilgrims to

Palestine on six different occasions; each time he had them visit the plain of Dothan and its hill. Finally, in 1953, he was able to negotiate a contract. He paid the rental fee and the high costs of excavating out of his own pocket.

EXCAVATION RESULTS

Do we not at times find the same enmities and jealousies between Christians as between Joseph and his brothers? Joseph, after all, was not completely blameless. He was pampered and given better clothes, so naturally he aroused some antipathy. And he was not very prudent in telling his dreams to his brothers. Undoubtedly he was aware of the strained relations and should have realized that his stories would scarcely win people over. The enmity of the others, although understandable, does not excuse their plan of murder. One brother, who shared the enmities of the others toward Joseph, did not wish to take part in the deed and strove to save his brother's life at least. Only their father, who loved all of them, pondered over the meaning of Joseph's dreams. Does not our common Father embrace us all in spite of our enmities?

This rather sentimental digression was prompted by my recollection of the excavator. Doctor Free is a Fundamentalist, and a man who has lived up to the name of Christian by his charity to visitors of every confession and by the religious attitude with which he has approached this work.

He was not there during our visit because he takes off during the summer. But our guide was able to tell us of these two traits. When our tour was over, the foreman brought out a small unpretentious guest book which all thirty-two of us signed.

One could justly say that Doctor Free's piety has been rewarded by the rapid progress and the fine results of the excavation.

Our first view of the excavation was something of a surprise. In other places we would usually have to climb a hillside to look down on the various levels burrowing into the rock. Here we find a smooth slope with a newly built staircase providing easy access to the different levels excavated so far. The levels are in excellent condition and arranged neatly along the slope. In a short time the excavator was able to draw conclusions which would have demanded months of comparative testing in other sites.

But archaeological levels are not new to us, so we are not especially attentive to them. The novel sight for us is the wide ladder which mounts toward the wall and turns off to the right. The pottery remains prove that this stairway was in use in Joseph's day. It would be too much to say that Joseph himself went up and down these stairs. But it would not be rash to suppose that his brothers used it in visiting the city.

THE COUNTRYSIDE AROUND DOTHAN

The most interesting sight is not what has been unearthed in the *tell* by picks and shovels, but the view from atop the hill. We have journeyed here from Judea, a barren region of rocky mountains quite unsuited for livestock. Joseph came the same way in search of his brothers, but he came from Hebron farther south, a region just as barren as this one.

Jacob had sent his sons out to pasture the flock in the north. He then sent Joseph to see how they were doing. The herdsmen had halted for awhile on the plain of Shechem; we too had stopped there and enjoyed the change from Judea. Our eyes, dazzled by the glaring sun in Judea, were able to relax in the green countryside of Samaria.

Joseph did not find his brothers at Shechem. Another herdsman tells him: "I heard them say that they were going on towards Dothan." Joseph continued northward — as we ourselves did — and his eyes came to rest on the plain of Dothan.

The plain itself is not very extensive but it has three appealing features: abundant grass for the herd to feed on and the shepherd to lay on; stout fig trees with burnished leaves untainted by dust; and gurgling water, bright blue and green, to quench the thirst. A thick pipe crosses the road and dumps a copious stream of water into a cistern large enough to bathe in. And a little farther on there is a well for the camels of a caravan and the flocks of the shepherd.

It is a pleasure to read the biblical account under the shade of a fig tree, while the waters gurgle pleasantly nearby. Joseph's brothers see him coming and say: "Here comes that dreamer! Let us therefore kill him and throw him into a cistern; we can say that a wild beast devoured him. Let us see then what becomes of his dreams." But Reuben intervenes to save Joseph's life. Instead of killing him they drop him down a dry well.

At that moment God's mysterious providence appears on the back of a camel. A caravan of merchants from the other side of the Jordan is approaching. They had started out from the region of Gilead around Lake Gennesaret, forded the Jordan near Beth-shan, crossed the plain of Jezreel, and headed south along the well-traveled central route. Dothan was one of the normal stopping places because it provided water and a pleasant rest. And so they stop as usual. But this time they are offered a business deal. They readily agree to buy the slave at such a low price. During the journey he will help with the work, and he will fetch a good price when they reach their destination.

So the Madianite merchants continue on their way southward (as we are doing) with their cargo of spices and their newly acquired slave. Little do they realize that the slave has an invisible companion: Yahweh's providence accompanies Joseph to give a sharp twist to the history of His chosen people.

II. *THE CHOSEN PEOPLE IN EGYPT AND SINAI*

When he called down a famine on the land
    and ruined the crop that sustained them,
He sent a man before them,
    Joseph, sold as a slave;
They had weighed him down with fetters,
    and he was bound with chains,
Till his prediction came to pass
    and the word of the Lord proved him true.
The king sent and released him,
    the ruler of the peoples set him free.
He made him lord of his house
    and ruler of all his possessions,
That he might train his princes to be like him
    and teach his elders wisdom.

Then Israel came to Egypt,
    and Jacob sojourned in the land of Ham.
He greatly increased his people
    and made them stronger than their foes,
Whose hearts he changed, so that they hated
        his people,
    and dealt deceitfully with his servants.
He sent Moses his servant;
    Aaron, whom he had chosen.
They wrought his signs among them,
    and wonders in the land of Ham.

He sent the darkness; it grew dark,
    but they rebelled against his words.
He turned their waters into blood
    and killed their fish.
Their land swarmed with frogs,
    even in the chambers of their kings.
He spoke, and there came swarms of flies;
    gnats, throughout all their borders.

For rain he gave them hail,
  with flashing fires throughout their land.
He struck down their vines and their fig trees
  and shattered the trees throughout their
    borders.
He spoke, and there came locusts
  and grasshoppers without number;
And they devoured every plant throughout the
    land,
  they devoured the fruit of their soil.
Then he struck every first-born throughout
    their land,
    the first fruits of all their manhood.
And he led them forth laden with silver and gold,
  with not a weakling among their tribes.
Egypt rejoiced at their going,
  for the dread of them had fallen upon it.

He spread a cloud to cover them
  and fire to give them light by night.
They asked, and he brought them quail,
  and with bread from heaven he satisfied them.
He cleft the rock, and the water gushed forth;
  it flowed through the dry lands like a stream,
For he remembered his holy word
  to his servant Abraham.
And he led forth his people with joy;
  with shouts of joy, his chosen ones.

And he gave them the lands of the nations,
  and they took what the peoples had toiled for,
That they might keep his statutes
  and observe his laws.

(Psalm 104[105])

Yet he saved them for his name's sake,
  to make known his power.
He rebuked the Red Sea, and it was dried up,
  and he led them through the deep as through
    a desert.
He saved them from hostile hands
  and freed them from the hands of the enemy.
The waters covered their foes;
  not one of them was left.
Then they believed his words
  and sang his praises.

[58]

But soon they forgot his works;
 they waited not for his counsel.
They gave way to craving in the desert
 and tempted God in the wilderness.
He gave them what they asked
 but sent a wasting disease against them.

They envied Moses in the camp,
 and Aaron, the holy one of the Lord.
The earth opened and swallowed up Dathan,
 and covered the faction of Abiram.
Fire broke out against their faction;
 a flame consumed the wicked.

They made a calf in Horeb
 and adored a molten image;
They exchanged their glory
 for the image of a grass-eating bullock.
They forgot the God who had saved them,
 who had done great deeds in Egypt,
Wondrous deeds in the land of Ham,
 terrible things at the Red Sea.
Then he spoke of exterminating them,
 but Moses, his chosen one,
Withstood him in the breach
 to turn back his destructive wrath. . . .

       (Psalm 105[106])

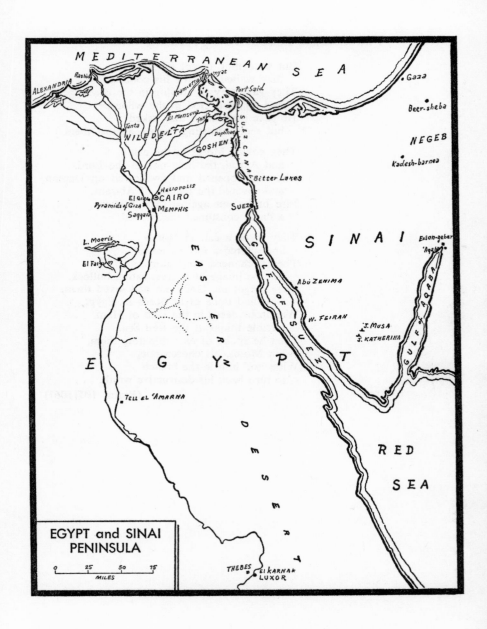

EGYPT and SINAI
PENINSULA

0   25   50   75
MILES

8. GIZA AND ALEXANDRIA: A STUDY IN CONTRAST

ONE of the preoccupations of present-day philosophers is technology. This man-made creation threatens to devour man himself. The individual worker is lost in the ranks of "mass" man and production rolls along the assembly line. As our train nears Giza (El-Gizeh), our eyes fall upon the pyramids and we cannot help but think about technology. After all, they are the products of technology, not of artistic creation. With the help of the imagination we examine the smooth marble slopes; but even with the setting sun reflecting off the four-sided mound of stone, it scarcely looks like a work of art. This geometrical mass is one of technology's boasts. And that is how it is described by commentators: "perfect symmetry of design, finely honed corners, accurate placement of the stone segments, etc." Egyptian engineers of forty-five centuries ago did not know about the pulley, still this ignorance did not hurt the technological aspects of the construction. For technological techniques are relative. Today we can still marvel at what the Romans accomplished without any knowledge of electricity. And in a few decades people will marvel at the things accomplished by our grandparents without any knowledge of electronic computers. In the more distant future people will sympathize with the engineering feats we achieved without the help of atomic energy. Technology continues to develop new techniques, but its inhuman laws remain. And if we decry the abuses of modern technology, we cannot be blind to the incomparable brutality of ancient technology, despite its achievement.

"Assembly-line production." A line of pyramids exemplifies the procedure. There is no testimonial to the countless workers who built them. Hundreds of thousands gathering rocks in the quarries (we visited the Aswan quarries to get a firsthand idea of this

[61]

terrible labor); thousands transporting them down the Nile and lifting them over the mounds of sand by rope; a more terrible form of anonymity could not be imagined. Although our system has flaws, the modern worker often enjoys the fruit of his labor, even if only indirectly. Today's dehumanized masses are producing useful objects which make our lives more comfortable or add pleasant complications. But in antiquity the anonymous masses toiled to erect a dwelling for a dead king, an uninspiring and spiritless dwelling. For me the pyramids are a cold testimonial to death, a piteous technological wonder.

ART VERSUS TECHNOLOGY

Behind the barefoot guide, who earns his piasters conducting the more stouthearted tourists, I have climbed the steep stairs leading to the top of the pyramid. From there I watched the sun set in the desert. It is a fine observation post in a level countryside. But this never occurred to the ancient engineers. Indeed, such an idea would be blasphemous, for the dead pharaoh lay buried inside. Those Egyptians were content to watch the shadow of the pyramid lengthening over the desert sands.

There is one thing which restores my faith in these ancient inhabitants of the Nile. In the many tombs at Saqqara I saw charming scenes of domestic life, men at work and animals at play, etchings and reliefs sometimes colored with genuine artistic intuition and marked by a love for expressive detail and a harmonious style. Inside these tombs, shielded from the fierce midday heat of the desert, I felt myself a true brother of the ancient artist. I strove to interest myself in the same things which interested him. I felt the heartbeat of our common life and our common humanity; and the tomb seemed to be anything but a tomb. I understood the real significance of the seemingly trite expression — "the enduring nature of art."

By contrast the pyramids are for me the most tragic and sepulchral thing imaginable. They are a geometrical memorial to the death of a pharaoh and to the piteous death of many workers. As a matter of fact, on my last free morning I did not go with my companions to "snap" the pyramids while the light was right. I chose to entomb myself in the dimness of the museum and to live with Egypt's real artists of old, her creative geniuses who continue to live even though they have not etched their names on rocks or reliefs.

And let us not praise the pyramids simply for having lasted all these centuries. To be sure, survival can be praiseworthy. The arched vault of a Gothic cathedral spanning the finely shaped columns is worthy of praise. One can justly delight in viewing the temples of Karnak. And our eyes and hearts can enjoy the sight of the Doge's palace at Venice mounted on a double row of gracious slender columns. But there is no merit or grace in this mass of rock standing in the desert. Indeed, it is easier for this inert mass of granite to perdure than it is for a slender palm tree. But the concrete blocks laid so symmetrically only add up to an inert mass.

ALEXANDRIA

In Alexandria one gets quite a different impression. There are countless memories a person would like to bring to life. Alexandria's significance for Western culture is incalculable. The school of Alexandria preserved and propagated the spirit and the substance of Greek culture. One has only to mention a few important names: Demetrius Falerius — the library's founder, Euclides, Apelles, Eratosthenes, the geographer Callimachus, Theócritus, Apollónius of Rhodes, and an army of students. Our Greek heritage comes to us in great part through Alexandria. But there is no palpable trace of all these memories in the city, save perhaps a street name here and there. There are no traces of the lighthouse, the library, or the museum. The tourist cannot even look at some designated spot and say: "here stood ——— "

Starting from the Christian era the memories grow in number. Besides noting the Septuagint translation of the Bible done in Alexandria, one can mention names like Panthenus, Origen, Cyril, and Athanasius. Alexandria is rich in memories of our Christian culture. But these geniuses have not left us any souvenirs.

This lack of souvenirs prompted our meditation in the city, for it stands in sharp contrast to the nearby pyramids. The spiritual heritage of Alexandria lives on throughout the world and suffuses every aspect of human life. It is a living force whose untapped resources are still discernible to men's eyes and hearts in times of crisis.

The great geniuses of Alexandria project a huge life-giving shadow over the face of the earth, in contrast to the mute lifeless shadow of the pyramids. Thus the absence of concrete memorials in Alexandria seems to be a vivid lesson in the true nature of culture.

AN ANCIENT EGYPTIAN OPINION

In a similar vein an anonymous Egyptian writer chants the glory of the scribe as opposed to that of the pyramids.

Now if you do these things, you will grow perfect in the art of writing. The wise scribes lived on after the divinities who predict the future, and left behind an imperishable name. They passed away, but they live a full life even when their parents have been forgotten.

They did not erect metal pyramids nor iron tombs. They had no heirs to mention their name to their children, except for their writings and their wise books. Papyrus was their priest, the writing board their beloved child; their books of wisdom were their pyramids, the red pencil was their child, and the etching stone was their wife. The great and the small were their children.

Other men constructed gates and buildings for themselves, but these have crumbled into dust. Their funeral obsequies have died away; their gravestones are covered with dust and their tombs are forgotten. But the scribe's name is still uttered in the fine books he wrote, and his memory endures forever.

Resolve in your heart to be a scribe so that your name will rank among theirs. A book is more enduring than a stone engraving or a lofty tomb. Men erect tombs and pyramids so that their name will be recorded in history. And certainly in the eyes of men this is a fine monument. But man dies, his body returns to dust, and his relatives descend into the grave. Only the written word continues to live on the lips of men. A book is more enduring than the work of a builder of tombs, better than a huge palace or a temple monument.

. . . The sages foretold the future. Their predictions came true and were recorded in their books. The children of other nations inherited their words, as if they were their own children. Although they have disappeared, the written word keeps their memory alive. (Circa 1300 B.C.)

THE BIBLE: A CASE IN POINT

From Alexandria we can broaden our meditation to include the people of the Old Testament whom we have been following on our journey. The Jews once constructed a magnificent temple to match those of Babylon. And they had an almost magical trust in it (something akin to the pharaohs' attitude toward their pyramids). But God permitted Nebuchadnezzar's general to raze this temple. The Jews built another temple, more modest in scale. Later kings added to it, and looked on it as something indestructible. To regard it as perishable was considered blasphemous. But its total destruction, as predicted by Jesus Christ, came to pass. Stone was not the true base of this religious culture, nor was the temple the keystone of this religion. However, successive generations of Jews did build a written monument — the Bible. Some rabbis distorted it with their arbitrary interpretations. But God would not allow them to alter its substance, and in His own way He preserved the sacred text for us. Then came the Roman emperors. They took these sacred books and burned many of them. But again God did not permit His own book to be destroyed. Today some commentators still strive to efface the profound spiritual and religious content of this written monument. But God still prevents it. He will never permit it to happen because this spiritual monument still sheds its salvific light on our religion. With its profound religious core, it still speaks to us in readily understandable human tones. It remains a work of eternal religious value and enduring artistic worth.

A BIBLICAL OPINION

Approximately 1000 years after the Egyptian writer cited above, one of the sacred authors also spoke of the excellence of the scribe, who contemplates truth and shares his wisdom with others.

The scribe's profession increases his wisdom; whoever is free from toil can become a wise man. How can he become learned who guides the plow . . . fashions carved seals . . . toils away in the furnace heat . . . molds the clay. . . .

All these men [the artisans] are skilled with their hands, each one an expert at his own task; without them no city could be lived in, and wherever they stay, they need not hunger. They do not occupy the judge's bench, nor are they prominent in the assembly; they set forth no decisions or judgments, nor are they found among the rulers; yet they maintain God's ancient handiwork, and their concern is for exercise of their skill.

How different the man who devotes himself to the study of the Law of the Most High! He explores the wisdom of the men of old and occupies himself with the prophecies; he treasures the discourses of famous men and goes to the heart of involved sayings; he studies obscure parables, and is busied with the hidden meanings of the sages. He is in attendance on the great, and has entrance to the ruler. He travels among the peoples of foreign lands to learn what is good and evil among men. His care is to seek the Lord, his Maker, to petition the Most High, to open his lips in prayer, to ask pardon for his sins. Then, if it pleases the Lord Almighty, he will be filled with the spirit of understanding; he will pour forth his words of wisdom, and in prayer give thanks to the Lord, who will direct his knowledge and his counsel, as he meditates upon his mysteries. He will show the wisdom of what he has learned and glory in the Law of the Lord's covenant. Many will praise his understanding; his fame can never be effaced; unfading will be his memory, through all generations his name will live; peoples will speak of his wisdom, and in assembly sing his praises. While he lives he is one out of a thousand, and when he dies his renown will not cease (Sir 38:24–39, 11).

9. REVOLUTIONARY INNOVATIONS
AT EL AMARNA:
A DIFFICULT CHOICE

OUR stay in Egypt did not last long, but it covered much ground. In a couple of weeks we spanned almost fifty centuries.

Egypt's long history and her enduring splendor in the plastic arts forced us to make a choice as to what we would see. Besides the quantity and the quality of her art works there was one more factor involved — the sand. Who would imagine that this same sand, which covered our compartment, our baggage, our clothes and our skin, would prove to be the capital element in preserving Egyptian antiquities? Even papyri, which fade so quickly in the heat, have survived in Egypt.

Unlike Greece, Egypt never had a group of experts who selected the finest works and sought to preserve them for posterity, thus making our choice for us (even though, strangely enough, these Greek experts worked in Alexandria). Here in Egypt the sand has not been selective in its role of preserver. Only the grave robbers have been selective, stealing the best jewels and transportable objects.

So we must make our own selection. And in doing so we must remember the purpose of our trip — to visit Old Testament sites.

We can get an overall view of culture and art, thanks to that handy invention — the museum. (The word itself originated on Egyptian soil.) The Cairo Museum contains many extraordinary treasures, nicely mounted for the convenience of the visitor and arranged chronologically for the benefit of the scholar.

I am going to start out in a relatively cool section of the museum. Once there I begin to walk around slowly, starting from the most remote ages of antiquity. Imposing statues in diorite, with burnished surface and regal mien; the famous functionary KA-APER walking

[67]

with quiet dignity and holding his staff authoritatively, wearing a lofty, intelligent expression. Next comes the middle empire with its collection of woodcuts depicting scenes of everyday life: wooden puppets with movable arms; the hard, almost cruel, face of Sesostris; the finely carved body of young Amenhotep.

The corridor comes to a large hall off to the right. A strange feeling of something radically new overtakes us. Two large statues dominate the collection. We are in the fourteenth century B.C., the biblical era; it is the hall of the great reformer Akhenaton. Our choice is made.

JEWISH MONOTHEISM

The distinctive phenomenon in Jewish life as a whole was its monotheism. Its culture was subject to various influences, especially from Mesopotamia. One day the Israelites were overcome with the desire to have "a king as other nations do." They even could be affected by the idolatry of the Canaanites, their neighbors and predecessors in the land of Palestine. But the sacred books remain intact and offer undeniable proof of their monotheism. The exiles in Babylon who chose to return to their homeland were completely cured of their wicked idolatrous tendencies.

Some researchers refused to accept this strange historical phenomenon as irreducible. So they looked for different explanations. One such explanation pointed to polytheistic elements in the Bible. It refers, for example, to "the gods of other nations." However, such phrases can be readily explained and prove nothing. Some claimed that polytheism existed in the Bible, but that the prophets removed all traces of it. A fine example of assertions unsupported by proof. All we know for certain is that literary themes borrowed from other peoples were thoroughly purified before being incorporated into the sacred text. Others explained Jewish monotheism by the evolutionary dialectic. But it has been awhile since people accepted the evolutionary scheme in the area of religious thought. Indeed it seems to work the opposite way. Primitive peoples preserve a monotheistic religion much better than advanced cultures. The latter tend to develop polytheism for various reasons. Social functions become more specialized and new independent states are created. These developments tend to foster a polytheistic form of religion.

Finally, some prefer to look for monotheistic precedents in other countries. And in this attempt they are especially attracted by the great enterprise of the visionary pharaoh who smiles down on the visitor from his stone pedestal.

THE GRAND ADVENTURE

Inheriting an empire greater than any ever known before, this descendant of the great warrior and organizer Thothmes III, with his prominent chin and curious wide eyes, strove with all his might to force monotheism on his subjects. Until then, the chief god had been Amon, thanks to the efforts of his priests. Among the people themselves Osiris held a special place because of his well-known feats recorded in legends and myths. The young king declared every cult to be heretical save that of Aton, and he began to extirpate the names of the other gods. However, his own father, Amenophis III, bore a heretical name derived from that of Amon. The Pharaoh, scorning the duty of filial piety, erased his father's name from stelae, obelisks, and inscriptions. To make matters worse he too was called Amenophis, after his father; so he changed his name to Akhenaton. At that time the capital of the kingdom was Thebes, a city dedicated especially to Amon. The young Pharaoh did not want to destroy the splendid city (so every winter Luxor, situated near ancient Thebes, is full of tourists). He decided to build a new capital dedicated to the one God. It was called Akhetaton and was located halfway between the capital of the ancient kingdom, Memphis, and that of the newer kingdom, Thebes. But his religious ideas were too radically different from those of old. The new faith did not take roots and grow among the people. The courtiers devoted to the person of the emperor, the inhabitants of the newly erected city, and public officials either embraced the new faith or compromised. But outside this area the new cult exerted no influence, and the enmity of Amon's priests grew fiercer. One day Akhenaton disappeared from the throne, but we do not know if he died of natural causes. He suffered the same fate as that which he imposed on his predecessors. His name was scraped off inscriptions; documents signed with his name were glossed "the wretch of Akhetaton," and the new sovereign returned to the ancient capital. His second son-in-law and heir had to change his name from Tutankhaten (= Aton's life is beautiful) to Tutankhamon. The old way of life was restored. But the newly built city was respected and still survives as testimony to a strange unsuccessful religious adventure.

AN INSTRUCTIVE FAILURE

Why did this venture fail? It is difficult to form an idea about the exact nature of this religion. But it seems to have been a true monotheism, not a henotheism. The difference between the two is quite simple. In every city there is only one mayor; but in a nation there are many mayors and only one president or king. According to henotheism, every nation has only one God, its own god; according to monotheism, there is only one God over the whole world and the whole cosmos. Apparently it is not exact to say that this one God was the sun; rather, the sun was the incarnation of this one God. We feel sympathetic to Akhenaton's aim because it seems to be a step forward in religious thought, a sincere attempt at purifying religious worship. But it was a purely human effort and it failed. This failure points up the difficulties encountered by monotheism in these civilizations. And it highlights the amazing phenomenon of Jewish monotheism.

By this time the Jews had been in Egypt for two centuries. They continued to grow in numbers, but to all appearances had little contact with the Egyptian court. It is scarcely probable that Akhenaton's reform exerted much influence on them. They continued to worship the God of their forefathers, the God of Abraham and Jacob. Moses, who was steeped in Egyptian culture, probably heard stories about the great reformer. But if our chronology is accurate, these stories would have reached him distorted by the hatred of Amon's priests. Historically it is very risky to say that Akhenaton's monotheism was responsible for that propounded by Moses. No proof can be presented in support of this claim. On the other hand, we do have an historical document which affirms the opposite. The monotheism of Moses triumphed in spite of his people's fickleness, because God intervened directly and personally. What a pharaoh could not accomplish with the resources of a vast empire was accomplished by a daring chieftain who launched his people on a nomadic life leading ever so slowly to the promise.

ARTISTIC REVOLUTION

Akhenaton's religious reform caused an artistic revolution as well. The court painters and sculptors had mastered all the traditional techniques of style. They are revealed in the balance and equilibrium of some of their more finished works. But the most interesting techniques of this school are revealed in their less finished work. When this court inaugurated its new style, it apparently provoked a scandal; and when the treasures of El Amarna were discovered in the past century, the general public did not know what to make of this art. Today we are fully prepared to appreciate these works.

Some of their characteristics would fall under the heading of "realism." In representations of animals we find a keen feeling for nature which surpasses mere decorative intent. And there are paintings of scenes which one would scarcely expect to find in the tomb of a pharaoh, scenes which one would expect to find in the servants' quarters.

Perhaps the most revolutionary innovation is a kind of expressionism. Today we have learned the value of deliberate distortion for expressing interior or transcendent realities. In some of the El Amarna works this distortion almost reaches the point of caricature; in other works the effect is extraordinary. One example is the large statue of Akhenaton standing in the right-hand corner. The face is elongated; the high cheekbones and the hollow cheeks break the unity of the curve and extend almost beneath the chin. The lines are clearly and finely drawn, and more expressive than a simply drawn line. It is as if they are trying to catch light and shadow exactly right. The eyes, almost unseeing, are narrowed to reveal the inner spirit, distant and remote. The lips are full and prominent, hinting at a mixture of sweetness and disillusionment.

One can have aesthetic reasons for leaving a statue unfinished. Sometimes it seems that certain techniques which strive for absolute perfection actually deprive a work of its expressive force; while the sketchy outline conveys the emotion of the artist or the subject directly and completely. Consider how much interest the scholar and the general public have in the sketches of the great artists; take, for example, the extraordinary popularity of da Vinci's sketch for the Christ of the Last Supper.

The El Amarna artists have left us a series of studies in plaster and other unfinished pieces. And the unfinished head of Nefertiti in the Cairo Museum, with guidelines traced in pencil, is more readily convincing than the other head, finished and colored, which is preserved in Berlin. A series of chalk masks somewhat akin to pencil sketches possesses great vitality and character. They are, perhaps, the most modern, the most contemporary of Egyptian art works.

LITERARY REPERCUSSIONS

The literature of this period also reflects this profound interest in nature. In the hymn to the sun which a priest had engraved on his tomb, we find a simple but joyous delight in nature, unembellished by purple patches. It is a pleasant meditation, rich in detail and incorporating every aspect of creation into a magnificent symphony. It is really a hymn to creation, somewhat reminiscent of the Pastoral Symphony. But it does not have the sonorous solemnity of Haydn's hymn to nature; rather it has an air of placid tranquility with everything fitting into place in perfect harmony.

> You shine brightly in heaven's horizon
> Living Aton, source of life.
> When you arise in the East,
> You fill the earth with your beauty.
> . . . .
> Your beams flood the ends of the earth which you have created.
> . . . .
> When you set in the West,
> The Earth is in darkness, as if in death.
> Men lie on their beds with heads covered,
> They do not see each other.
> If their goods were stolen from under their noses,
> They would not notice it.
> The lion leaves his cave,

All the reptiles start to kill,
Because darkness rules; the earth grows still,
When its creator sets in the sky.

In the morning, when you appear in the sky,
Shining as the day-star,
You drive away the night and send out your beams,
And the two kingdoms rejoice;
Men get up and stand erect,
Because you have awakened them.
They wash and dress,
And raise their arms to praise your appearance.

All the animals feed in their pastures,
The trees and fields come to flower.
Birds fly from their nest
And praise your name with wings outstretched,
While the flocks gambol in the fields.
Every living thing on land or in the air
Awakes when you arise for them.
Ships plow back and forth:
Their course is clear when you appear.
Even fish in the river rejoice.
Because your beams pierce the sea.

You create the ovum in the woman, the seed in man.
You make the embryo leap in the womb,
And dispel its tears
And nourish it even from the womb.
You vivify everything you have created.
On the day it leaves the womb
You open its mouth and satisfy all its needs.
When the chick peeps inside the egg-shell,
You give it nourishment.
And when the time comes to break the shell
It sallies forth into the light of day,
Standing bravely on its own two legs.

How varied are your works: hidden from the face of man.
You alone are God, without any equal.
You, and you alone, create the earth according to your plan:
Human beings, tame animals, and wild beasts:
Everything that walks the earth,

Everything that flies in the air.
Every land and nation: Syria, Nubia, and Egypt.
You give every man his proper place,
And everything he needs.
Each one gets his food, and the days of his life are numbered.
Their tongues are different,
Their features and their skin;
You mark off the different people.
You create a Nile in the lower world,
And let it gush forth to feed the people of Egypt,
When you will.

You have created Egypt for yourself.
Lord of all those for whom you care;
Lord of the lands over which you shine;
Majestic Aton of the day.

You also vivify the most distant lands;
For you have set a Nile in the heavens, which descends on them,
And sweeps over the mountains, like a huge green sea,
To irrigate their fields and towns.

How wise are your designs, Lord of eternity:
You give the heavenly Nile to every land,
And to the animals which roam through the desert;
But the Nile which springs from the bowels of the earth is for
    Egypt alone.

Your beams nourish the fields;
When you rise, they live and grow through you.
You send the seasons to preserve your creatures;
The winter cools them; in the summer they can enjoy you.
You set the heavens at a distance so that you could rise in it.
And contemplate all your works.
You are one alone, and show yourself as the living Aton,
Shining, spinning, rising and setting;
You take on a million shapes.
Towns, cities, fields, roads and rivers:
All eyes look toward you
For you are the day-sun. . . .

THE BIBLICAL VERSION

By retouching this poem and interpreting the sun as a symbol, we could easily apply it to the true God. And in fact, this Egyptian hymn did exert direct or indirect influence on Psalm 103, the exquisite chant which is usually called "the psalm of creation." It exhibits the same gentle interest in nature, the same balanced religious fervor; but it is more tightly knit and constructed with greater stylistic perfection. It was not in vain that the Hebrews were endowed with more literary talent than any other people in the ancient Orient. And in this psalm God's transcendence over creation is clearly expressed:

> Bless the Lord, O my soul!
> O Lord, my God, you are great indeed!
> You are clothed with majesty and glory,
>   robed in light as with a cloak.
> You have spread out the heavens like a tent-cloth;
>   you have constructed your palace upon the waters.
> You make the clouds your chariot;
>   you travel on the wings of the wind.
> You make the winds your messengers,
>   and flaming fire your ministers.
>
> You fixed the earth upon its foundation,
>   not to be moved forever;
> With the ocean, as with a garment, you covered it,
>   above the mountains the waters stood.
> At your rebuke they fled,
>   at the sound of your thunder they took to flight;
> As the mountains rose, they went down the valleys
>   to the place you had fixed for them.
> You set a limit they may not pass,
>   nor shall they cover the earth again.
>
> You send forth springs into the watercourses
>   that wind among the mountains,
> And give drink to every beast of the field,
>   till the wild asses quench their thirst.
> Beside them the birds of heaven dwell;
>   from among the branches they send forth their song.
> You water the mountains from your palace,
>   the earth is replete with the fruit of your works.
> You raise grass for the cattle,
>   and vegetation for men's use,

Producing bread from the earth,
  and wine to gladden men's hearts,
So that their faces gleam with oil,
  and bread fortifies the hearts of men.
Well watered are the trees of the Lord,
  the cedars of Lebanon, which he planted;
In them the birds build their nests;
  fir trees are the home of the stork.
The high mountains are for wild goats;
  the cliffs are a refuge for rockbadgers.

You made the moon to mark the seasons;
  the sun knows the hour of its setting.
You bring darkness, and it is night;
  then all the beasts of the forest roam about;
Young lions roar for the prey
  and seek their food from God.
When the sun rises, they withdraw
  and couch in their dens.
Man goes forth to his work
  and to his tillage till the evening.

How manifold are your works, O Lord!
  In wisdom you have wrought them all —
  the earth is full of your creatures;
The sea also, great and wide,
  in which are schools without number
  of living things both small and great,
And where ships move about
  with Leviathan, which you formed to make sport of it.

They all look to you
  to give them food in due time.
When you give it to them, they gather it;
  when you open your hand, they are filled with good things.
If you hide your face, they are dismayed;
  if you take away their breath, they perish
  and return to their dust.
When you send forth your spirit, they are created,
  and you renew the face of the earth.

(Psalm 103[104])

Revolutionary Innovations at El Amarna

POLITICAL CONSEQUENCES

Akhenaton's religious reform also had political consequences. Thothmes had organized his domains in Syria and Palestine. These smaller kingdoms were ruled by vassals loyal to Egypt out of fear or personal convenience, the two motives utilized by the ruling power. Egyptian officials and military garrisons insured the success of these two coercive forces. To the north of these vassal states lay a weak Hittite kingdom; to the northeast, a strong Mitanni kingdom ruled by a powerful Indo-European tribe. As long as Egypt was ruled by capable pharaohs, the Mitanni kingdom had to fall back discreetly. But when weaker pharaohs came into power, the Hittites conquered the Mitanni, put pressure on Syria, and the vassal states in Syria began to fold. The petty kings became jealous of one another and accusations flew back and forth. Intrigues, accusations, flattery, and graft keynoted this era. Egypt would have to step in if her prestige and respect were to be restored. But Egypt was ruled by a pharaoh who had devoted himself to a religious reform; he paid no heed to these political events. Meanwhile, in the royal archives of Akhenaton (El Amarna) this correspondence piled up. It was written in the *lingua franca* of that day, Accadian, in cuneiform characters. This collection was discovered by a woman who was digging in this spot; today it is parceled out among the museums of London, Berlin, and Cairo.

When the Israelites were ready to invade the Promised Land, they would find a similar situation. After the restoration of Rameses II, there is another period of decadence and the region is divided into petty kingdoms. But a new factor of great historical importance enters the picture: the great migrations of the seafaring peoples and the Aramean tribes.

The political and artistic testimony of El Amarna is well worth a long stay in the museum. There is more to examine here than at the excavation sites or the ancient capital. The most valuable finds have been parceled out among the different museums.

This museum tour helps us indirectly to understand some elements in the Old Testament. The religious and political failure of El Amarna contrasts sharply with the silent growth of the chosen people moving toward their dramatic debut in history.

[77]

10. *IN THE NILE DELTA*

THE palm tree is the distinctive tree of Egypt. Magnificent groves of these trees guard the Nile and its canals. But it stands out even better when it stands alone — with its slender upright trunk and its palm leaves waving tremulously. In one of its finely curved branches some birds have built a nest. Oblivious to the vital activity running through the trunk and to the men who seek its shade and dates, the birds live on, singing and procreating, until it is time to fly elsewhere. Then they leave, and scarcely a trace of the abandoned nest remains.

If you examine a wall map of the Nile, you might well imagine it to be a tall palm tree. Its trunk of water ascends upward decorated with sand and orchards. At the top we find a fan — the Nile delta with its winding canals and green fields, where agriculture flourishes.

THE TRUNK OF THE NILE

Almost all the important events of Egyptian history have occurred along the trunk. Its northern and southern extremes are key points in history. In remote antiquity they lived an independent existence. When they were united, Egypt began to exist as a nation; and the pharaohs were called the "kings of the two regions." In the era of pyramids the center of gravity was in the north. In the golden age the center of gravity was in the south: Thebes and Luxor. From the south the great conquerors, Thothmes III and Rameses II, set out on their campaigns. The dream of one pharaoh to set up a capital in the center (El Amarna) lasted only for a short while.

Today the artistic centers of interest in Egypt are concentrated in the two extremes. In Luxor we find the best preserved monuments of antiquity and the objects maintained *in situ*. At Cairo we find the gigantic museum which houses many outstanding artistic works of old.

In its long history this nation has been affected by movements which started in the south and worked their way up, like insects invading a plant from the roots. These were the pharaohs from Ethiopia.

Another invasion, that of the hated Hyksos, swooped down from above. But we must go up to the delta to tell this story.

IN THE GREEN TRIANGLE

The Hyksos are remembered in Egyptian history as birds of prey, vultures who wreaked havoc on the country. It is almost certain that they came from Asia. They yoked horses to their war chariots — a device unknown in Egypt — and built sloping walls to defend their cities. The Hyksos drove down the Nile, sacking cities and conquering the people. But they set up their capital by Lake Menzaleh in the far north, near the Mediterranean.

We set out in taxis from Cairo to visit Tanis, formerly Avaris, the capital of the Hyksos. The cars are big and comfortable, and the highway is excellent. Taking full advantage of the route, we stop first at Tel-el-Yehudiye, the refuge of those Jews who fled from the persecution of Antiochus in the days of the Seleucids. It is a sandy spot whose chief merit, as far as we are concerned, is the memory of the great archaeologist, Petrie. All the interesting objects were removed years ago, and the sand has again covered the excavations. A fox darts away when we appear at the top of the mound.

Next we visit Tel Basta, ancient Bubastis. It is a large field covered with archaeological debris: truncated columns, capitals, cornerstones bearing inscriptions. It is as if a giant had hurled pieces of rock over the area. In fact there was a giant, the excavator who removed the stones and carried the best off to Cairo for exhibition. In particular there was a magnificent collection of bronze cats and bronze statues of the cat-headed goddess (Pasht).

We skip on from rock to rock rather disrespectfully, peering inquisitively at the finely engraved hieroplyphs. Bubastis reminds us of the pharaoh who invaded Palestine after Solomon's death.

The Chosen People in Egypt and Sinai

It seems that the biblical events connected with Egypt are all stored in the delta.

We continue along the fine highway to Faqus; there a lesser highway leads to the north. The countryside turns yellow and all we can see is sand. Only in the distant horizon can we glimpse a few strips of water and green vegetation.

The first to sound the alarm is Vidal, the photographer. His sharp eyes discover that there are no lakes or palms at all. It is a mirage. Another Spaniard rejects his opinion sarcastically. But the driver, whose best language is Arabic, confirms Vidal's view laconically: "No water." He could explain the mirage better in Arabic, but we would not understand it so clearly.

Sure enough, as our auto continues on, the palms disappear. The lakes seem to lie farther on, surrounded by blue shores; and bright pebbles seem to glisten in the waters. But suddenly the whole scene disappears into thin air.

Everyone has heard about mirages. But it is quite an experience to encounter them on a large scale for the first time. I must confess that I had never expected to encounter them in this form. In the future, when I come across the phrase — "It's a mirage" — it will have a very distinct meaning for me and will remind me of an unforgettable sight.

ZOAN = AVARIS = TANIS = SAN EL-HAGAR

At last we reach the sandy enclosure and slowly gaze around at the impressive ruins. As the tour is set up, we have not yet visited Luxor or Saqqara; so this is our first close contact with antiquity, apart from the pyramids, which are of a different order.

We move around at a leisurely pace, and a guide comments on the different objects. I remember certain things very vividly. The monumental entrance gate flanked by huge statues; a short tunnel running down to the water level of a well; green and blue streaks of light and a touch of dampness in the midst of all the sand. Rameses' name engraved everywhere, almost obsessively — on every column, obelisk, statue, and columnar capitals. And most impressive of all is a colossal statue of Rameses II which has toppled over. The legs are broken, the eye sockets stare emptily at the sky, the impotent closed fist hangs alongside his thigh, and the hieratic beard rests on his chest. What a fine image for the vision of Daniel!

According to the most probable theory, Joseph's arrival in Egypt occurred during the period of Hyksos domination. This would explain the cordial reception granted to those Asians who came to Egypt in search of food and land. Joseph becomes the nation's overseer and lives in a palace here at Avaris. His family settles down a little farther south, in the region of Goshen. The story of Joseph (one of the favorite stories in our Western culture) unfolds here: his temptation, his steadfastness, his imprisonment, and his dream interpretations. Soon his brothers come to Avaris from Hebron. By rushing home on their camels, they could have told Jacob the news within two weeks.

In our visit we have learned that the records preserved at Tanis correspond to the reign of Rameses II and to biblical events. But now we must interrupt our visit.

THE LAND OF GOSHEN

We head back along the same road. The mirage returns to play with us: "Catch me if you can." But this time we know the game and let it bounce around in front of and behind our car. We are anxious to get on the fine highway which will take us to Ismalia. Once again the countryside becomes a rich verdant green; once again we pass the bird's nest.

The Israelites spent several centuries in this region. What did they do here? Egyptian life and history were unfolding along the Nile trunk. The fight for national independence succeeded in driving out the Hyksos. But the Israelites, living right in the path of these events, stood apart and continued to grow in this fertile region.

Such was the plan of God. He was going to give the Promised Land to His chosen nation. But Abraham's grandchildren were only a group of families. If they were to grow into a nation, they would have to spend some time in a quiet fertile region. The chosen race would grow in numbers over the course of generations.

Thus the descendants of Jacob, living freely as the birds and keeping aloof from the problems of other men, prepared for the moment when God would intervene. Now they had grown into maturity and were ready to take possession of the Promised Land. Their present home had only been a temporary nest.

Before their departure other events were to take place, which bring us back to Tanis once again.

RAMESES II — THE ARCHITECT

It took a persecution — the first "pogrom" in Jewish history — to make the Israelites leave Egypt; for they were reluctant to leave such a fine land.

The one responsible for this persecution seems to have been Rameses II. The title "architect" is a misnomer; actually, building was an obsession with him. His gigantic statues were scattered all over Egypt. He expropriated buildings constructed by his predecessors and had his name inscribed on them. He set out to build new cities or enlarge existing ones, even in the Nile delta, far from the traditional capital, Thebes.

It was here that he came face to face with the Jewish people. He tried to tax them with hard work, to extinguish their male children, and to oppress them in every way he could. In Tanis we saw some ramparts. The sand is swept back only on one side, and in certain areas one can still see the lines between the adobe bricks. One of the tasks forced on the Jews was to make a certain number of bricks each day. And they themselves had to find the straw.

The situation became unbearable. Then came the plagues. And one historic day this great people set out for the land which God had promised. The Pharaoh tried in vain to stop them. The fallen statue with its hand closed impotently symbolizes the first victory of the chosen people. It is the best souvenir of our visit to Tanis.

"Before their fathers he did wondrous things, in the land of Egypt, in the plain of Zoan" (Ps 77:12 [78:12]) .

But before we accompany the Israelites on their trip out of Egypt, we must travel along the trunk of the Nile to learn the history and the culture of this nation so often mentioned in the Bible.

11. *BY THE SUEZ CANAL*

THE usual route of the crowds leaving the Nile delta is toward the northeast, through the isthmus of Pelusium. Using this route they would come out on the seacoast of Palestine.

The sacred author knew this full well, and so he explains to his readers the reason which prompted the strange route of the Israelites. "God did not lead them by way of the Philistines' land, though this was the nearest; for he thought, should the people see that they would have to fight, they might change their minds and return to Egypt. Instead, he re-routed them toward the Red Sea by way of the desert road" (Ex 13:17–18).

We might add a few more reasons. God wanted His people to undergo a period of intensive training, separated from the surrounding cultures. For awhile they were to be alone with God, apart from the world. So He opens up a path through the sea to insure their escape, then closes it again to prevent them from backtracking.

By the time they reached the Promised Land, they will have seen the powerful arm of God at close range and should be purified of pagan influence.

But, whatever God's reasons may have been, the route of the Israelites determines ours.

A MILITARY ZONE

The magnificent highway cuts through the ancient land of Goshen and curves toward the south, just before reaching Ismalia. Then it runs parallel to the canal. It is a quiet, peaceful region. But this peace is maintained and preserved by military installments along the highway. Barbed wire, machine-gun nests, jeeps, guard posts; army tents being aired in the sun; and now and then a pleasant park with ball fields, soldiers bathing in the sun, and convoy trucks parked nearby. Our taxi speeds along and we are unable to examine the view closely. But the overall impression is that we are looking at a well-organized military setup, on the scene and ready for immediate action.

Then we come to the Bitter Lakes. Many are of the opinion that the Israelites passed over the sea at this point. How worried they must have been! Here they were, as yet unaccustomed to long marches and God's prodigies, pursued by Egyptian war chariots.

The landscape is very beautiful. Dusk is falling and the light pattern is clear and simple. The colors do not fuse or blend but rather stand out in contrast with one another. White mountains, yellow sand, blue sea and sky. Colors unadorned by adjectives, like the glow of a stained-glass window in a cathedral. It is not the scene for an impressionist, but for a primitive or medieval spirit.

THE HAND OF GOD

Some scholars place the crossing point at Lake Timsah near modern Ismalia. We cannot pinpoint the exact spot but that does not matter. We still can contemplate on the rod of Moses extended toward the waters, and the hand of God stretched out over this rod.

This miracle was the basis for the subsequent history of the chosen people, and they never forgot it. It became the symbol of liberation and a type of the future redemption.

I will sing to the Lord, for he is gloriously triumphant; horse and chariot he has cast into the sea. . . . The Lord is a warrior, Lord is his name! Pharaoh's chariots and army he hurled into the sea; the elite of his officers were submerged in the Red Sea. The flood waters covered them, they sank into the depths like a stone.

Your right hand, O Lord, magnificent in power, your right hand, O Lord, has shattered the enemy. In your great majesty you overthrew your adversaries; you loosed your wrath to consume them like stubble. At a breath of your anger the waters piled up, the flowing waters stood like a mound, the flood waters congealed in the midst of the sea . . . (Ex 15:1 ff.).

This was the song of Moses, and it was echoed many centuries later by the prophet Habakuk: "You tread the sea with your steeds amid the churning of the deep waters. I hear, and my body trembles; at the sound, my lips quiver" (3:15–16).

It is evening when we reach Suez to rest from our hard journey and to prepare for tomorrow's long trek.

12. *IN THE SINAI PENINSULA*

AN EXCURSION to Mount Sinai in 1954 was a real adventure. Cars made the trip quicker than camels could, but they demanded closer attention. In Sinai there would be no food, no gasoline, no post office, no telegraph, no drugstore, no repair shops. In other words, we would have to provision ourselves for the trip, bringing spare auto parts and matches for cooking.

It is a very complicated endeavor. The many details involved can be handled by a special agency or by one of the touring guides who has made the trip many times.

There are seventeen in our group: ten Americans, six Spaniards, and one Hollander. Only one is not a priest, so we must include portable altars in our equipage.

During the night the drivers complete the final preparations. Our alarm clock goes off at 3 a.m. We take turns celebrating Mass on the portable altars set up in the hotel lobby.

All our excess baggage has been left in Cairo, as we are taking only the essential items with us. The taxis are at the door at 5:30. We tend to the last detail: filling our canteens with fresh water or hot coffee. The trip will prove that the coffee lovers were right.

The morning air is cool and the city is silent. We head northward along the coast. Soon we begin to doze off. Then we are awake once again. We have reached the crossing point and must wait awhile. It is an unavoidable delay in our trip — the minister's permission is needed to enter the peninsula.

But we clear the checkpoint without any difficulty and meet on the other side.

Our car takes the lead and rolls along a fairly decent highway parallel to the coast. The highway is kept in good shape because it connects with the oil fields and manganese mines. Industry exerts more influence than the tourist trade.

The Chosen People in Egypt and Sinai

THE FIRST STOPS

We soon reach our first stopping place. According to the Bible, the Israelites left the Red Sea and journeyed three days without sighting water. Then they came upon an oasis. Excitedly they threw themselves on the ground and started to drink. But the waters were bitter to the taste. Moses cast a piece of timber into the water and it turned sweet. By calculation this little oasis would be three days distant from the Red Sea; so it has been pinpointed as the oasis mentioned in the Bible. We approach one of the pools approximately 32 feet in circumference and topped by a double crown of palms. Water gushes up continually from the bottom; it is not drinkable but we succumb to the temptation to savor it with our tongue.

The photographers test the light on the peninsula for the first time. But I am satisfied to enjoy the impressions awakened within me. There is a certain inconvenience in not being able to preserve this fleeting view for others; even the snapshot cannot capture certain elements: the clear bright light, the pleasant scents, the wonderful air. And the photographers have no time or desire to savor these fine elements.

I feel a sense of well-being deep within me, and it grows as we go on.

We continue along the coast. The mountains on the left are still distant and low. Nothing blocks our view.

Our next stop is at a point where the highway skirts the sea. It is an unexpected pleasure. We find ourselves bathing in the salt water and tasting the watermelons which scatter black seeds over the sand near the highway. Our bathing suits dry quickly in the hot sun and the desert air.

GOOD-BYE TO CIVILIZATION

A lane cuts off from the highway to the right and leads toward the petroleum tanks in the distance. The coast line has curved away from the highway; but we go on looking at the opposite shore, glistening in the sun which is still over Asia.

Around Wadi (stream) Garandel the highway grows worse. The

mountains to our left begin to take on color and shape. And when we reach the stream itself, the pleasant countryside draws our attention from the sea lying off to our right.

According to most commentators, this is the second stopping place of the Israelites. "Then they come to Elim, where there were twelve springs of water and seventy palm trees . . ." (Ex 15:27). I would say that there are more than seventy palms, and several tamarisks of a paler green. I begin to fall under the spell of the green. My eyes drink in the pure color and my body feels refreshed. The heat has already become a nuisance and the coffee in our canteens is disappearing.

The distant landscape is quite suggestive. The highway cuts a little way into the interior, and follows the meanderings of the wadi. The sides of the pass grow narrower and finally become the white walls of a gorge. Already we are leaving the small prairie on which the village of Abu Zenima is located. A few houses, a mosque, stores, and an enormous extensive mound of blackish earth. It is manganese which has been brought down by cable cars from the mountains eighteen miles away.

This is the last village bearing evidence of our modern civilization. It is the last place where we shall find gasoline, Coca-Cola, and — wonder of wonders — a ball. I see a child running after a bouncing ball, embodying in his play the human condition. We still have our pleasant, refreshing games; adults still know how to pass time playing with their children. It is the last sight I recall before we plunged toward the interior.

UNCONQUERED NATURE

The highway continues to skirt the sea for a short while, but now it runs along the mountain spurs sloping to the shore. The terrain becomes rough and uneven. It is as if we had landed on some wild, unexplored coast. The cars swerve left and climb a smooth slope. They leave the sea behind and come to a halt on a narrow esplanade.

Now we must get out of the cars. Once they are lightened they will be able to climb a steep, crooked stretch of uneven road which runs for 160 feet. We walk up and in a moment the four cars are ahead of us. From now on the road is all uphill and could scarcely be called a highway. We must climb over 5000 feet on a stretch of road which is part dirt and part sand, partly rocky and partly smooth. And all along this mountainous road there are countless curves.

The next official stop will be at the oasis of Feiran — for a meal. Even though we are behind schedule, we have decided to wait for the oasis where we can have water and shelter. The stretch of road between the sea and Feiran is the roughest. The heat is fierce. Our auto has yielded the lead to that of our guide who knows every inch of this road.

I would like to mention only the most striking impressions of this part of the trip.

"SPINGERE!"

We come to what is considered a trail. It consists of stone piles or erect posts indicating impassable sections. If it were not for these stone markings, we could not pick out the highway amid the sandy and rocky ground. However, at times the sandy area is more unstable and requires closer attention. It is interesting to watch our guide attack these stretches. He knows the precise angle and the proper speed to take. And when he crosses the shifting section, he stops to watch the progress of the other cars. He is like an expert seamstress threading the needle on her first try, or a bull thrusting expertly at the cloth provoking him.

But our auto is not so deft in its movements; perhaps because the driver is not so expert, or because the motor does not give the necessary velocity, or because there are two canons inside. At any rate, the car stalls in the sand. Our driver tries vainly to get traction. Then we hear a single Italian word from him, probably the only one he knows — *spingere* (push) ! We have to get out of the car, clear the sand from behind the wheels, and put our shoulder to the task. We must push until the wheels catch hold and roll over the sandy area. There is a certain fun in our first attempt. Then Don Vidal, the photographer, leaves us to do the pushing while he takes a few feet of film. By the third try there is no fun in this business at all. It is just a pain in the neck. A nimble auto with a skillful driver — he knows a fair number of Italian words — comes up behind us to help in the attempt. The car stalls again and Felipe, a native of Leon, comes to help us push. When he puts his weight behind the job, the wheels begin to turn. After we have crossed the treacherous area, the next car follows without any trouble. "There's nothing to it." Only once have we had the dubious pleasure of being stalled thus far; and this time we didn't mind giving the car a push.

More complicated mishaps soon follow. Some part of the motor refuses to shut off; it has been overheated or forced in some way. We make our first unscheduled stop and spend the time stretching our legs, looking at the scenery, and acquainting ourselves with the desert inhabitants: Bedouins and camels. Camels with their awkward gait and dull-witted eyes; boys with big timorous eyes; a little girl who clambers over the rocks, barefoot, to make a path for the goats; women shrouded in black with heavy scarfs covering their head and face, bedecked with brightly colored earrings, necklaces, and beads. For a nine-year-old boy whose ordinary diet consists of little more than milk and cheese, a caramel is a new taste experience; it is enough of a bribe to get his permission for a "snap." And soon his companions are ready to pose for the camera of their own free will.

The trip continues. We fall farther behind schedule and there is no hope of making up the time. We come to another tourist attraction: the "Valley of Inscriptions." On a large rock surface near the road the pilgrims of old inscribed their name or some comment or the picture of a camel. These inscriptions have been preserved for seventeen centuries.

At certain turns of the road we catch a glimpse of Mount Serbal, the colossus which stands guard over the Feiran oasis. We are getting close to our destination. But the cars stall a few more times and we have to push — now without any trace of enjoyment or good humor. The most serious mishap occurs at one stopping point where the water spouts from the motor and scalds the arm of our driver. A bandage of sorts is put on it, but there is not much else we can do except to continue.

The Chosen People in Egypt and Sinai

THE PASSING VIEW

We are worn out from the traveling, the heat, and the unforeseen delays. But the scenery does not bore us at all. The whole time we are traveling through a mountainous region completely devoid of vegetation. The roadway is nothing but rocks and sand. One would think that this would be very monotonous. We pass alternately from narrow gorges to open stretches varying only in length or width. Yet we are not bored.

It reminds me of the sea crashing against a rocky coast. I often spent several hours on the northern coast of Spain watching the waves batter the cliffs. It was a simple game repeated over and over again. But one never tired of looking at it. The next evening I returned to watch some more.

If you take away the motion and depict the same scene on a large canvas, you will never tire of looking at it. Here in Sinai it is the mountains which delight you. There are no extraneous elements like the woods in Germany or the lakes in Switzerland. There are no villages or fields, just mountains. But you never tire of watching the interplay of shapes and colors, and the peculiar aura of light throughout this region.

It is impossible to describe in detail the rise and fall of the crests; and it is also impossible to describe the succession of forms and colors. But I can say that anyone who wants to enjoy the simple unadorned beauty of a mountain region should come to the Sinai peninsula.

THE DESERT OF FEIRAN

On the last leg of the trip, we play a game with the sun. The mountains hide it and then show it in turns. At times it appears above a high peak, at times it gleams through a crevice, at times it is completely hidden behind a crag.

The first palm tree appears. We have reached the outskirts of our oasis and rest is near. We pass small groups of palm trees growing in narrow rows, then full groves of them, and finally we come to a stop in front of a house and garden. We enter through a garden path, loaded down with different food containers, and drop everything on a stone table in the terrace. Here we find a Greek monk who tends the garden with some Bedouins. The food is cold, the typical fare to be found in tin cans. It has a clinical aroma and the vapid flavor of homogenized food. The Americans are able to adapt to this kind of food but we Spaniards concentrate on the melon. The only hot fare is coffee and tea prepared by a servant. It is almost 7 p.m. when we begin to eat. The sun has dropped behind Mount Serbal which looks down on us through the trees in the terrace. But we are already so far behind schedule that there is no sense in rushing. The last leg of the journey will have to be made in the darkness of night.

TRAVEL BY NIGHT

It is almost 9 p.m. when we start out again. We stall one more time in the sand not far from our starting point. Our car takes the lead, and the others follow close behind so as not to get lost in the dense labyrinth of palm trees. We glance back now and then to make sure the headlights of the next car are still behind us. It is a slow, eerie trip. The headlights gleam through the columns of trees and reflect off a brook which we pass. The tires make more noise on the sand by night. After several miles amid palm trees the four cars turn into a broad road. The stretch of road ahead is quite safe, so we do not have to keep our eye on the cars behind us.

THE STARRY SKY

Night has blotted out the mountains. The earth is but a monotonous noise beneath our tires. We can do nothing but look at the sky. I have never seen such a sky before. People have talked about the night sky in the Orient and its countless stars. And I myself have seen the night sky in Damascus, Amman, Jerusalem, and other cities. But nothing compares with the view in Sinai. Here there are no clear-cut constellations or single stars twinkling in the distance. Here there is but one mass ensemble of light covering every inch of sky, countless beams brightening the whole area. There are no dark patches of sky. The whole sky shines with a pleasant glow. Unlike today's cities which turn on their many lights frantically to catch the attention of the traveler, the sky has lit its many lamps and placed them all in this vault above us as an invitation to pleasant contemplation. It is truly a pleasant celestial sight, a decorative display beyond the power of man, a fitting accompaniment to Dante's verses or Beethoven's Ninth Symphony.

It sets us thinking and several biblical verses come to mind. We recall the night on which Yahweh called Abraham from his tent and said: "Look at the heavens and, if you can, count the stars . . . so shall your posterity be" (Gn 15:5).

We softly chant several hymns to Mary: *Salve Regina, Salve Mater.* And under this soothing sky we arrive at the Monastery of St. Catherine. It is past 11 o'clock. Our car has made up ten minutes of lost time. At last we are all inside the monastery, more than four hours behind schedule.

A Greek monk, who speaks French, kindly attends to us. He puts us four in a room, asks if there is anything else he can do, then disappears until morning.

After the lengthy journey we find ourselves with soft beds and a pleasant duty: to get up when the sleep wears off.

13. *FIRST DAY IN SINAI: TOURING THE MONASTERY*

I WAKE up refreshed, much earlier than I had expected. I look out the exquisite balcony to contemplate the mountain which stands opposite. It is a wondrous display of colors. I would like a color photo of this display, but not the ordinary kind which loses so much of the original. Even a painter would have great difficulty in capturing these colors and the surrounding aura of light. The objects stand out sharply and there does not seem to be any atmosphere; but the light conveys a mysterious presence which is clearly perceptible to the eye, indeed, one might say to the whole body.

Once again I sense the feeling of well-being which I had yesterday morning, but which faded in the heat of the day and the wearying journey. It is a strong feeling pervading everything, a pure sensation of well-being which cannot be localized in the sense of touch or hearing or sight. Usually a person drinks water with his meals and pays no attention to it. Then, all of a sudden, one day he notices that the water tastes delicious, unlike anything he has ever drunk. It is not cold, just cool. But somehow he experiences its crystal purity in a vivid way and the sensation seeps through every pore in his body. Something similar happens to me on this first morning in Sinai. I feel the keen pleasure of breathing, seemingly for the first time. The air is not scented but it is pure, free from dust, heat, and odors. This seems to be a negative quality but I experience it as something positive. It is a delicious feeling which suffuses my whole body, a pure sense of well-being.

We celebrate Mass on our portable altars in three shifts. Our breakfast consists of items which we have come to know well — melon, eggs, canned ham, canned marmalade, canned cheese, and instant Nescafe. It is a very good breakfast.

In the late hours of the morning we tour the monastery. The

monk who looks after visitors is our guide. He speaks in French, commenting laconically on the various sights. He is content to tell us the date of each object or section we visit.

I shall just mention a few of the more striking sights and my overall impression.

The basilica is a mixture of elements, styles, and tastes, the kind of amalgam which displeases our generation. Magnificent columns painted a drab color, silver reliefs, fine inlaid works, two bronze lions, many icons of no special value. In short, the basilica contains some exceptional pieces but there is no overall organization. We are not accustomed to view a church as a museum housing many different kinds of objects. We enjoy a church as an artistic unit; even though our concept of unity is rather elastic. It is not a question of prejudice against the Greek churches. For we also are somewhat annoyed with the Basilica of St. James of Compostela, with the tombs which disfigure the Holy Cross in Florence, and with the display of sepulchers which detract from the beautiful architecture of Westminster Abbey.

In this basilica there are two things which deserve special mention.

A PAGE FROM HISTORY

The monk leads us through a dim corridor and low doorways. In a small vestibule we all take off our shoes in accordance with an historical custom. We shall do this many times in visiting mosques. But here in the tapestried vestibule we do it out of a deeper inner conviction. We are going to enter a venerable spot.

Before the Israelites fled Egypt en masse, Moses himself had to flee. In defending or avenging another Israelite, he had killed an Egyptian, and the news came to the ears of the pharaoh. According to tradition, Moses took refuge in the mountainous reaches of Sinai where the pharaoh would have difficulty in trailing him. He spent several years there tending flocks and acquainting himself with its roads and water holes. This knowledge would serve him in good stead later on, when he was the chief of a wandering people.

One day, while he was pasturing the herd, he penetrated deep into the mountainous region and found himself at the foot of a high mountain (precisely where this monastery is located, or so some good scholars maintain). Suddenly he saw a bush which was burning but was not being consumed. And he said to himself: "I must go over to look at this remarkable sight, and see why the bush is not burned." When he got nearer, he heard a superhuman voice: "'Moses! Moses!' He answered, 'Here I am!' God said, 'Come no nearer! Remove the sandals from your feet for the place . . . is holy ground. I am the God . . . of Abraham . . . of Isaac . . . of Jacob.' Moses hid his face, for he was afraid to look at God" (Ex 3:4–7).

In memory of this event, we too have taken off our shoes in reverence. Then we enter the sacred spot. It is a semicircular room. The floor is covered with tapestries, the wall with glazed tiles and paintings; many lamps hang from the ceiling. The dim light which creeps through three chandeliers is an inducement to meditation.

In the background there is an arched niche. Once a year the sun's rays, piercing through a mountain crevice, focus here on the site of the bush. Just in front of the niche stands a simple altar with a magnificent slab of chiseled silver. This is the site of the apparition.

"'But,' said Moses to God, 'when I go to the Israelites and say to them, "The God of your fathers has sent me to you," if they ask me, "What is his name?" what am I to tell them?' God replied, 'I am who am.' Then he added, 'This is what you shall tell the Israelites: I AM sent me to you'" (Ex 3:13–14).

Let us not go into a discussion of the different problems involved. We are content to relive mentally this transcendent event in which God shows Himself and reveals His name to men. The supreme being deigns to manifest Himself to man, a finite spiritual being, in this secluded spot isolated from human history and culture.

A visit to this cave is a moving experience for every Christian. Once upon a time pilgrims came here to visit the tomb of St. Catherine rather than the cave, because there was little interest in the Old Testament, and they preferred a New Testament saint to an Old Testament prophet.

Today we know enough to set aside private devotion for the sake of the religious significance of this spot. It does not just commemorate an historical event, but a transcendent theological event. We shall appreciate this better as we walk around the church.

The Chosen People in Egypt and Sinai

In the apse of the church a magnificent sixth-century mosaic depicts the Transfiguration against a gold background. Apart from its value as an antique, it is a true work of art. It did not impress me so much as the mosaics in St. Mark (Venice) which held my attention for a whole morning while I gazed at them with the aid of binoculars. But the theological import of this mosaic was more striking.

A beardless Christ hovers in the center, flanked by Moses and Elijah; at the bottom are Peter, John, and James. The scene is rimmed by a series of medallions representing the prophets, David, the Apostles, and the evangelists. There are thirty-two medallions in all, the remaining ones depicting people involved in the construction of the basilica. And in the front of the apse Justinian and his consort Theodora stand guard.

It would not be surprising to find such a scene in the church on Tabor. But here, at the site of Moses' vision, it seems strangely out of place. But these mute figures provide us with a lesson in theology.

Yahweh's appearance on Mount Sinai (or Horeb) is projected toward the future divine manifestation in which God comes down to live with men and reveals His full majesty on Mount Tabor. Christ is the new Moses who fulfills the laws, the greatest Prophet, who fulfills the prophecies embodied by Elijah. Elijah also was once in Sinai and was visited by God. (We shall visit the spot tomorrow.) Thus the two prophets of Mount Sinai point toward Christ who has now descended in the fullness of time.

It is worthwhile recalling that St. Matthew presents Christ as the new Moses. Christ's five discourses correspond to the five books of the Pentateuch. Matthew's Gospel begins with the phrase "the book of the generations," as do many chapters of Genesis. It, like Deuteronomy, is replete with blessings and curses. The baby Christ is persecuted like Moses, flees to Egypt, and then proclaims the new law on a mount. In short, Matthew selects those events in Christ's life which will point up the parallelism.

By contrast, Luke presents Christ as the new Elijah. Moved by the Spirit of God and acting as a prophet, he restores life to the son

[96]

of a widow, even as Elijah did. He begins his journey toward the Ascension as Elijah did. And so the parallelism continues.

Christ is the central figure in the scene. But the artist was not content to depict the historical figures present at the Transfiguration, because he wished to show us the deeper meaning of the event. So he depicts all the prophets, apostles, and evangelists. The last two people commemorated by medallions represent the ecclesiastical power; Justinian and his spouse represent the civil power.

OTHER OBJECTS OF INTEREST

Curiosity more than devotion leads us to take a peek at a withered branch lying inside a small grating. The monk explains that this branch is a direct descendant of the miraculous burning bush. One scarcely has to believe in the accuracy of the genealogy. We are pleased to read the nice Greek inscription: "in the burning bush which was not consumed, we hail your glorious virginity, O Mother of God." The burning bush was made a symbol of Mary's virginity in early antiquity, and the first monks consecrated their first basilica to Mary Most Holy.

Outside the church we are shown a well which is worked by a lever. This could be the well used by Jethro's daughter, although there is no certainty about the identification. At any rate it is a hot day and the water is refreshingly cool. So we drink heartily while one companion works the pump and another photographs the scene. The biblical story commemorated here is as pleasant as the water. I take the liberty of telling the story (Ex 2:15–22) in my own words.

Moses is fleeing from Egypt and sits down to rest near a well. In a short while seven young girls come along to water their flocks. They are all sisters, the daughters of Raguel (or Jethro). Moses, the fugitive, watches the girls draw water and pour it into the troughs for the sheep. But at that moment some shepherds come along, chase the girls away, and try to use the water. Moses comes to the aid of the girls and helps them to water the flock.

The seven girls are impressed with the stranger. They break the daily routine and hurry home to tell the story. Their father looks at them questioningly. "What are you doing home so soon?" — "Well, an Egyptian man delivered us from the hands of the shepherds and helped us to water the flock." — "Then why didn't you invite him here? Go and invite him in for a meal." Moses accepted the invitation to dwell in this man's house, and Jethro gave him his daughter Sephora as a wife.

It is a pleasant chapter out of pastoral life, a scene without any transcendent meaning. Jethro's treatment of the stranger was a little out of the ordinary, but the marriage deal was typical. In giving one of his daughters to the stranger, Jethro got two more hands to help him with his work. He did not see anything extraordinary about the man who was now tending his flocks, just as we did not see anything of religious significance in those Bedouins who passed us on the road. Yahweh knows how to direct the course of history with poetic simplicity; but He also can reveal His awesome grandeur.

One day He orders Moses to return to Egypt. Moses pretends to be homesick and departs from his father-in-law. Once in Egypt he begins a difficult and active life; so he bids his wife to return to Jethro's house with their children. Sephora returns to sheep-herding and her children already know how to help her.

Then one day Jethro hears of the prodigies worked by God through his daughter's husband. Taking Sephora and her two children, he comes to the Israelite encampment to greet his former herdsman.

"Moses went out to meet his father-in-law, bowed down before him, and kissed him. Having greeted each other, they went into the tent. Moses then told his father-in-law of all that the Lord had done to Pharaoh and the Egyptians for the sake of Israel, and of all the hardships they had had to endure on their journey, and how the Lord had come to their rescue. Jethro rejoiced over all the goodness that the Lord had shown Israel. . . . 'Blessed be the Lord,' he said, 'who has rescued his people from the hands of Pharaoh. . . . Now I know that the Lord is a deity great beyond any other; for he took occasion of their being dealt with insolently to deliver the people . . .' " (Ex 18).

How easy it was for these desert folks to meet God. Isolated from the high cultures of Egypt and Mesopotamia and unaware of the great works of man, they can recognize God's hand in the course of events. What a wonderful afternoon it was for Jethro. Sitting in his son-in-law's tent, he hears Moses' vivid account of the events which he will later describe for future generations. (Meanwhile, the Israelites are encamped in tents on the plain.) And Moses' wife and children will listen to the tale of his exploits with no less enthusiasm. This friendly, informal session was the first version of the Exodus.

Now, many centuries later, we find it easy to relive these ancient scenes evoked mysteriously by the surrounding landscape. And we are touched by their simplicity and profundity.

TREES AND BONES

A visit to the cemetery is absolutely necessary. But since it preserves no biblical memories, we shall make it a quick visit. The cemetery is small and very plain. The cadavers are placed in the earth without coffins. On one of the crosses we read the name of a lay worker: this monk, four years ago, was alive and eighty-two years old. He served as a guide for our caravan chief in an ascent of Gebel Musa. And it was an effort for the robust, 34-year-old American to keep up with the old man. Now he has probably scaled his last peak. At any rate we say an Our Father at his grave.

When the bones have been stripped clean, they are taken from the grave, classified, and put in their proper place in the ossarium. The big bones are put in one place, the ribs in another, and the skull is neatly placed on the large pile. The quantity and neatness of the display diminishes its macabre aspect. It is impossible to estimate the number of bones. Suffice it to say that in its golden days the monastery counted more than 200 monks.

An exception to this display is the skeleton of the holy miracle-worker Stephen who was a doorkeeper in the sixth century. There his skeleton rests, seated at the door with arms crossed on the chest and head bent, wearing a white cassock and a purple skullcap.

From the ossarium we go to a beautiful garden, bright and pleasant. The cypresses lose their gloomy aspect, here between the olive trees. Some turkeys wander awkwardly between the trees, sporting their gaudy red color and their raucous voice; guests for a few years alongside the ossarium which preserves the bones of many centuries.

14. *ON GOD'S MOUNTAIN*

Our initial plan had been more romantic, but it fell through. We were going to climb the mountain in the late afternoon and spend the night there. We would watch the sunrise from the peak and celebrate Mass there. But we could not climb the mountain without a monk to guide us, and they all counseled against it.

We set out shortly before eight o'clock. The night coolness still hangs over the valley. The sun's heat will grow stronger as we move farther from the shady area. Usually travelers make the ascent over the three thousand steps cut out of the mountain. It is an arduous climb and serves to remind people of the trek made by the wayfarers of old. But we prefer to save this route for our descent.

We head southward and find ourselves on a good pathway sloping gradually up the mountain. The only hardship is the heat. One could hardly say we were scaling or climbing. We are simply walking up a winding road. Little by little we are scattered into smaller groups: two Americans in the lead, behind them three Spaniards, then some other groups and a few loners. In one of the groups farther back is the monk who is guiding us; and, along the rocky terrain so well known to them, two Bedouins are carrying the food and water containers. The distance between the groups gradually lengthens.

The group of Spaniards joins the Americans at the top of the road. We stand before a huge wall of sheer granite, over 600 feet high. It glows resplendently in the bright sunlight.

The road continues parallel to the granite wall, and then narrows between two walls. It is a cool passageway aired by a nice breeze, a good spot to take a brief rest. At the end of this passageway the road breaks off. The Americans choose to wait for the others; the Spaniards choose to pick up the road once again. We know that the road joins the last series of 700 steps for the final stage of the ascent, a boring monotonous climb.

On God's Mountain

We approach the summit and one Spaniard takes the lead. Our pace quickens and we lose all sense of fatigue. The steps are of uneven size but firm: smooth stones set into larger blocks along the irregular slope. It is a job which took years, but has lasted for centuries. A final push and we are at the top, about 7500 feet above sea level and 2300 feet above the monastery.

It took our group an hour and a half to make the ascent. The two Americans arrive eight minutes later. And other groups arrive at intervals of fifteen minutes, thirty minutes, or even longer. The summit is a fairly extensive level area which permits us to contemplate the view on all sides. There is a small chapel on it and a small mosque. In the shade it is quite cool. Our fatigue and perspiration disappear quickly and our eyes take in the splendid panorama.

Instead of describing the view, I shall try to meditate on it in much the same way as a classical symphony would. Beethoven introduces some descriptive elements into his Pastoral Symphony, but he is mainly concerned to express his own emotional reactions. I know that it is impossible to paint this panorama in detail; the most I can do is make a few brush strokes. But it will not be too hard to write down the high points of my meditation.

PRIMORDIAL GEOLOGY

Undoubtedly God knows how to pick a proper setting for His activity. Some thirty-two centuries ago, God intervened dramatically in the history of man. The course of human history was radically altered and the repercussions of this intervention are still being felt. For this irruption God chose a spot bypassed by history. The cradles of civilization lay elsewhere; in the narrow region around the Tigris and Euphrates, along the shores of the Nile, and along the narrow stretches of Syria and Palestine which connected these two regions. Poised between these two regions lay the inverted triangle of Sinai. One would think that if history should pass through any area, it should pass through here; but it did not. To be sure, many people passed through its upper area, the region bordering the Mediterranean: merchant caravans, diplomats, armies, and war chariots; migrant Asians seeking Egyptian wheat, the Patriarch

Jacob and his family, the Holy Family fleeing to the traditional refuge from persecutions in Syria and Palestine. But all these people passed along the upper rim of the triangle.

Other activities took place along the left side of the triangle where copper, malachite, and turquoise were mined. The pharaoh shipped slaves to this region and they collapsed in the heat trying to augment the riches and splendor of his empire. From the time of Menes the great pharaohs continued to work these mines, and some established colonies containing wells, cisterns, and temples: Cheops, builder of the great pyramid; Amenhotep in the ancient empire; the vigorous and glorious Queen Hatsepsut in the middle kingdom; Rameses II and Rameses III; Rameses V who closed the mines during a period of decline. But some poor slaves buried in the bowels of the earth can scarcely be considered history.

Countless pilgrims also have passed through Sinai since the beginning of the Christian era; they, like the tourists of today, have left their names or thoughts inscribed on some rock. But this shifting tide of travelers is not history either. There are certain places that are pregnant with history, for example, the plain of Esdraelon which was a perpetual battlefield, or the ancient city of Jericho, or the disputed fortress of Cadiz. In these sites the traveler has trouble recalling all the events which took place. But in Sinai it is a different story. The mountains seem to be completely devoid of history.

We can even go a step farther. In Sinai there seems to have been no prehistory either. We find ourselves in the pre-Cambrian age, in the second day of creation, before men, animals, and plants were created.

Many simple men and poets have felt the splendor of creation as they stood atop a hill.

Here in Sinai there is only the bare earth. The trembling has been petrified in stone, and nostalgia turns into awe at God's nearness. The moving finger is now the arm of the Almighty, piling huge rocks over the earth's surface and punching gaping crevices in the lofty peaks.

A phrase from Antonio Machado describes it well: "a glistening bolt of rock appears." It is not really a bolt but a wave of rock, frozen forever at its crest high above the earth; tongues of fire transformed into red granite and the deep rich colors of gneiss, porphyry, diorite, and slate. Here we cannot utilize the music of Wagner: it has too many hints of fantasy, legend, and mythical human characters. Nor can we profit from the discordant tones of Stravinsky's *Sacre du Printemps:* it is too suggestive of plant and animal activity. Here on this peak only the voice of God will help us, sounding in the fury of a storm or in the pages of a book.

Psalm 28 describes the voice of God in powerful strokes:

> The voice of the Lord is over the waters,
>   the God of glory thunders,
>   the Lord, over vast waters.
> The voice of the Lord is mighty;
>   the voice of the Lord is majestic.
> The voice of the Lord breaks the cedars,
>   the Lord breaks the cedars of Lebanon.
> He makes Lebanon leap like a calf
>   and Sarion like a young wild bull.
> The voice of the Lord strikes fiery flames;
>   the voice of the Lord shakes the desert,
>   the Lord shakes the wilderness of Cades.
> The voice of the Lord twists the oaks and strips the forests,
>   and in his temple all say, "Glory!"
>
> (Psalm 28:3-9 [29:3-9])

In this setting we should overlook the references to place names and plant life. We must feel this powerful voice causing the mountains to spring up, the desert to tremble, and the waves to crash on the shore. Then we can open to the first chapter of the Bible and read it in its true setting.

I am convinced that many chapters of the Bible are pieces of sublime poetry. To read them properly one must be in the right mood and in the appropriate surroundings. The third verse of Genesis should be read at dawn in a tropical region where the sun comes up at once: "God said, 'Let there be light,' and there was light. God saw that the light was good. God separated the light from the darkness, calling the light Day and the darkness Night."

The eleventh verse should be read during the spring when nature restores life to all the plants and covers the frozen earth with greenery. "Then God said, 'Let the earth bring forth vegetation: seed-bearing plants and all kinds of fruit trees that bear fruit containing their seed.' And so it was. The earth brought forth vegetation, every kind of seed-bearing plant and all kinds of trees that bear fruit. . . . God saw that it was good."

One should read about the creation of the stars on a summer night, when one is on a plateau such as ours, looking up at the sky. And only a young man in love can fully appreciate the verses which tell of the creation of woman.

On Sinai we would read about the second day of creation (verses 9 and 10). "Then God said, 'Let the waters below the heavens be gathered into one place and let the dry land appear.' And so it was. God called the dry land Earth and the assembled waters Seas. And God saw that it was good."

How close to us these divine words sound, here on these lofty heights. The thrill of creation, antedating man himself, has perdured on the Sinai peninsula. There is no lack of history or prehistory here. We pass beyond vegetation and reptiles to reach the primordial geological stratum. The earth is not yet teeming with life, but stirs only at the voice and hand of God.

This was the setting for God's magnificent appearance. But before we review this event, we shall close this meditation in a more quiet vein. It was a wearying climb and we must refurbish our strength with a restful meditation. This mountain stands at the bottom of the inverted triangle and looks out over two bodies of water to the right and left: the gulf of Suez and the gulf of Aqaba. On the far side of each gulf there are continental mountain ranges: the African chain in Egypt and the Asian chain in Arabia. This moutain has seen the trading ships of Egypt sailing in the west and those of Solomon sailing in the East. They plowed a furrow through the waters for a moment or two; then the waters covered their tracks once again and assumed the same appearance as they had at the dawn of creation. One day men linked the two seas by a canal. But the canal is in the north, beyond our range of vision from this peak. When the sun rises in Asia, the peak casts its thin shadow over the coast of Africa for a long time. When the sun sets in the Atlantic, the peak casts its shadow over the mountains of Asia. Millions of times has this game been repeated.

On God's Mountain

For one brief moment the full force of history struck this bypassed spot. From then on it would be a spot rich in human history and divine history. Our religion is supernatural, surpassing the confines of time and space. But it is also an historical religion inserted into creation at a specific time and place. God, from His eternity outside time, directs temporal history and breaks into it. The first and most spectacular of these irruptions took place here.

"THIS IS THE BLOOD OF THE NEW TESTAMENT"

Different people offered to carry the portable altars and set them up on the peak. They are in small lightweight valises. Everyone would have volunteered, but we came to an amicable agreement.

The altars are set on stone blocks. The backdrop is formed by the lofty primitive mountain scenery; the canopy is the clear deep sky. An American priest says Mass and the ceremonies are outlined against the sky. Photos are taken to preserve this most memorable scene in color. Five of us form an impromtu chorus and sing several Eucharistic chants: *Adoro te devote latens Deitas, quae sub his figuris vere latitas . . . Jesu quem velatum nunc aspicio, fac ut fiat illud quod tam sitio, ut Te revelata videns facie, visu sim beatus tuae gloriae.*

The moment of consecration arrives. The priest elevates the Host — above the mountains, toward the heavens. We kneel in silence while the movie camera clicks away. Then the consecration of the wine: "This is the chalice of My blood, of the new and eternal covenant." Here on Sinai these words are especially moving.

They refer to a solemn covenant between God and men. God in His mercy and love invites men to enter a solemn pact of friendship. However, the pact is restricted to a single nation which He Himself chooses. They are free to accept or reject this offer. Then God sets His conditions. They must guard and keep the Commandments which He personally gives to Moses. In return He promises them a lofty gift: "You will be my people and I shall be your God."

When Moses came to the people and related all the words and ordinances of the Lord, they all answered with one voice, "We will do everything that the Lord has told us." Moses then wrote down all the words of the Lord and, rising early the next day, he erected at the foot of the mountain an altar and twelve pillars

[105]

for the twelve tribes of Israel. Then, having sent certain young men of the Israelites to offer holocausts and sacrifice young bulls as peace offerings to the Lord, Moses took half of the blood and put it in large bowls; the other half he splashed on the altar. Taking the Book of the Covenant he read it aloud to the people, who answered, "All that the Lord has said, we will heed and do." Then he took the blood and sprinkled it on the people, saying: "This is the blood of the covenant which the Lord has made with you in accordance with all these words of his" (Ex 24:3–8).

Thus was the first alliance solemnly promulgated at the foot of the mountain. But it was not perfect or eternal. And when the fullness of time came, God sent His Son to seal the new and eternal alliance. And His Son sealed it with His own blood on another sacred mountain near Jerusalem.

Shortly before He died, He instituted an eternal sacrifice in which He repeats His own sacrifice in all times and places. This is the sacrifice being offered by our companion.

Here in Sinai, the place where the old alliance was sealed, we feel the deep significance of Christ's spilled blood and God's alliance with us His children.

The next Mass is celebrated by Canon Alberto Vidal, canon and lector from Gerona. Again the familiar actions are repeated against the exceptional backdrop. This time, however, we sing a popular Spanish hymn: *Cantemos al Amor de los amores, cantemos al Señor; Dios está aquí . . . cielos y tierra bendecid al Señor.** Never have these words been so pregnant with emotion.

A HEBREW RECITATION

When the Masses are finished, we each spend our free time as we choose. The canteens have been empty for some time, so the Bedouins bring up a huge tin of fresh water. Some take photos in any direction the sun permits. Don Vidal, with his sharp eyesight, is the first to glimpse a strip of the gulf of Aqaba to the east. Once it has been pointed out, we all can spot it. Some of us are content to contemplate the incomparable scenery. A few hours of quiet

---

* Let us sing to the greatest love of all,
  Let us sing to the Lord;
  God is here. . . .
  Heaven and earth, bless the Lord.

contemplation will not tire me. And we must take advantage of the morning because it is not easy to return to Sinai.

The caravan chief takes a small book out of his pocket. It is a pocket edition of the Hebrew Bible. He picks out the most appropriate sections, Chapters 19 and 24 of Exodus. Readings *in situ* will be a delightful ritual throughout our journey.

Father reads the text according to modern Hebrew pronunciation. Now and then he stops to clarify some point. Even those who understand little or nothing listen attentively. In this spot the original language has a sacred value: *"wayehi bayyom hašliši bihyot habboqer wayehi qolot ubraqim. . . ."*

> On the morning of the third day there were peals of thunder and lightning, and a heavy cloud over the mountain, and a very loud trumpet blast, so that all the people in the camp trembled. But Moses led the people out of the camp to meet God, and they stationed themselves at the foot of the mountain. Mount Sinai was all wrapped in smoke, for the Lord came down upon it in fire. The smoke rose from it as though from a furnace, and the whole mountain trembled violently. The trumpet blast grew louder and louder, while Moses was speaking and God answering him with thunder. . . .
>
> Then God delivered all these commandments: "I, the Lord, am your God, who brought you out of the land of Egypt, that place of slavery. You shall not have other gods before me. You shall not carve idols for yourselves. . . . You shall not take the name of the Lord, your God, in vain. . . . Remember to keep holy the Sabbath day. . . . Honor your father and your mother. . . . You shall not kill. . . . You shall not commit adultery. . . . You shall not steal. . . . You shall not bear false witness against your neighbor. . . . You shall not covet your neighbor's house. You shall not covet your neighbor's wife. . . ."
>
> When the people witnessed the thunder and lightning, the trumpet blast and the mountain smoking, they all feared and trembled.   (Ex 19:16–20, 18.)

The shade has retreated along the walls and hidden between the two buildings. Only a thin slice remains on the ground, cast by the jutting roof. Wearing helmets to ward off the sun, we eat the sardines and the melon. The pure poetry of the mountain is stained with drops of oil and human words.

15. *THE DESCENT*

WE WILL descend by the steps. The path carved out in the gorges will provide us with a few shady nooks. We soon notice that we are often between two fires, the sun above and its rays reflected off the rocks. Going down a long series of steps is often more tiring than going up. I doubt whether many people have ever descended a series of 500 steps. Their irregular shape increases the fatigue. At times the knees almost seem to buckle, and a feeling of vertigo runs through the body. Then the sensation disappears until we have gone 100 or 200 steps farther down.

We make our first stop in the grotto of Elijah. It contains a small unimposing shrine. In the early afternoon heat this shady refuge is refreshing for our body. So it must have been for the spirit of Elijah many centuries ago.

He was fleeing from a persecution. Jezabel had come down from Phoenicia to be queen of Israel. She dominated her husband and insisted on propagating the religion of her native land. Her fiercest enemy was the prophet Elijah, and she decided to eliminate him. Elijah discovered her plan and fled southward. His first stop was at Beer-sheba, on the outskirts of the desert. There he separated from his followers. He then continued through the desert for one day "and he said: 'It is enough; now, O Lord, take away my life, for I am no better than my fathers'" (1 Kgs 19:4). It is a state of complete exhaustion in which one feels all his strength gone. Life itself is a burden.

An angelic vision and a meal provided miraculously will restore his strength and enable him to continue his journey. After "forty days" he reached the mountain of God (Sinai) where the solitude brings one close to God. Unlike Moses he only went halfway up and hid himself in a grotto.

"But the word of the Lord came to him, and he said to him: 'What are you doing here, Elijah?' 'I have been very jealous for the Lord, the God of hosts,' he said, 'for the Israelites have forsaken the covenant with thee, thrown down thine altars, and slain thy prophets with the sword; and I, even I only, am left, and they are seeking to take away my life.' 'Go forth,' he said, 'and stand upon the mount before the Lord.'

"Now behold, the Lord was passing by, and a great and mighty wind was rending the mountain and shattering the rocks before the Lord; but the Lord was not in the earthquake. After the earthquake a fire; but the Lord was not in the fire, and after the fire the sound of a gentle whisper. Now as soon as Elijah perceived it, he wrapped his face in his mantle and went out and stood at the entrance of the cave. Then there came a voice to him . . ." (1 Kgs 19:9–13) .

What a contrast between this appearance and God's appearance to Moses! Here, the gentle murmur of a soft wind; there, peals of thunder and lightning! But in both cases it is the same God who knows how to adapt circumstances to His purpose. In one case He is trying to instill the fear of God in men; in the other He is consoling a persecuted prophet. This gentle wind felt by Elijah prefigures the meek Master who passed by like a breeze doing good.

We make our second stop several yards below. It is a delightful oasis buttressed by granite shelves. Over the centuries the south wind gathered sand and earth in this spot. Then one day a strange wind brought seeds. The water tended them maternally and soon this patch of green appeared: a group of medium-sized poplars topped by a giant cypress.

Seated in the circle of rocks we enjoy a little bit of the scanty shade and fresh well water. We read a few verses of the Bible and pass a few comments back and forth while the sun moves lazily in the heavens. Then we hold a brief discussion. (It is said that the seventy ancients stayed here while Moses went on to the peak.) Our discussion ends in a cowardly decision.

From this point a path leads up the rear of Ras Safsafa, the triple-peaked collossus which looks out over the encampment area below. From this spot Moses communicated God's commandments to the people. Ras Safsafa is much lower than the Sinai peak. To climb it you must first descend into a gully and then start the steep climb. It takes about an hour and a half. Our legs and our breath might hold out, but at 2:30 in the afternoon the heat is intolerable and dissuades us from this project.

We start down a new series of steps and stop briefly at a little shrine to the Virgin. It stands under an arch where pilgrims used to go to confession before climbing the mountain. Nearby there is a spring and a poplar tree.

We have reached the bottom of the 3000 steps and find ourselves before the imposing wall of the monastery. We circle it and go inside with no more immediate thought than to rest.

16. THE ISRAELITE ENCAMPMENTS

IN MANY of our trips by touring car we have crossed camping areas ringed by mountains. But none can compare with the great plain of Er-Raha. We decided to cross it at dusk. Leaving the monastery we travel in the shelter of the sacred mounts and head for a far corner of the esplanade. From there we can see the rolling plain stretch out before us. We travel slowly, unhurriedly. The ground is a series of irregular undulations. At a certain point we turn to view the scene. The mountains stretch out on both sides, sloping upward gradually at first and then cutting up almost vertically. They are the walls of this great theater. Directly ahead looms the triple-headed mound of red granite. This was the sight which the Israelites beheld. Their chief disappeared over one of these hills to keep his appointment with God. Then suddenly he reappeared on a huge mound to communicate God's commands. Above this mound God unleashed a terrifying storm when He Himself promulgated His commands from the pedestal of Sinai. Then one day the man of God disappeared beyond the mound, leaving his brother Aaron in charge. Several days passed and he did not reappear. The people became impatient and turned this spot, hallowed by God's appearance, into a carnival arena.

The people wanted to have a visible image of Yahweh, the God who brought them out of Egypt. They wanted to adore it, as other people adored images of their gods. So they petitioned Aaron: "Come, make us a god who will be our leader; as for the man Moses . . . we do not know what has happened to him" (Ex 32:1). Aaron orders them to collect all gold objects, while he himself or some artist prepares the mold of a calf. He sets up the statue, builds an altar, and proclaims the next day as a day of solemn feasting.

The people gaze at the golden calf, saying: "This is your God, O Israel, who brought you out of the land of Egypt" (Ex 32:4). They begin the celebrations on the following day with many sacri-

[111]

fices to the calf. After the religious ceremonies there is a great banquet: "Then they sat down to eat and drink, and rose up to revel." The banquet may well have had a ritual character. Finally, the feast ends with a ritual dance around the golden calf.

Within the brief space of a few days this site is the scene of the tragic interplay between divine mercy and human sinfulness. Within a few hours we have relived God's offer of an alliance and the people's faithlessness.

Then God proposes to reject this nation which He liberated so recently, and to choose another nation for a new alliance. But the old alliance, transitory though it be, is meant to last for a few centuries: the new garment is not to be cast off so quickly. Moses is the one who must reconcile the people with God. And he does so in a prayer which is one of the most sublime and touching passages in the Old Testament.

"Why, O Lord, should your wrath blaze up against your own people, whom you brought out of the land of Egypt with such great power and with so strong a hand? Why should the Egyptians say: 'With evil intent he brought them out, that he might kill them in the mountains and exterminate them from the face of the earth'? Let your blazing wrath die down; relent in punishing your people. Remember your servants Abraham, Isaac and Israel, and how you swore to them by your own self, saying: 'I will make your descendants as numerous as the stars in the sky; and all this land that I promised, I will give your descendants as their perpetual heritage.' So the Lord relented . . ." (Ex 32:11-14).

The interplay between mercy and sin contains a third element — punishment and pardon. It crops up here for the first time, but it will reappear throughout the history of the chosen people.

While the dancing and the singing were going on, Moses was coming down the mountain with Joshua, holding the two stone tablets in his hand. Joshua hears the shouts of the people and says: "'That sounds like a battle in the camp.' But Moses answered: ' . . . the sounds that I hear are cries of revelry.' As he drew near . . . he saw the calf and the dancing . . . so that he threw the tablets down and broke them. . . . Taking the calf . . . he fused it in the fire and then ground it down to powder, which he scattered on the water and made the Israelites drink" (Ex 32:17-20).

Then Moses demands an explanation from Aaron and prepares the final stage of this drama. The great plain which we are now crossing, to return to the monastery and which had been the site of God's awesome appearance and man's sacrilegious dances, becomes the scene of bloody chastisement.

"When Moses realized that, to the scornful joy of their foes, Aaron had let the people run wild, he stood at the gate of the camp and cried: 'Whoever is for the Lord, let him come to me!' All the Levites then rallied to him, and he told them: 'Thus says the Lord, the God of Israel: Put your sword on your hip, every one of you! Now go up and down the camp, from gate to gate, and slay your own kinsmen, your friends and neighbors!' The Levites carried out the command of Moses and that day there fell about three thousand of the people" (Ex 32:25-28).

The people lived in this region for a year. But this does not mean that they stayed in this plain all the time. Five valleys lead into it, and the area around the Feiran oasis (about thirty miles) is the most fertile in the peninsula. This spot would serve as a place for reunions. The people would gather here for general assemblies, to hear the instructions of Moses and to celebrate religious rites. For the rest of the time they would live like seminomads, grazing their flocks like today's inhabitants. This is the way the Israelites spent their religious novitiate. They experienced the period of initial fervor and learned what their God wanted of them and how He acted. When the proper time came, God gave the order to move on. The Israelites left this area once and for all, but now it was a sacred site hallowed in the memory of all succeeding generations.

17. A SPEEDY RETURN TRIP

WE MUST leave soon because we have a long journey ahead. But it will take more than a little time for us to digest the extraordinary impressions gleaned during our brief stay. Indeed, we shall have to wait until our journey is over because new impressions pile up one after the other. We have seen many things in a short space of time. Our attitude has been one of detached meditation or scholarly interest, and we have kept a distance between the objects viewed and our own mental attitudes. In some cases we have felt ourselves immersed in the countryside. But nowhere have we felt ourselves so deeply immersed in the events of long ago as in Sinai.

We speed toward our destination on the return trip. But we stop for a long time at the Feiran oasis, eating and waiting for our companions who set out to climb Mount Serbal in one day. While we wait, two Spaniards are royally entertained with tea and songs in a Bedouin tent.

It is already dusk when the cars start out. At first we proceed slowly along the rough trail. Night is a better traveling companion and we avoid many potential troubles. The motors do not overheat and give us more thrust on the sandy stretches.

The driver points to the right. Two phosphorescent eyes are following us. Perhaps it is a jackal attracted by the headlights. We can make out his curved outline and watch him retreat into the darkness, his glowing eyes staring after us.

I manage to have a fitful sleep. In Abu Zenima we get out to stretch our legs and meet the Coca-Cola sign once again. Civilization makes its appearance once more. It is hardly a very tasty debut. Only my fierce thirst can reconcile me with this beverage which is trying to supplant beer. I do not want to insert the considered opinions of myself and my companion Javierre on beverages. They are, of course, a part of the travelog, but it would be improper levity to recount them on this solemn night.

A Speedy Return Trip

We continue to travel along the coast. My sleep varies as does the trip itself. It has ups and downs like the highway, sudden jolts like the motor, and then smooth stretches of uninterrupted ease. We stop once more before leaving the peninsula. It is a dark cool night. Once again I feel the pure sensation of well-being engendered by the environment. It is my last sensible impression of the peninsula.

We celebrate Mass in Suez and come face to face with a full-bodied breakfast, quite unlike the ones put up in tins. In Sinai the Americans performed yeoman's service in trying to make the rations more appetizing. They provided us with hot meals. Our menus were far superior to those of other pilgrims who travel several weeks by camel. But it is still a pleasure to see silverware instead of tins, to smell the aroma of cooked food, and to experience the clean freshness of a well-set table. Recall how the Israelites longed for Egypt while they were wandering in the desert (Ex 16:3).

After breakfast we take the highway which links Suez and Cairo through the desert. We pass English military warehouses, huge oil trucks, and, once in awhile, a touring car.

Toward noon we reach the Egyptian military installations, quite similar to the English ones in outward appearance. Then we pass the houses of a beautiful city, modern Heliopolis with its broad streets, its stately buildings done in classical Arabic style (as our driver notes), and its many fancy cars. This city adjoins Cairo; and so, before we realize it, we are at Holy Family College. It is almost noon. Our trip to Sinai is over.

III. *ON TO THE PROMISED LAND*

They angered him at the waters of Meriba,
  and Moses fared ill on their account,
For they embittered his spirit,
  and the rash utterance passed his lips.
                      (Psalm 105[106])

. . . dear to God and men, Moses, whose
memory is held in benediction. God's honor
devolved upon him, and the Lord strength-
ened him with fearful powers; God wrought
swift miracles at his words and sustained
him in the king's presence. He gave him the
Commandments for his people, and revealed
to him his glory. For his trustworthiness
and meekness God selected him from all
mankind; he permitted him to hear his
voice, and led him into the cloud, where,
face to face, he gave him the Commandments, the law of life and understanding,
that he might teach his precepts to Jacob,
his judgments and decrees to Israel.
                      (Sirach 45)

18. BETWEEN EGYPT AND PALESTINE

AFTER traveling through Egypt from south to north, we were to have passed through Sinai into Palestine by land. Thus we would have followed the tracks of the ancient Israelites. But circumstances have changed greatly, and such a course was impossible. The primitive geological surface of Sinai was a severe test for our cars. We followed the footsteps of the Israelites along the Suez from Goshen to the Bitter Lakes. A ferry brought us to the other side. Then we continued our journey through a territory without good roads or water. It became increasingly difficult for the autos, and more than once we had to push them out of sand traps or holes in the road.

We could not complete the journey along this route. Instead we had to return to Cairo. At Alexandria we now board a ship for Beirut. And as we sail along, we pass the time meditating on this thin slice of land called Palestine.

PALESTINE, A THROUGHWAY

Palestine seems to have been made so that different peoples might pass through her. Consider how God's mind works! He chooses one nation out of many to preserve intact a particular religious tradition, a new outlook on life. And yet He places this nation in an area frequented by all sorts of people and coveted by all the great empires. The Hebrews, who are supposed to maintain their unique position in isolation, end up in one of the busiest spots of the ancient world.

The commercial and military routes of the ancient Orient passed through Palestine. If we look at a map of the entire area, we shall see that the southern tip of the Nile delta and the northern tip of the Persian Sea — Abraham's homeland — are almost parallel. But the trade route between the ancient empires of Babylon and Egypt cut at a right angle. It stretched north from Babylon toward

[119]

Harran (which means "road") and then cut southward through Palestine into Egypt.

PALESTINE, A COVETED LAND

Babylonia did not have trees, metals, or rock formations. All it had from the very beginning was canals, and these were the source of its urban culture. But without raw materials it could not become an empire, because it could not construct things or wage war. The Babylonians hunted for metals in the north, in the region of Subartu; but the best timber was in the "white" mountains, the mountains of Lebanon. Even today this small nation sports its cedars in seals, flags, and national emblems, although it has only a few dozen left. And these are preserved as a national monument in a conservation area where there is snow the year around. In the days of antiquity the long double chain of mountains was probably covered with cedars. If our interpretation is correct, the ancient governor of Lagash, who carved inscriptions on the shoulders of his statues, boasts that he succeeded in linking the southern sea (the Indian) with the northern sea (the Mediterranean). (This would have been more than forty centuries ago.) And he also explains how the trunks were transported down the Euphrates on rafts.

The Egyptians had productive mines in Sinai and good quarries in Aswan. But they too wanted the cedars of Lebanon and the ports of Palestine.

PALESTINE, IN THE MIDDLE

Palestine was not especially wealthy or powerful. But in the game of empire-building it was a decisive pawn and represented the balance of power for Egypt and Babylon. Both wished to dominate it or at least have it as an ally, mainly because of its geographic position. We who live in an era of international conflicts can appreciate this fact.

There was one period during which the Israelites were tragically aware of their tenuous position between East and West. We too can appreciate their feeling because we have West Berlin. In the days of Jeremiah there were two political factions; one favoring

Egypt, the other favoring Babylon. Both factions sought to save Israel by allying her with one empire against the other. Neutrality was impossible. The eastern empire of Babylon was a greater threat; and the western one offered its help and protection out of fear and self-interest. But through the voices of the prophets God announced that Israel's salvation did not lay in human alliances, but rather in fidelity to God's covenant. "It is neither East nor West, but God who governs."

PALESTINE, A PORT OF REFUGE

Palestine is a bridge. And in times of peace as in times of war bridges are passageways and sources of dispute. But we are going to consider another aspect of Palestine, its value as a harbor, a port of entry and departure. How often we have heard it called "the land of promise." And we tend to attribute this expression solely to the chosen people wandering in the desert. Theologically this is correct. But we forget the immense geographical value of this verdant strip for the vast arid peninsula of Arabia.

Draw a large parallelogram somewhat irregular in shape with the top sloping toward the left. Now mark a sea on the left side and on the bottom. Then put a sea on the right side and link it with the Euphrates river. At the top mark a large green strip. This enormous peninsula has two spots where the sea is blocked: the far side of the Euphrates, seat of the great cultures of antiquity; and the far side of the Jordan, facing the Mediterranean.

The Bedouin feels free living in the desert under the open sky. But sometimes he is tempted by the green fields he passes. The fertile regions promising permanent security almost win him over to a sedentary existence. But then one day he leaves this quiet life and returns to his roaming ways. These ancient peoples, like the tides, ebbed and flowed continuously even as they do today. They are like the desert sands, scattered in every direction by the wind. One day they find a rocky stretch and settle to form a sand dune. If a green thicket is able to take roots in the dune, the ensemble solidifies permanently. But if not, another wind will lift the sand and scatter it once again.

One day the Israelites left their sedentary life in the Nile delta and set out to wander in the desert. After forty years, the span of one generation, they began to encounter the green stretches of Palestine. It was easy to settle on the right bank of the Jordan. Then gradually they began to cross over and establish pockets among the Canaanites.

While the Israelites were establishing settlements, new bands from the desert swept up periodically to devour their crops. These were the Madianites whom Gideon defeated by a clever stratagem, knowing full well that open battle was out of the question. When the great Babylonian emperor, Nebuchadnezzar, deported the Jews into exile, the surrounding peoples swarmed into the vacated region, greedy for its verdant pastureland. Later on, for different reasons, it would be the Greeks and Romans; then the Arabs; then the Mongols and the Turks.

PALESTINE, A VIEW FROM THE SEA

Palestine also was a port of disembarkation, and we are no longer speaking metaphorically. The sight which looms up ahead is strange and surprising. It is not surprising that Arabs from the desert would push up to settle in this verdant strip of land. But one can scarcely explain on natural grounds why groups of people living in more fertile regions should take refuge in this patch of earth.

Two events of suprahistorical import have taken place in Palestine, and both have spurred historical movements to conquer this region. First came the crusaders seeking to regain the land hallowed by Christ's presence. They felt that this land belonged to Christians. And they left impressive and enduring traces of their two-hundred-year stay.

But God also gave this strip of land to His chosen people. And so, in the twentieth century, a great movement arose which gathered Jews from the four corners of the earth and wafted them to Palestine like so many grains of sand.

Where did this wind arise? What course did it travel? It was an inner call echoing the divine call which Abraham heard so many centuries ago: "Raise your eyes, and from where you are now look to the north and the south and the east and the west.

Between Egypt and Palestine

All the land which you see I will give to you and your posterity forever. I will make your posterity as the dust of the earth; if anyone can count the grains of dust, your posterity can also be counted. Arise, walk the length and breadth of the land, for to you I will give it" (Gn 13:14–17).

As always, the rise of this new movement led to conflict. And the nations of the world have watched the battles. Now these grains of sand are gathered together and seek to take root. They are working to plant, to build, and to construct. They do not want a strong wind to scatter them once again.

19. *THE LUCKY MOSAIC*

How many times have we used such expressions as a mosaic of races, a mosaic of religions. The metaphor, on account of its frequent use, has lost its freshness. In such a case it is better to bypass the metaphor and look at a real mosaic.

Today we are going to visit a mosaic. There are many in Palestine, remnants of Byzantine churches and witnesses of an ancient veneration. The archaeologists are more interested in their historical significance than in their artistic value. "What does this mosaic, depicting this scene and located in this spot, tell us?"

The most important mosaic in Palestine is the one in Madaba, the one we are visiting today. It has received more important and more intensive visits; and it has been covered by a wooden frame for protection. Specialists have written detailed papers on it; and the last of these, written by Father R. T. O'Callaghan, S.J., occupies seventy-seven columns in the *Supplément au Dictionnaire de la Bible.*

Such tender care and attention are perhaps meant to atone for the ill-treatment accorded to it in the first years after its discovery. Eyewitnesses testify that it was almost completely intact. But more than half of it was destroyed during the building of a new church. The architect in charge of building the new church claimed that the whole mosaic did not deserve the attention being lavished on it. It was only twelve years after the discovery that a Greek monk, a devotee of Christian archaeology, discovered the exceptional importance of this mosaic.

Madaba borders the highway in the lofty tableland of Moab, parallel to the northern edge of the Dead Sea. It is a hot, dusty village, quite like any other. Groups of children stare at us with curiosity. One of them runs to find the sexton who has the keys to the church. A villager comes along, driving a donkey through the

[124]

rock wall which rings his plot of land. The sun's strong rays reflect off the white facade of the houses.

The church belongs to the Greek Orthodox. We hurry across the ancient patio, today attested to only by a low stone wall, and then the modern patio covered with white cobblestones. We are eager to see the great treasure. The guide lifts off the wooden planks and shows it to us.

PIECEMEAL GEOGRAPHY

What a delightful idea! — Drawing a map of Palestine in a mosaic. For some inexplicable reason it strikes me as the work of a child, or a man with a simple poetic soul. Even today it would be a good way to teach geography to children. Have them arrange the pieces correctly to form a map. "This red piece represents the mountains of Sinai, this green piece represents the Dead Sea, this maroon piece represents one of Jericho's palm trees and also the B of Bethlehem." So the children would go on, piecing the map together and learning the geography of Palestine at the same time.

Such a game is impossible with the maps of today. They stress accuracy and precision, but all the imagination is gone. Only maps displayed at exhibitions or found in statistical works still contain descriptive or symbolic markers. The maps which I had to study as a child were as serious and monotonous as grown-ups. The only attractive feature was the color variety representing different nations. Why is France blue and Italy green?

But geography is brought to life in this mosaic at Madaba, because the artist had a poetic soul and really knew his craft. The result is a delightful combination of colors and harmonies; and the details could occupy us for several hours. (Later on I had the opportunity of examining a good reproduction hanging in a room at the Pontifical Biblical Institute at Jerusalem. On this second occasion I was not forced to hurry or to bend down.)

The cities are not marked simply with a dot and a name. They are depicted according to their geographical or botanical characteristics, and identified by some brief text referring to them. The Dead Sea has some dark ripples and two elegant ships; the sails are furled and one of the occupants is rowing; there are no fish.

[125]

The Jordan has lighter, smoother ripples and a fish is crossing the surface. The Nile opens its branches at the delta and the fishes are angling their way through it. But the most enchanting animal is the swift-footed gazelle turning fearfully to look at the lion already leaping at him. (Only the lion's tail and hind paws are still intact.) The most frequent plant depicted is the palm tree, slender and almost always loaded with two bunches of dates. Most of them are in Jericho. There are other shrubs and bushes, not readily identifiable, on both sides of the Jordan.

The artist has devoted special attention to the mountains. One would say that he never visited Sinai because he depicts its mountains as being lower than those in Moab. The mountains have pronounced curves with a few patches of vegetation, and the slopes glisten red or yellow as if the sun were shining on them.

The cities are depicted in a delightful way. Small villages are represented by a house or a wall with a certain number of towers. But the important cities are depicted in a way similar to that of medieval miniatures. It is a view from above, looking down on the city and the wall surrounding it. Jerusalem occupies a disproportionate amount of space because the artist wants to indicate its religious importance, not its actual size. In Ashkelon we see two avenues join together at a magnificent city gate. Through Gaza runs a single street flanked by porticoes with columns. Nablus is interlaced with buildings, while the walls of Kerak, on the other side of the Dead Sea, rise on a sturdy hillside.

OLD TESTAMENT MEMORIES

On the map the territory belonging to each of the twelve tribes is marked in red: "Kleros Simeon, Kleros Jouda, Kleros Dan. . . ." And here and there are verses of Jacob's blessing on his sons. This would be the proper place to recount the second last chapter of Genesis in which Jacob blesses his sons before his death in Egypt. But for several reasons I have decided to recall another famous set of benedictions.

The incident took place quite nearby, in the mountains of Moab. And it had overtones of splendor and triumph. Like the mosaic it was done in brilliant, controlled strokes.

The Lucky Mosaic

But, above all, these blessings were voiced by a man who was able to look down on the chosen people and see them as a huge and beautiful mosaic. "From the top of the crags I see him, from the heights." Before the chosen people had spread through Palestine, he saw them camped below, distributed "tribe by tribe."

It is a pleasant story in which a donkey reproaches his rider, a fortune-teller mocks his client, and God pronounces a blessing through the mouth of a sorcerer.

When Balak, the king of Moab, saw the Israelites encamped in his territory, he did not dare to attack them openly. So he sought the aid of a sorcerer. Balaam was a seer noted for the success of his curses.

We know the system employed by the Egyptians. They would write the name of their enemy on a piece of pottery and then dash it against the ground. We also know some of the ritual formulas: "May all those who rebel, or practice sorcery, or do battle, or speak of doing battle, or speak of rebellion in the land . . ."; "Ameni, son of Hetep and Sen-Usert, must die." Balaam had his own secret formulas which assured him a reputation and a good clientele.

Summoned by the king of Moab, he sets out on his donkey. We know how the story goes. An angel of God plants himself in front of the donkey, and the poor little animal gets off the road and heads for some vineyards in a field. But the angel plants himself between two sides of a stone enclosure and the animal brushes the wall, bruising his rider's leg. The rider beats her three times before she turns and reproaches him: "What have I done to you that you should beat me these three times." — "You have acted so willfully against me that if I but had a sword at hand, I would kill you here and now." — "Am I not your own beast and have you not always ridden upon me. . . . Have I been in the habit of treating you this way?" — "No." (Cf. Num 22:28–30).

Then Balaam saw the angel and heard God's orders: "Go with Balak, but say only what I tell you to say."

Balak received him royally, offered him burnt oxen and sheep, and on the following morning asked him to perform the service requested.

They ascended the mountain dedicated to Baal. The sorcerer

had seven altars built, and sacrificed a lamb on each one. Then he set off alone toward a barren headland to seek inspiration. "And God . . . put an utterance in Balaam's mouth." When he returned, he found Balak with the princes of Moab. And he began to speak: "From Aram has Balak brought me here, Moab's king, from the Eastern Mountains: 'Come and lay a curse for me on Jacob, come and denounce Israel.' How can I curse whom God has not cursed? How denounce whom the Lord has not denounced? For from the top of the crags I see him, from the heights I behold him. Here is a people that lives apart and does not reckon itself among the nations. Who has ever counted the dust of Jacob, or numbered Israel's wind-borne particles? May I die the death of the just, may my descendants be as many as theirs!

" 'What have you done to me?' cried Balak to Balaam. 'It was to curse my foes that I brought you here; instead, you have even blessed them.' Balaam replied, 'Is it not what the Lord puts in my mouth that I must repeat with care?'

"Then Balak said to him, 'Please come with me to another place from which you can see only some and not all of them, and from there curse them for me' " (Num 23:7–13) .

He took him up to the summit of Mount Phasga. Again the sacrificial rites were performed; again Balaam went to meet Yahweh. Then he pronounced his message:

"It is a blessing I have been given to pronounce; a blessing which I cannot restrain. Misfortune is not observed in Jacob, nor misery seen in Israel. The Lord, his God, is with him; with him is the triumph of his King. It is God who brought him out of Egypt, a wild bull of towering might. No, there is no sorcery against Jacob, nor omen against Israel. It shall yet be said of Jacob, and of Israel: 'Behold what God has wrought!' Here is a people that springs up like a lioness, and stalks forth like a lion; it rests not till it has devoured its prey and has drunk the blood of the slain" (Num 23:20–24) .

Again there is a discussion and they climb to the peak of Phogor. The sacrificial rites are repeated and Balaam pronounces an even greater benediction: "How goodly are your tents, O Jacob; your encampments, O Israel! They are like gardens beside a stream, like the cedars planted by the Lord . . . his king shall rise higher . . .

[128]

and his royalty shall be exalted. . . . He lies crouching like a lion . . . who shall arouse him? Blessed is he who blesses you, and cursed is he who curses you!" (Num 24:5–9.)

(Reading this benediction as we look at the mosaic, we can see its full significance. The extensive valley, the long river, the pouncing lion, all convey vividly the sentiments of joy and beauty.)

But this third benediction infuriates the king: "It was to curse my foes that I summoned you here; yet three times you have even blessed them instead! Be off at once, then, to your home. I promised to reward you richly, but the Lord has withheld the reward from you!' Balaam replied to Balak: 'Did I not warn the very messengers whom you sent me. . . . Whatever the Lord says, I must repeat' " (Num 24:10–13).

And giving answer once again, Balaam prophesied the victories of the chosen people over their neighbors and enemies. "A star shall advance from Jacob, and a staff shall rise from Israel. . . ."

The mosaic dates from the end of the sixth century A.D. At that time the Holy Land was enjoying a long era of peace. The Christians felt that they were the heirs of the divine promises and dotted the landscape with beautiful churches adorned with mosaics. The earth was not very fertile, but there were many villages and a few walled cities. The great saints of the New Testament and the illustrious men of the Old Testament were venerated equally.

This aura of political peace and religious piety is reflected in the mosaic at Madaba. Soon after would come the Arab invasions and countless tragic incidents: Byzantine basilicas destroyed, medieval churches leveled to the ground or converted into mosques.

Today the land of benedictions is shattered and mutilated, like the beautiful mosaic of Madaba.

20. *MOAB, THE BURIAL PLACE OF*
TWO PROPHETS

TODAY we are taking an impressive trip. The tomb of the first prophet, Moses, and that of the last prophet, John the Baptist, await us in the highlands of Moab. We would have to recollect ourselves to appreciate fully the importance of this pilgrimage. But the hot climate of Amman makes inner recollection impossible. The thermometer reads 120° in the sun and the bus we are riding breaks up any attempt at inner concentration. Sitting in the rear of the bus is like riding a bucking bronco. As soon as we get off the highway proper, it kicks and bucks impudently.

TOWARD THE PROMISED LAND

Our return trip has approximated the route of the Israelites. We followed the lofty plateau of Moab to the highlands of Aroer. Then we hit the deep canyon through which flows the Arnon river. The mountainside dips sharply to the river almost 2500 feet below. The Israelites had to clear this formidable obstacle on their way to the Promised Land. But even from this height they could not yet catch a glimpse of their destination. The most they could see was a dense cloud hanging over the steaming waters of the Dead Sea. Their caravan mounted northward, overcoming any resistance offered by the small pockets of native inhabitants. Finally, they reached the northern end of the Dead Sea. There the plateau starts again, its headlands surging up over the valleys below. And finally the long-awaited moment arrived.

A PLACE OF OBSERVATION

We too have left the highway and mounted the slight elevation. A grating opens up and offers us our first view of the "Holy Land."

Moab, the Burial Place of Two Prophets

The summer mist enables us to glimpse only outlines. We cannot see the Jordan entrenched in its bed. We catch a glimpse of the gray fringes of the Dead Sea. With the aid of binoculars we finally pinpoint the tall tower built on Mount Olivet by the Russian Orthodox Christians. And without being able to see any details, we scan the mountain ranges of Judea. The view in itself is not spectacular; but it is our first glimpse of the Holy Land and is, therefore, somewhat moving.

A similar view, perhaps on a bright sunny day with the wind sweeping the heavens, was the last thing seen by Moses before his eyes closed forever.

A PLACE FOR CONTEMPLATION

We soon complete our observation; but there is much to think about. It is not easy to re-create the sad keen gaze of Moses or to fathom its significance.

Here was a man of gigantic stature, one of God's chosen intimates. Supported by God he devoted his qualities of leadership to one endeavor: uprooting a nation from its sedentary way of life and leading it through countless difficulties to a narrow strip of verdant land, the land of promise.

In this endeavor he had to endure their discontented murmurs and their idolatrous practices. He had to intercede on their behalf before God. He saw a whole generation of Israelites perish in the desert. Even though "his eyes were undimmed and his vigor unabated" (Dt 34:7), he is weighed down with weariness and many burdens. His heart is set on one thing: to lead his people into the Promised Land, see them settle down, and then die. He wants to reach his earthly and sacred goal, and then die. But God, as a punishment for some sin of his, denies him this wish. The sacred author discreetly passes over the details of this sin. All we know is that it happened in a moment when the people were rebellious. At any rate, God punishes Moses by refusing to let him enter the Promised Land. He leads him to the edge of a mountain, lets him look at the surrounding panorama, and then shuts his eyes forever.

It must have been a sight full of melancholy and resignation for this giant of history. "Since then no prophet has arisen in Israel like Moses, whom the Lord knew face to face" (Dt 34:10), says the brief eulogy in the Bible.

His body was buried reverently in an unknown tomb somewhere in a valley. The exact spot has never been found. The streams meander irregularly through this region. The mountains slope thousands of feet to the ground and a gray vapor hangs over the Dead Sea. Somewhere in this somber region lies the burial place of the first prophet.

THE LAST PROPHET

The last, but not the least, of the prophets was John the Baptist. He pointed out the promised Messiah. From the banks of the Jordan he could contemplate the front of Mount Nebo. He whom Moses had glimpsed dimly, the one who would conquer and sanctify the Promised Land in a definitive way, was seen in the flesh by John. He entered the waters of Jordan with the mountains of Moab rising in the background.

Once his job is done, John too retires from the scene. The line of Old Testament prophets is at an end. John completes the cortege begun by Moses and, like Moses, entrusts his young healthy body to the mountains of Moab.

Secluded some 2700 feet above the Dead Sea stood Herod's castle. In the dungeon of the castle lies enchained a youth with a far too courageous tongue. And during a night of feasting and dancing, John's head was brought out on a plate. Down below the Dead Sea was a mute witness of the scene and still sends up its somber vapors. Up above, the highlands of Moab heard the sounds of music which were soon dispersed by the wind. The castle of Macheronte had been the scene of murder. John's disciples took the body and buried it in some anonymous spot.

21. MANUFACTURING ANTIQUES

By now it is a well-known anecdote. The foreman was explaining his job to a visitor. "Now we are constructing a fifteenth-century bridge; when we finish it, we shall build another one, even more ancient." This procedure is such a commonplace today that the restoration work on the Palatine hill in Rome is called "the antique factory."

Some of this work has to do with smaller objects — not bridges or columns but small decorative pieces, statuettes, and bronzes. Many times these pieces are so skillful and graceful that they require a warning sign: "copy" or "imitation."

In Luxor we are besieged by the wandering antique vendors with their wares: scarabs with hieroglyphic inscriptions, small stone busts, figurines of sacred animals. They ask for twenty piasters (50 cents) and settle for four. In front of the temple of Hatsepsut a Bedouin approaches stealthily and draws one of our group to the side. With an air of mystery he draws from his pocket a stone tablet bearing pictures and whispers in broken English: "An authentic piece, I found it right here, don't let anyone see it — 200 piasters." The potential client shakes his head and offers him ten piasters. The Bedouin calls over another member of our group and repeats his secret offer. I think he would have called each of us in turn; but just then a group of young ladies, tourists from Scandinavia, came on the scene. The vendor left us and headed toward them, hoping to make a better deal.

The bad point about a new piece is that its price is lower. The same bronze piece, made two or three thousand years ago, is worth much more. Time adds a luster to the object, and its age adds to its cost.

Certain places and times are well suited to the invention and sale of phony antiques. Students, for example, might want to have a joke at the expense of their professor of archaeology or prehistory.

More than two centuries ago, the illustrious Beringer proudly displayed the finds which his own students had buried. And later he published them in a book.

Another spot well suited for this type of trick is Dibon, a region in Moab which we have just visited. We climbed a mound to take a look at the excavations. The finds are not very ancient but the method of excavation is quite patent. Here we found everything mentioned in our class lectures: ditches, wells, walls, pavements, etc. Here these terms came to life. And, furthermore, our guide excavated here to learn the techniques of archaeology.

There is a good reason for picking this place to study archaeology. It is the site where the famous stele of Mesha was discovered. Various nations fought for it and it ended up in fragments. It is an old story by now, but it is worth recalling. We are on the other side of the Jordan, like the Israelites before the conquest of Palestine. This was the scene of many infamous forgeries at the time when archaeology had begun its conquest of Palestine. Recalling these events will shed some light on the difficult early stages of this science. As I indicated earlier, archaeology is going to be one of our most important companions on this journey. Today, just before crossing the Jordan, I am going to recount the colossal fraud which was perpetrated about eighty years ago, and which involved so much bitter controversy and high finance.

SHAPIRA

The setting for our story is a side street in Jerusalem, near the Spanish consulate, where there is a small antique shop run by one Mr. Shapira. He is a shrewd and crafty businessman capable of all sorts of fraud and trickery. The time is just after the discovery of three great archaeological finds: the temple inscription forbidding gentiles to enter under pain of death, the inscription at the pool of Siloam, and the disputed stele belonging to the king of Moab. After these three authentic finds, Europeans are inclined to be gullible and to accept fakes as authentic. Shapira, who is well aware of this, displays a series of objects purported to be from Moab: a small collection of statuettes and somewhat larger figurines, some vases, and several ceramic pieces similar to

[134]

medallions or coins. Many bear cryptic inscriptions in an alphabet similar to that on the stele of Moab. The dealer has been wise enough to win the friendship of the German ambassador, named appropriately enough, Baron von Münchhausen. Americans examine the display and, on the basis of paleographic analysis, decide it is a forgery. So they refuse to buy it. But in Germany the collection finds an enthusiastic supporter in the person of Professor Constantine Schlottmann. For this reason the new Imperial Government of Prussia buys the collection of Moabite antiques for its museum. The Americans are stunned, the English are unconvinced, and the great French archaeologist, Clermont-Ganneau, discredits the collection in private utterances. In Germany too the collection meets opposition. Two young philologists, Socin and Kautzsch, lead the attack against the renowned professor. (Kautzsch was to become the foremost authority in his own special field.) Their analysis of the inscriptions finally leads them to reject the authenticity of the collection. Since they are young men, they have to be cautious in their statements. But there are plenty of professors who continue to work feverishly at deciphering the whimsical series of famous letters. The translations reveal the ingenuity and erudition of their authors.

Two other persons, Lieutenant Conder and Mr. Tyrwhitt Drake, are willing to accept the authenticity of the collection and go so far as to make copies and facsimiles. Their principal argument is based on the state of the material in the objects. The pottery is encrusted with saltpeter which cannot be washed off. It looks as if the pottery had lain for centuries exposed to the corrosive action of water.

The controversy rages openly and eventually reaches the ears of Shapira. He graciously declines to sell a second series of antiques until the authenticity of his merchandise is proved. And he offers to prove his case to two people, a German Protestant minister named Weser and M. Dinsberg. Both are invited to the site of the finds. It is, as it were, a hunting party tracking buried pieces of pottery. The generous invitation is a shrewd move and is readily accepted. The group reaches the chosen site and the visitors are permitted to dig around for several days. While they work, Shapira offers coffee to his Bedouin hosts. The expedition has two results.

On to the Promised Land

First, the visitors find a series of objects bearing the same kind of inscriptions and mysterious symbols in groups of seven. A crust of saltpeter guarantees their antiquity. Second, this discovery restores Shapira's reputation. In his report, dated 1873, Lieutenant Conder says that the authenticity of the finds is beyond any doubt, and goes on to transcribe and sketch the figures.

ENTER CLERMONT-GANNEAU

One person still doubts the authenticity of these antiques. His instinct and his reasoning tell him that they are forgeries. But since he has no tangible proof, he does not want to attack them openly. Finally he comes to Jerusalem to gather proof, unconvinced by the booty from the expedition. He starts a private inquiry, like the amateur detective in our crime movies. He is looking for the "third man" in the plot. He already has two, Shapira the dealer and Selim el Kari the artist, whom he regards as the real creator of these antiques. The "third man" would be the potter whose furnace was used in baking the "antiques."

Scene I. A visit to Shapira's shop. The dealer is reluctant to let the Frenchman see the collection. But at Drake's request he finally allows him to see the second series. As he leaves the shop, Clermont-Ganneau comments laconically: "The only authentic piece from Moab is the live ostrich they brought back!"

Scene II. In his apartment Clermont-Ganneau reviews the facts. Selim el Kari is an expert designer, trained in sketching neo-byzantine models for devout pilgrims. It would be easy for him to sketch the rough statuettes. Selim had also copied various fragments of the Moabite stele and knew the alphabet. He could easily have made the inscriptions. The Frenchman takes two sheets of paper out of his files. One is a drawing by Selim el Kari, a woman holding a child in her arms — Lot's wife fleeing from Sodom. The other is a fragment of the stele copied by Selim. He has a distinctive way of forming the letter *m,* and it matches the *m* on the disputed antiques. Clermont-Ganneau puts the papers back in his files and smiles confidently to himself.

Scene III. Clermont-Ganneau pays a casual visit to the potters' ovens in Jerusalem and strikes up a conversation with various apprentices and officials. He passes from one to the other, trying to fit the jigsaw puzzle together. Finally, one worker tells him a secret. One day, when he was an apprentice in the house of Ahmed Alamiye, a stranger (who later turned out to be Selim el Kari) showed him the location of his own house. Soon after this the apprentice began a new routine. After dusk he would take a well-concealed vessel from the potter's house to Selim's. It contained the molding clay. Selim would give him a series of unusual figurines which he would carefully conceal. On the following day he would return with the now baked figurines. Selim would be waiting for him by a large tub filled with rather murky water. He would carefully dip the figurines in the tub and leave them there.

The triangle is closed: Shapira, el Kari, Ahmed Alamiye. Clermont-Ganneau is able to publish his incontrovertible findings. The question is settled as far as Clermont-Ganneau is concerned.

INTRIGUE AND INSULTS

However, neither Schlottmann in Berlin nor Shapira in Jerusalem are ready to admit defeat. They launch a counterattack. Schlottmann accuses the Frenchman of "chauvinism." Shapira lays his plans carefully. The German consul has interrogated the band of potters involved in the undertaking directly or indirectly. He also has interrogated Selim. The testimony of these people is conflicting. Then one day there is a cross-examination in Clermont-Ganneau's presence. This time the witnesses are in perfect agreement. The young apprentice in our story swears that the Frenchman had locked him up, beaten him, and forced him to memorize the account. The others give similar testimony. Selim tells a less violent version of the affair. He says that Clermont-Ganneau had offered him 100 pounds sterling to declare himself the creator of these forgeries. So now the Frenchman himself is reputed to be the author of the hoax. He, of course, defends himself before the general public. And in scientific circles the antiques are already falling into great disrepute.

But Shapira is not finished yet. No damaging evidence has been found in Selim's house. So Selim extends two invitations. First he invites the Scandinavian, Professor Almkvist, to pick out some spot and then excavate. As it turns out, Almkvist removes a heavy rock in one spot and, lo and behold, there is a figurine bearing inscriptions on it! It is a real stroke of luck because Almkvist had chosen the spot. Next Selim invites the German consul, Baron von Münchhausen, to dig in some spot which he, Selim, would choose. The area is covered with moss and tiny channels made by insects. Apparently men have not tampered with it. The excavators find a cavern, and in a niche they discover a statuette with the familiar inscriptions. Everything has been done on the up and up. Selim has won and Shapira receives a letter of recommendation from the German consul which tells of the authentic finds. Upon arriving in England Shapira hastens to publish the letter.

But Clermont-Ganneau is not taken in. In one case there is too much coincidence involved. In the other case, moss can grow very quickly and insects can make tunnels overnight. Other specialists add their support to the negative view. Scarcely anyone believes in the authenticity of these antiques.

THE ANTICLIMAX

The whole affair ends gradually on a quieter note. One day Clermont-Ganneau receives an unexpected letter from Selim el Kari in which the latter confesses his part in Shapira's plot. The Frenchman does not make too much of the letter, but keeps it in his files for the opportune moment. Meanwhile Lord Kitchener obtains three statuettes of the same type, expressly presented as forgeries. And in Selim's house they find an unbaked statuette of an idol. In 1878, after six years of dispute, the whole affair is brought to a conclusion. But even as late as 1883, there are some naïve people, such as the elderly American consul, Frank S. Dehass, who can celebrate the magnificent find of some 15,000 objects. By that time the last echoes of the debate have died down. The antique makers, who have been forced into temporary retirement, are now preparing to make another sensational find: the Ten Commandments written on a parchment by Moses himself or by one of his secretaries. But we shall save this fantastic story for the next chapter.

22. *HUNTING FOR ARCHAEOLOGISTS*

THE reader should not be frightened by the title of this chapter. We are not going to describe scenes of fierce cannibalism. That is the concern of the ethnologist.

Our title refers to a different situation. When the archaeologists went hunting for famous objects of the past, the native inhabitants went hunting for the archaeologists. Their bait was the antique being sought; the catch they hoped for was money. The Europeans were interested in antiques, the natives were interested in negotiable currency. It was, after all, a fair exchange. And the nice thing about antiques was that they could be counterfeited by someone with a little skill.

The antique makers usually followed this pattern. After some authentic find had been made, they would produce some variations of the same find. For example, the famous stele of King Mesha, dating from the early part of the eighth century B.C., gave rise to a whole series of antiques bearing inscriptions in the same alphabet. Roman and Maccabean coins began to multiply like so many cells. And the great temple stone with its menacing inscription produced a series of stones bearing similar inscriptions.

We are going to devote our attention to some of these antiques. The Jewish merchant Shapira has already entered the story because of his famous collection of Moabite antiques and the controversy occasioned by them.

MOSES' MANUSCRIPT

The *coup de grâce* was delivered to Shapira's Moabite collection around 1878. But the merchant did not shuffle off with his tail between his legs. Instead he decided to get revenge with an even more sensational find, one so sensational that it was no sensation at all.

On to the Promised Land

On the morning of July 20, 1883, Shapira knocked at the door of the English Archaeological Society and asked to speak with the secretary. He informed him that he had brought a manuscript to England. It was a fragment of Deuteronomy written in Moabite characters on parchment and containing important variants. The secretary asked to see this manuscript but Shapira refused. He agreed to show it only if Captain Conder, our lieutenant in the last chapter, were present; so they agreed to meet on July 24. The three men met on that day and Shapira showed them the find. He modestly pointed out that the find would be most important if it proved to be authentic, and demanded the less modest sum of a million pounds sterling.

Accompanying the manuscript was a document describing its initial discovery and acquisition, and the first attempts at selling it.

SHAPIRA'S DOCUMENT

Around the middle of July, 1878, I was sitting in my office with a sheik and a group of Arabs. They knew little about antiques and were telling me about some black fragments found near the Arnon river. One of them added that they seemed to be talismans and smelt like asphalt.

The next day the sheik invited me for a meal. During it he gave me more information. During the persecution of 1865 a group of Arabs took refuge amid the rocks. In one cavern they found some bundles wrapped in linen. Inside the bundles they found several black fragments. Dismayed, they cast the fragments aside. But one of the group held on to them, thinking that they were talismans. The Arab grew rich and attributed it to the talismans.

I promised to recompense the sheik if he would send me an Arab who might be able to obtain the fragments for me; but the sheik fell sick and died soon after. Ten or twelve days later, an Arab brought me one fragment containing four columns. Only a few words were legible. As time went on he brought me more fragments. After the third set, I did not see the Arab again.

I spent the next four weeks copying the legible columns. I sent a copy to Professor Schlottmann in Berlin, my defender in the ceramics dispute, and Professor Rieu. Schlottmann gave his categorical answer. They were forgeries and it would be a shame to call them the "sacred text." Not content with that, the professor sent a warning to Baron von Münchhausen, the German consul in Palestine who also had been duped by the ceramic collection. I meekly accepted his conclusion and wrote another letter to Doctor Rieu, admitting that I had been deceived by the Arabs. I then deposited the manuscripts in a bank at Jerusalem.

But I could not get the fragments out of my mind. As time went on, I began to think that Schlottmann's decision might have been based on errors in my transcription, since the professor had not seen the parchments firsthand. I took them out of the bank and proceeded to decipher them anew. I began by showing them to the German consul in Beirut, Professor Schröder, who considered them genuine and expressed a desire to buy them. Then I journeyed to Leipzig to photograph the manuscripts. In Leipzig I showed my treasure to two professors, Guthe and Hermann. Both regarded them as genuine and Guthe was eager to write an article on them.

This was the story Shapira told in London. It was passed on to the men in charge of the British Museum and published in the *Times.*

The manuscripts were brought to the British Museum and exhibited to the public. Crowds of people passed before the glass case. Among them was an interested visitor who spent two whole days in front of the case. It was the great detective of the scholarly world, Clermont-Ganneau.

THE MANUSCRIPTS ON TRIAL

Professor Ginsburg began to study the manuscript and publish translated fragments with notes. Ambassador Schröder wrote to the *Times,* denying Shapira's account. Professor Neubauer called them phony on the basis of Hebrew grammar and lexicography. Clermont-Ganneau wanted to examine them before reporting his opinion. But he already doubted their authenticity. A meeting was arranged, but on the scheduled day Clermont-Ganneau was politely rebuffed. After all, he had been the one mainly responsible for unmasking Shapira in the previous affair. So the persistent bloodhound had to be satisfied with scrutinizing the manuscript in the glass case and bucking the crowd of curious visitors. This

[141]

examination was enough to enable him to publish a damaging report. The lines were written in horizontal columns. The lower margin was uneven, torn, and trimmed; the upper margin was cut with a pocketknife. From top to bottom ran fine lines traced with a sharp instrument. At one point the parchment was stitched to the next piece.

In short, the forger had bought a roll of parchments sown together (such as the rolls used in synagogues, between 100 and 130 feet long), and had carefully cut the lower margin. On it he had written Moabite characters and added some strange variants. And for his work, i.e., his discovery, he was asking a million pounds.

Along with his report Clermont-Ganneau made the following offer: "Give me a synagogue roll and permission to cut it. I will transcribe some text such as Leviticus in archaic characters. It will be a good follow-up to the Deuteronomy text offered by Shapira and it won't cost a million pounds."

The authorities did not accept this offer, nor that of Shapira. Other negative reports followed, with the result that the great antique maker had to pack his merchandise and return to his little shop in Jerusalem. His dream of making a quick million fell through, but he has gone down in history as the most genial forger.

ANOTHER FORGER

His name was Martin Bulos, no less; a name which would immediately arouse suspicion in a Spaniard. What's more, he was a Christian Arab. And to top it all, he had helped Clermont-Ganneau to get the famous stele of the temple in Jerusalem bearing an inscription in Greek which prohibited Gentiles from entering the temple under pain of death. The archaeologist worked very enthusiastically on the find, and his Arab assistant took mental note of the interest aroused. The Turkish governor was interested in the project, and so were some foreign powers. One day the stele was shipped to Constantinople from Jaffa, but it disappeared mysteriously en route.

One day in Constantinople Clermont-Ganneau got a letter from a friend. The friend reported that one Martin Bulos had offered him a stele with an inscription quite similar to the earlier one. For the present he had given him a copy of it. Clermont-Ganneau saw through it at once. Bulos was cutting inscriptions on the cemetery stones. He was a stonecutter by profession and knew what would appeal to Europeans. Furthermore, he was probably the one who had betrayed the archaeologist in his attempt to get the original. Clermont-Ganneau decided to have a little fun at the expense of Bulos. So he wrote to his friend and told him to "play along with the scheme." Bulos fell for the bait. First, he brought a sketch of the stone. Then he gave some imaginary reasons for refusing to show the original. One day in November Bulos brought the European to the site of his discovery. They went at dawn, when it was dark and deserted. They entered a dark barn. A burro began to bray, but Bulos quieted him by pulling his tail. The two visitors feigned terror. It was an hilarious scene and it is hard to say who was enjoying it most. Finally the treasure was spotted, half buried near the wall of the house.

Several days later Bulos made his triumphal entrance with the treasure. It was the last act of the comedy. Clermont-Ganneau's representative sprung the trap and Martin was forced to confess. He departed, leaving behind the treasure which he had so carefully forged.

From then on Bulos looked for more gullible clients. The stele, with its incorrect inscriptions, was deposited in a convent at Jerusalem. Later he sold another stele to a Greek professor; but this time the inscription was untranslatable, just in case.

After another set, there appeared a grotesque head adorned with a Moabite inscription and offered for the modest sum of twenty pounds. Then came a porphyry column on which was narrated Moses' victory over the Moabites. Later there was a bilingual inscription in Moabite and cuneiform characters, and the head of some emperor with a Latin inscription:

AVSVITVSHASPIANVS

which should read:

AVGVSTVS HADRIANVS

Apparently this line of work provided Martin Bulos with more income than his simple work as a stonecutter. But at any rate, his name did not become as famous as Shapira's. And his stone-work turned out to be more expensive and troublesome.

Clermont-Ganneau was indefatigable in unmasking forgers. He performed a great service for archaeologists, epigraphists, and paleographers. In an enjoyable book he recounted the many forgeries which he had heard of or unmasked personally.

WHO CAN BE TRUSTED?

By now the reader must think that distrust is the guiding principle of archaeology. But this is not true today. Two factors have changed greatly. First of all, archaeologists no longer go hunting for precious objects (museum pieces); so the natives no longer are on the lookout for archaeologists. Second, eighty-odd years ago, epigraphy, paleography, and even semitic archaeology were infant sciences; and it is easy to fool an infant. Today, however, an attempt at forgery by the native inhabitants would soon be discovered by the team of experts involved in any given excavation. But let us not forget that even in those early days many scholars knew how to catch the forgeries and pinpoint the small handful of authentic archaeological finds.

IV. THE HEROIC AGE: CONQUEST AND DEFENSE OF THE PROMISED LAND

Valiant leader was Josue, son of Nun, assistant to Moses in the prophetic office, formed to be, as his name implies, the great savior of God's chosen ones, to punish the enemy and to win the inheritance for Israel. What glory was his when he raised his arm, to brandish his javelin against the city! And who could withstand him when he fought the battles of the Lord? Did he not by his power stop the sun, so that one day became two? He called upon the Most High God when his enemies beset him on all sides, and God Most High gave answer to him in hailstones of tremendous power, which he rained down upon the hostile army till on the slope he destroyed the foe; that all the doomed nations might know that the Lord was watching over his people's battles.

(Sirach 46)

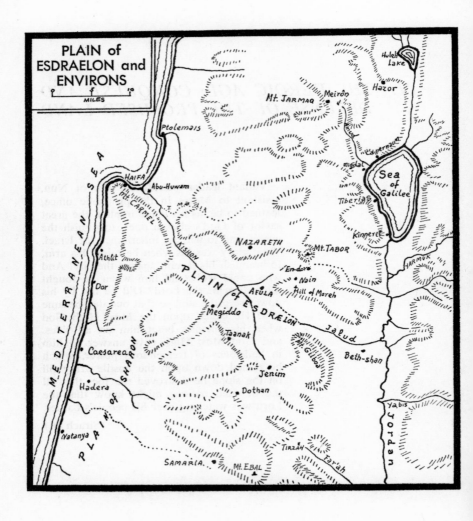

PLAIN of
ESDRAELON and
ENVIRONS

0 5 10
MILES

MEDITERRANEAN SEA

Huleh Lake

Mt. JARMAQ Meirôn Hazor

Ptolemais

HAIFA Capernaum

Abu-Huwam migdal Sea of Galilee

Mt. CARMEL MALIK

Athlit Kishon NAZARETH Mt. TABOR Tiberias Kinneret

Dor PLAIN 'En-dor JARMUK

AFULA Nain

of Hill of Moreh

Megiddo ESDRÆLON Jalud

Taanak Gilboa Beth-shan

Caesarea Jenim

PLAIN Dothan

of Yabis

Hadera SHARON Jordan

Natanya TIRZAH Farah

SAMARIA Mt. EBAL

[146]

Rock formation in the region around Sodom.

Along the shore of the Dead Sea.

Caves near Beer-sheba

A pipeline for irrigating the Negeb.

Two Arab refugees in a camp.

A Bedouin refugee and his pipe.

A general view of modern Hebron.

The sanctuary at Hebron.

Terrain in the Sinai Peninsula.

Terrain around the Dead Sea.

The River Arnon.

*Mountains and hills of
Galilee.*

Excavations at Jericho.

Mt. Gerizim towers over Nablus.

Mt. Tabor.

The fountain of Gideon.

Ain Sultan, the well of Elisha, near the ruins of Jericho.

Near the sources of the Jordan.

Landscape around Qumran.

The meanderings of the Jordan.

Panoramic view of Nazareth.

Mountains and hills near Safed in Galilee.

A view from Mt. Carmel.

The Pool of Siloam, near the end of Hezekiah's tunnel.

23. THE WALLS OF JERICHO

I THINK that few ramparts are as famous in history as the walls of Jericho.

The first scene in the drama takes place at night (cf. Jos 2). Rahab dwells in a house bordering the city wall. Several Israelite spies had entered her house in the late afternoon. They were followed by emissaries of the king ruling the city, but Rahab tells the latter that the spies left the city before its gates were closed. Now, in the dead of night, Rahab drops a rope through an opening in the wall, and the spies flee to safety in the mountains nearby.

The second scene lasts six days. It is almost a pantomime act. The Israelites have already crossed the Jordan and are encamped near the hill of Jericho. The city people have closed their gates and are preparing their defenses. The next morning their lookouts see a strange sight. A silent procession of Israelites is moving toward the city. In the midst of the procession a huge wooden chest is being carried by several men. Next to them seven men are blowing their trumpets. It is the only sound in the silent procession. The procession is led by armed men and at the rear comes the rest of the people. The procession marches around the city once and then returns to the encampment. The lookouts gaze at this procession in silent wonder. They presume that it is some cultic function and do not dare to provoke their peaceable enemy.

The next day the same procession takes place again. It is as if the Israelites are rehearsing for a great performance, or observing a series of religious ceremonies. This time, a crowd of townspeople watches the procession from the wall. On the following day the city folk are fighting for a place along the wall so that they can watch the proceedings. By the sixth day they are no longer interested in the simple repetitious ceremony. Once around the city, for six days. The air of silence and peace continues, broken only by the dull, hollow sound of the rams' horns.

The Heroic Age

On the seventh day the final scene is played. This time the procession circles the city six times. Then on the seventh time around Joshua raises a shout, as had been prearranged, and all the people join in. At the sound of the trumpets and the shouts of the Israelites the city walls totter, crumble at the bottom, and come crashing down. The peaceful-looking marchers pour into the city, sack and burn it, sparing only Rahab and her family.

A VISIT TO JERICHO

We too advance in silence toward this city, but for a different reason. The thermometer registers 110 degrees and we are more than 900 feet below sea level. The only one to speak — a peace-loving Joshua — is Father Robert North who took part in the recent excavations at this site. He is a perfect guide, and we listen attentively to his comments on this legendary spot, resigning ourselves to the oppressive heat. He relives the incidents connected with the excavation work, the failures and findings. And his deliberate commentary gives new meaning to mounds of brick and rock. Life stirs in the stucco pavements, the copper axes, and the skulls stuffed with cement.

Our guide tells us of the excavations which took place during 1952, 1953, and 1954 under the direction of Miss Kenyon. But he also makes references to the excavations of Garstang (1929–1936) and those of Sellin and Watzinger (1907–1909). It is significant how much vexation this little hillock called Tell el Sultan has caused the archaeologists. It is no more than 900 feet long, 450 feet wide, and 50 feet high. It should not be difficult to circle it seven times in one morning. But it has demanded repeated efforts to fathom its mysteriousness. And after all this work, it still remains an unsolved problem.

Joshua circled the city thirteen times. The archaeologists have waged thirteen campaigns for the scientific conquest of this city. Indeed, the walls of Jericho have known how to arouse and hold the interest of men.

The Walls of Jericho

Naturally the archaeologists use different tactics to conquer the coveted walls of the city. The outsider would regard them as a series of strange rituals: the long line of Arabs with their tire baskets full of earth, or the director prowling back and forth over the area. The archaeologists do not attack the walls from below as did the ancient warriors, but from above. The warriors strove to topple the wall and break it. The archaeologists want to preserve it intact, and work slowly down to its base; so they use technological aids when they have to. Anything which has to be destroyed to enable further digging is first photographed in full detail.

Sellin and Watzinger (1907–1909) discovered two distinct walls: an outer one lower down, forming a sloping rampart, and a double wall above. In the fine sketches accompanying their book on the excavations, the upper wall is done in blue and the lower one in red. The upper wall has a perimeter of about 2000 feet (whereas the Roman Coliseum has one of about 1700 feet). According to them, this would be the wall conquered by Joshua in the biblical account. The outer wall is much bigger and would encircle the fountain. According to the excavators, this wall was constructed by the Israelites in the ninth century B.C.; in short, it was the one attributed to Hiel by the Book of Kings. Sellin and Watzinger believed that they had conquered the mystery of the coveted walls. But they had no sure way of determining the exact chronology, and soon had to correct their conclusions.

When chronological dating had made some advances, Albright and Watzinger, working separately, attributed the lower rampart wall to the Hyksos (1600 B.C.) ; a change of eight centuries. Joshua's wall was still the double wall with fortifications, painted blue on Sellin's map.

Into the fray came Garstang who hit upon the solution to all the problems. The double wall was the wall of Joshua. Its fortifications fitted in with the data on Rahab's house which purportedly looked out on the wall. At some points the wall seemed to have toppled over due to some disturbance, and this coincided with Joshua's invasion. And in the city itself he found scraps of burned food: grain, lentil seeds, dates, etc. This would fit in with the biblical

[149]

report that Joshua burned the city. Finally Garstang was able to place these events in the fifteenth century B.C., contrary to the common view which dated the Exodus in the thirteenth century B.C.

These great finds aroused much enthusiasm among the defenders of the Bible. Sir Charles Marston, a great devotee of the Bible who has done much to subsidize the excavations, published a glowing volume entitled *The Bible Is True*. It was highly praised, translated into various languages, and read avidly by novices in this field. We believe in the veracity of the Bible, of course; but not because of Garstang's discoveries or his weighty hypotheses. But, for the moment, the walls of Jericho seemed to have been conquered. They had fallen under the weight of scientific evidence, and their fall seemed to fortify that other stout wall, the veracity of the Bible.

Then came a third attack launched by Miss Kenyon, a careful worker and a specialist in ceramics. In the ditches of her excavations she failed to find any remnants of Joshua's era. Everything there either antedated or postdated this epoch. She also discovered several other interesting things. The primitive city had been built at ground level; the successive layers of ruins had built the mound. Then there were the mysterious skulls and other objects of value. But the most impressive fact was the absence of remains dating from the biblical epoch. Joshua, the trumpets, the fire — no trace remained. The walls still stood, invincible, and seemed to undermine the veracity of the Bible. Would the archaeologists retreat in defeat after so many supposed triumphs?

It did represent a defeat for archaeologists seeking to prove the veracity of the Bible, or for those who pinned their hopes on Marston's overconfident book. But it was not a defeat for those who came looking only for facts.

And the mystery of the walls? It still stands, waiting for new generations of archaeologists. Meanwhile, two hypotheses stand out. Either all traces of the biblical events have been destroyed, or else the city conquered by Joshua lies elsewhere.

24. THE "RUIN"

HÖLDERLIN once said that certain places have a fatal destiny. He was a romantic at heart, and loved ruins. Unfortunately he applied this statement to the ruins of Heidelberg. Somewhere I once saw a picture of Heidelberg and its castle rising high above the Neckar, its ruins glistening in the light of the moon. It would seem to prove the truth of Hölderlin's statement. But in reality the ruins of Heidelberg do not merit such a tribute. They are too recent, and are preserved intact to satisfy the romantic desires of tourists.

It would be different if Hölderlin had applied his statement to the ruins we visited today, or rather to "the ruin" we visited today.

It was a memorable visit, but hardly for archaeological reasons. Our director was an American who did not know about that marvelous Spanish custom — after-dinner conversation (*sobremesa*). And today's meal deserved a good after-dinner conversation, in the opinion of ten Spaniards at least. The Cistercians of Latrun are austere in their own eating habits, but lavish food on their guests. And they make a wine which is the best in this part of the world. But our director did not learn about the *sobremesa* during his three-month stay in Spain. So we were hustled into the bus right after dinner, and arrived at Ai around two o'clock of a July afternoon. However, the spot was so full of memories that we were quite willing to climb around in the heat.

ABRAHAM AND JOSHUA

First we climbed a nearby hill to study the lay of the land. One day, more than thirty-six centuries ago, a small band of Bedouins was passing through this region. They were just like the many other groups of nomads which passed by in search of good grazing land.

They had come a long way from the northeast, from a key city called Haran ("road"). It was the hinge point on the route between Mesopotamia and the kingdoms of the Mediterranean. The nomad leader had left a flourishing city south of the Euphrates where he lived a normal urban life. For God had ordered him to set out in search of a new land which He intended to give to him.

We must speak his name with respect and reverence because he is the natural father of the Jews and the spiritual father of all Christians. Abraham passed through this region and came to a city called Luz. In front of the city he saw a pile of ruins — off to our side — which the people called Ai. It had not been inhabited for centuries. The people now dwelt in the city of Luz. There Abraham encamped, saw a vision of God, and built an altar.

Four centuries went by and Ai entered history once again. First Joshua sent out a scouting party. Their report was favorable. The area could be taken with a small detachment of men. The inhabitants of the hill had probably heard of their impressive conquest of Jericho; but they still resolved to put up a fight. When the Israelites started up the hill on the following morning, the defenders launched a sudden attack, slew thirty-six Israelites, and scattered the rest. It was the first defeat inflicted on Joshua's army and caused consternation. It had been poor strategy to launch an open, frontal assault. But there was a deeper religious reason for the defeat. One of the Israelites had sinned. Until he was punished, the Israelites' relations with God would be strained. When the guilty one had been chastised, Joshua decided to capture Ai by a stratagem. A small detachment left the camp, crept close to the hill by night, and hid on the west flank behind the hillock where we are standing. The lookouts on Ai did not notice anything until the early hours of the morning. Then they saw the enemy forces advancing toward the city from the north and the east. The alarm was sounded. The defenders of the city sallied out, crossed the valley, and attacked the Israelites from below. The Israelites retreated, without losing altitude. At the prearranged moment Joshua turned around, set his bow, and shot an arrow in the direction of the mound. The guerrillas climbed the undefended slope and set fire to the city. The end came quickly. The pursued suddenly turned around. The stunned pursuers spotted the bright flames on the hilltop and saw another force attacking them from the rear. Hemmed in on both sides they surrendered and were put to death. The fatal destiny of the city comes full circle. Once again it becomes a pile of ruins. And the chronicler closes his story: "Then Josue destroyed the place by fire, reducing it to an everlasting mound of ruins, as it remains today" (Jos 8:28).

THE SECRET OF "THE RUIN"

After stopping to contemplate the topography and to recall the historical events which took place here, we descend our hill and climb to the ancient city of Ai. Few of the mounds we have visited are so rocky. Even the thistles, the only flower at these ruins, have little space in which to grow. All we can see above are rocks and more rocks. One can just imagine the work required of the archaeologists. Everything is confused and hard to explain. The only clear point is the condition of the excavated summit.

The Arabs call this hill *Et Tell* (a free translation of "rubble heap"), and it is said that some spirit guards the prophetic secret of these ruins. But, just as in the fairy tale, there is some girl anxious to discover the secret. The girl in the fairy tale fearlessly sets out to do battle with the guardian of the ruins. She opens corridors, penetrates caverns, and pries into the cursed city. The things she discovers will make the ancient city live once again. But the invisible guardian waits to take his revenge, kills the girl, and again conceals the data uncovered by her. It is one more layer added to the pile of ruins.

It happened much that way in reality. Judith Krause was born of Jewish parents. She studied in Palestine and France, specializing in archaeology and languages — French, English, German, Arabic, Syrian, and Accadian. She married a Frenchman but did not surrender her maiden name. Her name thus became Marquet-Krause. When Rothschild resumed his grants to archaeological work, Judith was chosen to head an expedition. She chose this mysterious hillside as the excavation site. Working at a feverish pace she directed three assaults on the hill, hiring eighty, ninety, and even as many as one hundred and fifty Arabs. The discoveries were not sensational, but surpassed the expectations of most people: temples, walls, houses, one strange two-story house, and a large quantity of well-preserved pottery. Day after day the lady director cataloged the finds in chronological order. Toward the end of the third campaign she had found the key to the mysterious city. The data had been formulated in her mind and she was preparing her description of the ancient city. It was a remarkable success for a young woman thirty years old. Then death overtook her and the "pile of ruins" was again shrouded in an air of mystery.

BAD LUCK TO THE VERY END

Bad luck followed her even after death. Her notes were gathered by friends and were to be published intact. The type was readied and one set of galleys was run off. She had died in 1936. The book was to appear in 1939. Then came the war and the invasion, and everything was requisitioned. The type was melted down and used for munitions. Once again in history the printed word was destroyed, to further the destruction of men and cities.

The one set of galleys which survived was the only record left. With it men were able to recapitulate the immense work of the young investigator. In 1948 two volumes of her notes and charts were published. Her findings were finally salvaged, and that was something. But it was only a partial victory. The "pile of ruins" had demanded a high price for victory.

25. MOUNT EBAL: THE NEW SINAI

WE SET out from Jerusalem very early in the morning. The highway twists and curves through this mountain region. Once we reach the province of Samaria the road curves even more so that we can descend gradually over the bumpy surface. As we lose altitude, we gain a pleasant landscape — verdant stretches of fertile land. Our destination, Nablus, lies in the very center of Palestine. It is near Shechem, the first stopping place of the patriarchs, and Sebaste (Samaria), the capital of the northern kingdom (Israel) shortly after its separation from Judah.

The present-day city of Nablus lies in a narrow valley. Little by little houses are going up along the mountain slopes, while other installations crop up through the valley.

We are at the center of Palestine. This valley cuts the great mountain range in half. Journeying to the west we would end up on the coastal plain; to the east lie the approaches to the Jordan. In short, nomads coming from the east could penetrate into Palestine through this region.

But this is hardly the place to spend time calculating one's position. To be sure, Nablus is about 1600 feet above sea level. But the two mountains encircling us are enough to suggest that we should consider this the center of Palestine.

THE CLIMB

The weighty recommendation of Adam Smith is a strong argument for climbing the slopes of Nablus. It is not a question of physical prowess because it is only a climb of some 1600 feet. But it is the end of July and weariness has crept up on us. We cannot make up our mind. But finally geography and history gang up on us and we push up toward the summit. Two policemen armed with shotguns quietly accompany us. When we have passed the last houses they politely take their leave and wait for our return. At dawn a thick white mantle covered the mountain, delaying the climb. Now the sun beats down and we are sweating profusely. It is not a lofty mountain but it is very tricky. Thinking we are at the top, we find ourselves in a pleasant grove of fragrant pines; but it is only a stopover. The peak lies above us. We descend a little way and then start to climb again. The slope is not too perpendicular, but the ground is rough and uneven. Rocks and thistles cover the trail. The rocks are really jagged boulders against which the unwary traveler might stub his toe. And the thistles get caught in our socks and prick the skin.

We finally reach the top of the slope. Fooled again! We have not yet reached the summit and we are beginning to get discouraged. Two of us set out alone. My companion, a native of Colombia, is a mountaineer and sets a quick pace. We pay no attention to several herdsmen grazing their cows. I don't know what the cows are doing here. I doubt that they have learned to eat thistles, as goats do. There isn't any water along the way either. And the water in our canteens has succumbed to the intense heat.

After an hour and fifteen minutes we reach a pile of rocks marking the summit — 3000 feet above sea level. We have climbed so fast that it is ten minutes before the next group arrives. And because of the fierce heat two of our companions have stayed behind at the pine grove.

GEOGRAPHY ON EBAL

The summit is a broad barren flatland covered with rocks and thistles. There is no room to roam around and no refuge from the heat. But there is a pleasant breeze which dries us off and soothes our weary limbs.

After our rest we can enjoy the only pleasure provided by the mountains — contemplation. Mountain peaks rise up all around us. Behind them the mist obscures the distant panorama and hides the sea from us. Between the mountains are crevices, slopes, and valleys; the paths of men and the courses of rivers.

To the south the first mountain is Gerizim, then come the

mountainous stretches of Judea. We can picture in our minds the location of Jerusalem. To the northwest a mountain chain stretches out toward the Mediterranean. It is Mount Carmel cutting across the passes running through Palestine from north to south. Behind it, we know, lies the magnificent plain of Esdraelon (Jezreel). To the east we can see the mountains sloping to the Jordan somewhere below. And farther on another mountain chain rises majestically toward the sky — the mountains of Gilead in Transjordania.

Amid all these mountains Ebal reminds us of a little bit of Sinai. It is only a slight resemblance, however, because the topography here differs greatly from the antediluvian wastes of Sinai. Sinai was the home of the chosen people during their novitiate; Ebal is the center of the Promised Land.

HISTORY IN EBAL

History too links Ebal with Sinai. We recall the scene of Moses climbing the sacred mountain, while the people were encamped below. And we remember the solemn moment in which the people ratified their alliance with God, the moment when the "ancient covenant" began.

Before dying Moses bade the Israelites to renew the covenant in a solemn way when they reached the Promised Land. The responsibility fell to Joshua, the successor of Moses. After their military victories had given the Israelites a certain measure of security, and before they dispersed in every direction, they held a great convocation. For this convocation Joshua chose the sacred city of the patriarchs, Shechem, located in the center of Palestine. The people encamped in the narrow valley where the present-day city of Nablus is located, and in the wide valley which stretches to the east. The Israelites took their places on the rocky slopes of the two mountains, six tribes on the slopes of Gerizim and six on the slopes of Ebal. It was an amphitheater provided by nature herself. Down below, in the middle of the valley, was the Ark of the Covenant and the priests.

Meanwhile, Moses' successor ascended the mountain to worship God, taking a select group of priests with him. On the summit of the mountain they erected an altar of unhewn stones. In those

[157]

days it would have been blasphemous to cut and shave these stones (Jos 9:31). Joshua did not have much trouble finding stone for the altar. (We can vouch for that.) On the altar Joshua sacrificed a peace offering. (We have seen how easy it is for flocks to climb the mountain.)

After the sacrifice Joshua descends and takes his place in the center of the proceedings. He begins to read the law. The people listen attentively and indicate their acceptance. When this is finished the levites rise and begin to intone these words echoed by the mountains. First they face Mount Gerizim: "If you continue to heed the voice of the Lord . . . all these blessings will come upon you and overwhelm you: 'May you be blessed in the city, and blessed in the country! . . . [and the people responded 'Amen'] . . . blessed be the fruit of your womb, the produce of your soil and the offspring of your livestock [Amen!] . . . May you be blessed in your coming in . . . and your going out!' " So the benedictions go. Next the levites face Ebal: "Cursed be he who dishonors his father or his mother!" And they answered "Amen!" And this time the chorus of shouts has a fearsome ring to it. It is their unanimous curse pronounced in full view of heaven and earth. "Cursed be he who slays his neighbor in secret! — Amen. . . . Cursed be he who fails to fulfill any of the provisions of this law!" And the narrow valley echoes the roar of the assembly (Jos 8:30 ff.; Dt 27:15 ff.).

Then the twelve tribes disperse from this historical spot in the center of Palestine and spread throughout the Promised Land.

26. MOUNTAINS AND HILLSIDES

In RECENT years two books on mountain-climbing have sold well on two continents: one on the ascent of Mount Annapurna by the Frenchman, Maurice Herzog; the other on the ascent of Everest by the Englishman, Hunt. The latter book had record sales in England. In May Hillary and Tensing reached the peak. The colonel edited his memoirs in the space of a few weeks. The book was put on sale in September. By November it had sold 150,000 copies.

It is quite obvious that the subject appeals to modern man. People not only want to read books and see films on mountain-climbing; they also want to engage actively in this pastime. These men are true adventurers in an age where there are no more islands left to discover. For the average enthusiast, mountain-climbing is an exhilirating pastime. By dint of skill and know-how he surmounts every obstacle until the mountain peak is a pedestal under his feet.

Many other people climb mountains in cable cars, lifts, and elevators. The only price they pay is a few francs, but they cannot taste the fruits of conquest or exercise. Atop the summit the surrounding countryside is a vast panorama, the air is purer, and the light is more dazzling. The thrill is undeniable, but one must experience it to appreciate it.

Do mountains evoke any religious sentiments in the observer? One of the most surprising things in Herzog's book was the fact that God was never mentioned. On the summit of Pilatus overlooking Lake Lucerne a Swiss boy, who was a total stranger, began to talk to me about the lure of the peaks. His eyes sparkled as he described his feelings. Here he felt far from the world of men and very close to God. It was a spontaneous emotion, and almost instinctive, to my way of thinking. Modern man has discovered the beauty and the challenge of mountains. But many have forgotten their religious value. Long ago men may not have realized the thrill connected with mountain-climbing or the pleasure derived from a mountain view; but they certainly understood their religious importance.

The Heroic Age

SACRED MOUNTAINS

Our journey has often taken us over mountainous regions and through mountain passes. Much of the time we have been traveling through hilly countryside. We could not stop to identify every piece of high ground or to admire every hillside. But neither can we pass by without making some comment. For the Hebrews, mountains, hills, and other high ground had religious significance. And if we do not dwell on this point for a bit, our trip will have been very superficial indeed.

Today we spent the morning on Mount Ebal and the evening on Mount Gerizim, contemplating the mountain panorama. So it is an appropriate moment to summarize these recollections and impressions.

On this earth inhabited by mortal men the ancients thought that the gods had hallowed certain spots, and dwelt there in a special way. These places were venerated; and pious men offered prayers and sacrifices at these spots.

In the basin of the Euphrates there were no mountains. The inhabitants had to manufacture their own. Using brick and earth they constructed the type of pyramid known as a ziggurat. These were fine symmetrical mountains (i.e., towers) on which the people erected sanctuaries reached by ramps and stairs. The ziggurat represented an ascent from earth to heaven in search of the divine. These towers climbing into the air, midway between earth and heaven, symbolized the elevation of the spirit.

One of these towers in Babylonia had a very significant name, *Esagila* (short for *E-sag-an-še-ila*); the Sumerian word means "temple whose top reaches the sky." Philologically it is the same as our word "skyscraper," but there is an important difference. Our sky is a secular, neutral sky (witness the German equivalent — *Wolkenkratzer* = "cloud-scraper"). For the ancients the sky was a religious entity, and "touching the sky" was a distinctively religious act.

Another example might clarify the point. We all would agree that the basic architectural lines of a Gothic cathedral give it a soaring appearance. So all extraneous embellishment is avoided. But to what does the cathedral soar? To a secular sky or a religious domain? In short, what we attempt to convey with a vaulted arch, the Babylonians and Assyrians attempted to convey with the terraced levels of a ziggurat.

THE HEBREWS ON THE "HEIGHTS"

When the Israelites began to invade the Promised Land, it was inhabited by the Canaanites. These people worshiped their divinities on hillsides and under trees. Near the end of our stay in Jerusalem we were invited to visit a small exposition of recent archaeological finds. The most interesting items were a set of silver figurines depicting some feminine deity, a collection of seven-branched candelabras, and a pottery wheel with a hole in the center and six holes ringing it. All of them had been found in one of the "heights" or sacred sites of the Canaanites.

The Israelites could not simply eradicate all the native inhabitants. They had to live side by side with these people. And in time they were attracted by their religious practices. The Hebrews had spread out through the many hills of Palestine. And undoubtedly these hills were just as appropriate for the worship of Yahweh as for the worship of the Canaanite gods. The Israelites had just come from their wanderings in the arid desert wastes. The green groves and murmuring trees of Palestine were a temptation. At first they worshiped Yahweh alone. Then, without abandoning Yahweh, they also worshiped the twin deities of the Canaanites. While Moses was spending those many days on Sinai, the people had become bored, and had built a golden idol to satisfy their religious yearnings. Now in Israel they had the many pleasant hills at their disposal. Here God was present and accessible to all, not just to one such as Moses.

THE KINGS OF THE TWO KINGDOMS

Throughout the history of the two kingdoms, Judah and Israel, the hills continue to seem accursed places. At first this form of worship was quite acceptable, because it was directed to Yahweh: "The people offered sacrifice in the high places because the house of Yahweh had not yet been built." Solomon built the temple, worshiped Yahweh, and fulfilled the commands of David, his father. But he also offered sacrifices and burnt incense on the heights.

After Solomon's death the unity of the kingdom could not be preserved. In the north the secessionist king inaugurated his own religious policy. He knew full well that the one sanctuary at Jerusalem was a strong inducement to political unity. If his subjects were allowed to go to Jerusalem, the two kingdoms would soon be reunited and he would lose his throne. So "the king took counsel and made two calves of gold, and said to the people: 'You have gone up to Jerusalem long enough. Behold your gods, O Israel, who brought you up from the land of Egypt!' So he set up the one in Bethel, and the other he put in Dan. . . . He also made sanctuaries at high places . . . and priests from all sorts of people" (1 Kgs 12:28–30).

In the kingdom of Judah to the south, the magnificent temple erected by Solomon stood in Jerusalem. But, strangely enough, the green trees and pastures on the hillsides were more enticing than the gold and marble of this temple. People still worshiped in these places; and Solomon's successor, Rehoboam, sanctioned this perverse practice.

From then on, idolatrous practices increased throughout Palestine, moving alternately from north to south and from south to north. Even pious kings, who introduced severe measures to curb idolatry, did not dare to destroy the privileged sanctuaries on the hillsides, where some worshiped Yahweh and some worshiped Canaanite gods.

Asa was bold enough to revoke his mother's title of queen because she had made an idol; but he did not touch the hillside altars where the people offered sacrifice and incense. His son, Jehosaphat, followed his rule, and the same is true of Joah, his son Amaziah, his grandson Azariah, and his great-grandson Jotham.

THE BUGBEAR OF THE PROPHETS

The distorted religious practice connected with the hillside altars was one of the sins most vehemently denounced by the prophets. "The sin of Juda is written with an iron stylus, engraved with a diamond point upon the tablets of their hearts, and the horns of their altars . . . beside the green trees, on the high hills, the peaks in the highland" (Jer 17:1–3). "On the mountaintops they offer sacrifice and on the hills they burn incense, beneath oak and poplar and terebinth, because of their pleasant shade" (Hos 4:13).

Today the hills of Palestine have less trees than in ancient times and the Israeli colonists are trying to grow them once again. They are marking off terraced areas with rows of rock, and clearing the soil to plant fruit trees, olives, and pines. Pipelines carry water where it is needed.

But in areas which the colonists have not touched, the hillsides are sparse and unkempt. It is as if they were still under the curse pronounced by the prophet Ezekiel: "So will I spend my fury upon them. Then shall they know that I am the Lord, when their slain shall lie amid their idols, all about their altars, on every high hill and mountaintop, beneath every green tree and leafy oak, wherever they offered appeasing odors to any of their gods. I will stretch out my hand against them, and wherever they live I will make the land a desolate waste, from the desert to Ribla; thus shall they know that I am the Lord" (Ez 6:13–14).

The most heartrending threat was pronounced by Hosea. One day the very sites of idolatry will be invoked, when only one desperate remedy remains: death. "The king of Samaria shall disappear, like foam upon the waters. The high places of On (Aven) shall be destroyed, the sin of Israel; thorns and thistles shall overgrow their altars. Then shall they cry out to the mountains, 'Cover us!' and to the hills, 'Fall upon us!'" (Hos 10:7–8.)

THE DAYS OF PURIFICATION

Hezekiah was the first king to challenge the idolatrous practices on the hillsides. The twenty-eight years of his reign were peaceful, and he was quite successful in his project. But his son Manasseh, who reigned for fifty-four years, reversed the whole situation. He promoted idolatrous practices and set aside the cult of Yahweh. Once again altars sprouted up on the hillsides, and the air was filled with the odor of burnt incense. His successor, Josiah, initiated a thoroughgoing reform. Idols and altars were banned once again. But this reform was not completely successful. The unbridled fanaticism of Manasseh had affected several generations of Israelites. So when Josiah died tragically in Megiddo, idolatry sprouted up once again. Religious principles declined steadily in Judah from then on, until finally the kingdom was defeated and destroyed by Nebuchadnezzar's general, Nabuzaradan.

The exile accomplished what Hezekiah and Josiah could not. When the Israelites returned from Babylon, the hills of Palestine were no longer a temptation to idolatry. The people remembered the sad result of their naturalistic religious practices, and were cured forever. But now there was a new source of temptation, the pagan culture of the new conquerors, the successors of Alexander.

THE EXALTED MOUNTAINS

We must not think that this desire to perform religious rites in the mountains and hillsides was a sign of outright depravity. Indeed, it seems to be a natural and fitting gesture. God, who inhabits every portion of His universe, can freely choose certain sites as His special dwelling place. What better place than the hills overlooking the land where His people live and work? And, as a matter of fact, Yahweh seemed to show a marked preference for mountains and hillsides. He sealed His alliance with His chosen people at the foot of Sinai. Atop this very mountain He spoke to Moses and revealed His Commandments. Joshua renewed the alliance on Mount Ebal. And Elijah passed judgment on the false prophets atop Mount Carmel.

The temple, God's special dwelling place, was built on a hill in Jerusalem. It came to be called "the Lord's mountain." So many lofty places had hoped to be given this honor! But God chose Zion; on the other side of Lake Gennesaret there were many mountains reflected in its waters. They all are "exalted" and "lofty." And the poet chides them: "Why, lofty mountains, do you look with envy on the mountain chosen by Yahweh?"

The psalmists and prophets sing a litany of praise to the chosen mountain: "His sacred mountain, his chosen hill, blessed above all the hills of earth, the citadel of the great King"; "it is unshakeable and endures forever.". . . .

The Israelis succeeded in having Mount Zion included in their section of Jerusalem. The boundary line swerves to bypass this hill. There we Catholics were allowed to pay a quick visit to the Cenacle, and to venerate the memory of the Blessed Virgin in the beautiful basilica which stands as her tomb.

To reach it we first had to descend to a bridge over the valley of Hinnom, a piece of burnt earth which is a no-man's-land for the most part. Then we climbed a long crooked staircase. On both sides the Jews have erected stones bearing texts related to Mount Zion. And at the top Jewish visitors pay their respects to the tomb of David. But scholars are certain that this is not Mount Zion and that it is not David's tomb. It is merely a concession to the nationalism of some and the curiosity of others. We too paid a visit, covering our heads before entering so as not to "desecrate" it.

But the real Mount Zion lies inside the confines of the temple, which today is a great mosque, second only to Mecca in the eyes of the Moslems.

THE MOUNTAINS OF THE NEW TESTAMENT

Jesus Christ also showed marked preference for mountains. He prayed and fasted on them. On a mount He promulgated His new law. Atop a hill He died. And from a mount He ascended into heaven. In this last act mountains achieved their ultimate religious significance. They became a means by which man ascends into heaven. In the highlands man is not meant to sin under the trees but to raise his heart to the Almighty.

The Christian people also have a predilection for mountains. They prefer to place their hermitages on hillsides and to build basilicas on hilltops.

It is not without reason that the prophet Isaiah viewed the future messianic kingdom as a great mountain. "In days to come, the mountain of the Lord's house shall be established as the highest mountain and raised above the hills. All nations shall stream towards it; many people shall come and say: 'Come, let us climb the Lord's mountain, instruct us in his ways, and we may walk in his paths.' For from Sion shall go forth instruction, and the word of the Lord from Jerusalem. He shall judge between the nations, and impose terms on many peoples. They shall beat their swords into plowshares and their spears into pruning hooks; one nation shall not raise the sword against another, nor shall they train for war again. O house of Jacob, come, let us walk in the light of the Lord!" (Is 2:2–5.)

27. WAR CHANTS IN ESDRAELON

The Judges, too, each one of them, whose
hearts were not deceived, who did not
abandon God: May their memory be ever
blessed, their bones return to life from their
resting place, and their names receive fresh
luster in their children.

(Sirach 46)

They did not exterminate the peoples,
  as the Lord had commanded them,
But mingled with the nations
  and learned their works.
They served their idols,
  which became a snare for them.
They sacrificed their sons
  and their daughters to demons,
And they shed innocent blood,
  the blood of their sons and their daughters,
Whom they sacrificed to the idols of
    Chanaan,
  desecrating the land with bloodshed;
They became defiled by their works,
  and wanton in their crimes.

And the Lord grew angry with his people,
  and abhorred his inheritance;
He gave them over into the hands of the
    nations,
  and their foes ruled over them.
Their enemies oppressed them,
  and they were humbled under their power.
Many times did he rescue them,
  but they embittered him with their counsels
  and were brought low by their guilt.
Yet he had regard for their affliction
  when he heard their cry.

(Psalm 105[106]:34–49)

But once the rest of that generation were gathered to their fathers, and a later generation arose that did not know the Lord, or what he had done for Israel, the Israelites offended the Lord by serving the Baals. Abandoning the Lord, the God of their fathers, who had led them out of the land of Egypt, they followed the other gods of the various nations around them, and by their worship of these gods provoked the Lord. Because they had thus abandoned him and served Baal and the Asthartes, the anger of the Lord flared up against Israel, and he delivered them over to plunderers who despoiled them. He allowed them to fall into the power of their enemies round about whom they were no longer able to withstand. Whatever they undertook, the Lord turned into disaster for them, as in his warning he had sworn he would do, till they were in great distress. Even when the Lord raised up judges to deliver them from the power of their despoilers, they did not listen to their judges, but abandoned themselves to the worship of other gods. They were quick to stray from the way their fathers had taken, and did not follow their example of obedience to the commandments of the Lord. Whenever the Lord raised up Judges for them, he would be with the judges and save them from the power of their enemies as long as the judge lived; it was thus the Lord took pity on their distressful cries of affliction under their oppressors. But when the judge died, they would relapse and do worse than their fathers, following other gods in service and worship, relinquishing none of their evil practices or stubborn conduct.

In his anger toward Israel the Lord said, "Inasmuch as this nation has violated my covenant which I enjoined on their fathers, and has disobeyed me, I for my part will not clear away for them any more of the nations which Josue left when he died." . . .

The following are the nations which the

> Lord allowed to remain . . . the five lords
> of the Philistines; and all the Chanaanites,
> the Sidonians, and the Hevites who dwell
> in the mountain region of Lebanon between
> Baal-Hermon and the entrance to Hamath.
> (Judges 2)

ESDRAELON has great geographic importance because of its central position. The traveler must survey it several times from different observation points. Our first glimpse was from the Arab zone. The highway skirts the southern border of the plain around the heights of Taanach. There, with special permission, one can climb a military observation post and take a look around.

Through misinformation or a misunderstanding we were denied this permission. But we didn't mind too much. It saved us a climb in the midday heat, and the guard post at which we stopped was situated somewhat high up on the slopes.

From there our director pointed out the sights of interest: Mount Hermon, Mount Tabor, Nazareth. We were satisfied to look at these sites from a distance because we couldn't reach them from here anyway. The vast plain is under Israeli control — they were wise enough to settle in the most fertile regions of Palestine. Although the mountains on the other side belong to the same government we would have to make a detour to reach them.

Lesson One in military strategy: whoever controls the plain can isolate the northern regions from the central ones. The situation is exactly the same as it was in the days of Barak and Sisera. Two Israelite tribes had settled on the other side of the Jordan. The mountains of Galilee and a strip of coastline were occupied by Asher, Zebulun, and Naphtali. Lower down Benjamin and Judah were fighting to consolidate their gains. But the plain of Esdraelon, which had been left to Issachar, was controlled by Sisera, the chief of Harosheth. The secret of his successful domination was his horse-drawn war chariots, which maneuvered very well on the vast plain. But to the east, near the Jordan, there was a pass which linked the two divided sections.

DEBORAH

A tree is a central point on a plain. We have noticed this several

[168]

times during our trip. This is especially true if it is a palm tree. A tall palm tree near Bethel was the central meeting place for the Israelite tribes in the south; under this tree the prophetess Deborah ("bee") sat down to pass judgment.

The inspired author pictures Deborah as an extraordinary woman, inspired in her military tactics, her political decisions, and her victory hymns. Truly the spirit of God resided in her.

From her palm tree she sent a message to the chief of the northern tribes. He was to draft troops and carry out the battle plan she had thought up. However, Barak demands that Deborah accompany him. He wants her there as a prestige factor when he begins to draft men and stir them up to battle.

THE STRATEGY

We took a careful look at the plain from the edge of the mountains of Galilee several miles from Nazareth. It is like a huge triangle with its base in the north. The eastern side cuts down almost at a right angle and the opposite side cuts down obliquely from the northwest to the southeast. We have traveled over this plain in different directions, so we can appreciate its compact size and the ease with which it can be crossed. And we have had a close-up look at the corners of the triangle.

In the southern corner are the gardens of Jenim, a pleasant place to eat, to rest in the shade of the palm trees, and to enjoy the plentiful supply of water. But it is hardly a military vantage point.

In the northeastern corner stands Mount Tabor, an excellent place to concentrate troops and then launch an attack on the plain. Tabor could hardly be assaulted from the plain by men or war chariots. But troops could pour down onto the plain like a stream of lava. (Today the Israelis have built a fine highway which can handle cars and light trucks.) Furthermore, Mount Tabor is a good place from which to observe the plain. Little Mount Hermon obscures one's view of the eastern side of the triangle; but, on the other hand, one has a perfect view of troop movements coming from the west along the edge of the plain or into its center.

In the northwestern corner lies a narrow pass between Mount

Carmel and the western extreme of the mountains of Galilee. We visited it during our trip from Nazareth to Haifa. From this point the inhabitants of the coast could descend onto the plain. Protected by the ridges of Carmel, they could easily control the entire plain.

The rivers were another important strategic factor. The Jalud rises on the right, is joined by several small tributaries, flows through the plain, and gathers force near Beth-shan as it rushes to the Jordan. We have seen it in midsummer rushing through a deep gorge. But the eastern section of the plain does not interest us at the moment.

The small stream of Kishon climbs along the oblique side of the triangle. It is almost completely dried up in summertime. At the northwest corner of the triangle it assumes a more important air. But we did not pay much attention to it during our travels. However, those who have lived in that area for a long time say that during the winter this stream rises considerably, especially after a rainfall, and could seriously hinder cavalry maneuvers.

Deborah's plan was quite simple. Barak was to assemble his troops at Mount Tabor in the north. From this point he could watch the movements of the enemy and wait for just the right moment. In the south, between Taanach and Megiddo, the central tribes would provoke the enemy to descend down the plain. Then they would wait for the forces of heaven to intervene and decide the outcome of the fight.

THE BATTLE

Our trip took place during the summer; and there were many days when there wasn't a cloud in the sky. Only near the coast or on a morning in Jerusalem would we see these familiar white formations in the sky. But don't think that they augured rain. In this region rain has its appointed times; and it never misbehaves in summer. No trip had to be postponed because of rain, and the phrase "weather permitting" never cropped up. As far as we know, Deborah chose a season when rain was a distinct possibility. Otherwise, it would have been pure foolishness to launch an attack against the chariots of the enemy. In the mountains the foot soldiers could prevail; but the chariots had the advantage on the plain, as long as it was passible.

We also examined the plain from the hill of Megiddo. It is not completely flat and smooth. It has undulations and rough spots. The highway brought us between the fields to the communication center, Afula. The plain could be treacherous if it were inundated. The only way out would be the mountains or the rushing waters nearby.

The battle unfolded as Deborah had hoped. Sisera's chariots rushed into the plain; Barak and his men descended from Mount Tabor; and rain poured down from the heavens. (The Bible does not say this explicitly, because it does not describe the battle in detail.) The apparent advantage of horses and chariots is turned into disaster. Sisera's forces retreat toward the northwest corner of the plain where their city is located. But the high waters of Kishon block their escape. Meanwhile, their general decides to head for the mountains. There, in the tent of some Bedouin, a woman hammers a nail into his head while he is asleep.

So the battle is decided in favor of the Israelites "and their power weighed ever heavier upon him, till at length they destroyed the Chanaanite king, Jabin" (Jg 4:24).

A VICTORY CHANT

From what we saw of Kishon, it is hard to see how it swallowed Sisera's warriors. The rushing waters of Jalud would seem to be a more likely setting. But it is very easy to picture both armies, swept up in the inspired lyrics of Deborah.

> Hear, O kings! Give ear, O princes! I to the Lord will sing my song, my hymn to the Lord, the God of Israel.
> O Lord, when you went out from Seir, when you marched from the land of Edom, the earth quaked and the heavens were shaken, while the clouds sent down showers. . . .
> In the days of Samgar, son of Anath, in the days of slavery caravans ceased; those who traveled the roads went by roundabout paths. Gone was freedom beyond the walls, gone indeed from Israel.
> When I, Debora, rose, when I rose, a mother in Israel, new gods were their choice; then the war was at their gates. Not a shield could be seen, nor a lance, among forty thousand in Israel! My heart is with the leaders of Israel, nobles of the people who

bless the Lord; they who ride on white asses, seated on saddle-cloths as they go their way; sing of them to the strains of the harpers at the wells, where men recount the just deeds of the Lord, his just deeds that brought freedom to Israel.

Awake, awake, Debora, awake, awake, strike up a song. Strength! arise, Barac, make despoilers your spoil, son of Abinoem. Then down came the fugitives with the mighty, the people of the Lord came down for me as warriors. . . .

The kings came and fought; then they fought, those kings of Chanaan, at Thaanach by the waters of Mageddo; no silver booty did they take. From the heavens the stars, too, fought; from their courses they fought against Sisara. . . .

Blessed among women be Jahel, blessed among tent-dwelling women. He asked for water, she gave him milk; in a princely bowl she offered curds. With her left hand she reached for the peg, with her right, for the workman's mallet. She hammered Sisara, crushed his head; she smashed, stove in his temple. . . .

From the window peered down and wailed the mother of Sisara, from the lattice: "Why is his chariot so long in coming? why are the hoofbeats of his chariots delayed?" The wisest of her princesses answers her, and she, too, keeps answering herself: "They must be dividing the spoil they took: there must be a damsel or two for each man, spoils of dyed cloth as Sisara's spoil, an ornate shawl or two for me in the spoil."

May all your enemies perish thus, O Lord! but your friends be as the sun rising in its might! (Jgs 5.)

The verses say a great deal about the active part played by the different tribes in the battle. The presence of Zebulun and Naphtali from the north; of Manasseh, Benjamin, and Ephraim from the south. The absence of Dan and Asher who stayed by the sea; of Reuben who remained in his pastures; and of Gilead who stayed on the other side of the Jordan. And the active participation of Issachar in conquering his assigned territory.

Indeed, the tribes which took part in the battle played a direct role in uniting all the tribes. This victory inaugurated a new epoch in the Promised Land. And Deborah realized this.

Today this region is under Israeli control. I don't think they were moved by sentimental reasons. Esdraelon is one of the most fertile areas in Palestine, and it still is very important from a strategic point of view.

28.   GIDEON'S FOUNTAIN

ONE OF the few passages of the Bible well known to many people is the story of Gideon. I remember reading it as a small boy. It was then a tale of adventure, and later on it took some effort to transform it into an historical event. A trip to the actual scene of the story helped immeasurably.

As indicated previously, the plain of Esdraelon is a large inverted triangle (almost a right-angle triangle). The base at the top is formed by the mountains of Galilee, and Nazareth serves as a lookout post. The rambling heights of Carmel form the left side of the triangle. And the right side is bordered by Mount Hermon and the mountains of Gilboa which hook toward the northwest. Between these two mountains the plain leads down into the deep valley of Jezreel adjoining the Jordan. In the center of the triangle is Afula, a communications center where the traveler can find a good restaurant.

Soon after eating we set out on the trail of Gideon. We crossed the fertile plains which lay dry and yellow under the August sun, inched our way between the cliffs of Gilboa on the right and Mount Hermon on the left, and descended into the valley of Jezreel.

THE PAST RELIVED

It was a period in which the Israelites had not yet consolidated their gains in the Promised Land. The new settlers were tilling the fertile fields of Esdraelon. Meanwhile, another tribe of settlers in the desert wastes of Transjordan were waiting for the harvest to ripen. When the time came, they crossed the Jordan on their camels, swept through the valley of Jezreel, and settled triumphantly on the plain of Esdraelon. Everything was ready for them. The Israelites had done all the hard work, and now they could reap the benefits.

In another valley farther south, the inhabitants threshed their

[173]

crop in caves and underground caverns. They did not want to leave it in the fields, exposed to marauding bands of Madianites. This had been going on for several years. The Israelites had had several skirmishes with the Madianites, and two young men, brothers of a man named Gideon, had been killed. But as yet no heroic figure had come upon the scene to unite the Israelite forces and launch a successful counterattack.

A DELIGHTFUL FOUNTAIN

Our bus comes to a stop near a pleasant pine grove situated at the foot of Mount Gilboa. The air is filled with the shouts of children and the noise of gurgling water. We take a few steps and find ourselves at the fountain. The fresh water flows out from a crevice in the huge rock. About thirty-five feet beyond lies a rivulet where the children can bathe without fear. It is a delightful spot, a real picnic ground where one can stroll around and enjoy the pine-scented air.

But amid this pleasant landscape we are going to film a reenactment of events which were scarcely idyllic. To set the stage for the story of Gideon, we must first clear away the children in their bathing suits. The photographers and the movie camera prepare to act out the story.

A STRANGE SCENE

The actors bend over to drink the spring water, as the camera grinds. One player bends all the way over and puts his lips into the water to drink deeply. A bad move! He forgets that the enemy is encamped on the mountain in front of him and on the plain behind. In this position he could not ward off a surprise attack. The other actors — go down on one knee and cup the water in our hand. That way we can keep our eyes on the heights above us, and have one hand free to grab our weapons in a hurry.

We get our fill of water before the photographers have had their fill of photos. When the scene is finished, the children return and we sit down in the shade to read a passage from the Bible. It is the one which tells how Gideon picked out a mere 300 men from his army and set out for the decisive battle.

Gideon's Fountain

SURPRISE BY NIGHT

We hop on the bus and ride away from the grove to a clearing. Here we can survey the whole scene and populate it with biblical characters. On our right are the mountains of Gilboa. Gideon has left with his force of 300 men. The rest have headed for their houses or tents.

To our left lies Mount Hermon and the major part of the valley. There the Madianites are encamped. The area is dotted with tents and camels.

In back of us is the vast plain of Esdraelon, and the Jordan lies before us. The scene is set. Night is falling. A bonfire flickers nervously in the Madianite camp. One Madianite is telling the lookout about a terrible dream he had: "A round loaf of barley bread was rolling into the camp. . . . It came to our tent . . . and . . . turned the tent upside down." The lookout gives his interpretation: "This can only be the sword of the Israelite Gideon. . . . God has delivered Madian . . . into his power" (Jgs 7). Gideon, hidden in the darkness nearby, overhears the conversation and hurriedly slips back to his mountain encampment. The 300 soldiers are ready; each one carries a candle covered with a pitcher and a ram's horn strapped to his neck. Gideon divides them into three groups, leaving an escape route open to the Jordan. They begin to descend the mountain slope at the changing of the guard, when the fresh lookouts are still wiping the sleep from their eyes.

Suddenly the mountains reecho with what seems to be the sound of trumpets. And the plain is flooded with light, as if hundreds of lamps were glowing in the mountains. This must be the spearhead of a huge enemy army — so the Madianites think. The enemy is advancing nearer; the Madianites hurriedly fold their tents, leap on their camels, and flee toward the Jordan. A fair number reach the far shore, but others get to the river too late. For Gideon has sent a message to the Israelites telling them to take the riverbank. Three hundred men and a stratagem have liberated the Israelites, at least for a few years. But Gideon does not want to accept the role of king offered to him by the grateful Israelites (cf Jgs 6:8).

I open my eyes and return to the here and now. Only the setting of Gideon's exploit remains. But how easy it is to relive the story in fantasy, when the proper setting is at hand!

29. ON THE TRAIL OF SAMSON

TODAY we have come down from Jerusalem to the region frequented by Samson. He is such a popular hero that it is easy to evoke the memory of his exploits. They constitute the most exciting pages of the Book of Judges. They are read by children in condensed versions. His name is synonymous with great power and great weakness. Movies and operas tell his story. Indeed, he is one of the favorite biblical heroes.

But did you know that some scholars claimed that Samson never existed, that the Bible story was a solar myth? I was telling this to my companion as the bus was leaving Jerusalem to take us to the historical site.

Samson's name is suspicious, since it means "solar" or "sunny." And it so happens that in the vicinity of his home there was a city dedicated to a sun cult, Beit Shemesh (= "house of the sun"). These facts, combined with other data and the tendency of some to explain away everything as being some kind of astrological myth, led some scholars to formulate a theory which rejected the historical existence of Samson. But the giant, dead though he was, brought his exploits to bear against these hypothetical constructions and toppled them.

Curiously enough, the Jews have dedicated a cement factory to his honor. Now a warrior who plows straight ahead and topples a house when he is in a peevish mood hardly seems to be a proper patron for a cement factory.

THE SHEPHELAH

A mountain chain can border on a plain in one of three ways. It may suddenly loom up as a sheer sheet of rock. This is the most imposing posture, and it cuts the plains off from that which lies beyond. No contact is possible. But it may also slope down gradually to meet the plain. This is the least restrictive posture

[176]

and does not confine the plain dwellers at all. Finally, it may eventually splinter into hills and hillocks with exits and entrances scattered all around. This is the most picturesque kind of arrangement. Valleys are scattered here and there, and people can move around. And this is the shape of the Judean mountains as they slope down to the seacoast. This section of the mountains, lowly in stature when seen from above, is called *shephelah* (lowly).

One of these picturesque valleys, Sorek, was the birthplace of an exceptional youth. He grew up with a long head of hair and possessed extraordinary physical strength. Adam Smith likened him to a mountain stream. It rises somewhere above the valley, skips along playfully for awhile, and then flows down into the valley where men utilize its force to turn mills, etc. But then one day it overflows its bank and engulfs the village and its people.

The bus stops in the *shephelah* region. We are not going to look at ruins, but rather at the countryside. The latter is much more informative in the case of Samson. Looking southward we see on our left the lofty mountains inhabited by the Israelites of old. On our right lies the coast occupied by the Philistines, who were wont to make raids on their neighbors. And in the middle, where we are now, Samson appeared on the scene to avenge his fellow countrymen. He lived in the area which had suffered most at the hands of the Philistines, the region bequeathed to the tribe of Dan. And he took his revenge as he saw fit, adopting no methodical plan but utilizing the natural layout of the countryside.

It is now the month of July, so the plain is not covered with wheat stalks. But we can see how easy it would be to descend the hill, set loose a few foxes with lighted torches tied to their tails, and then climb back up the hill to watch the fields burning brightly. (I understand that in their skirmishes with the Arabs a few years ago, the Israelis adopted this tactic, using mice instead of foxes — more economical.)

We can also see how easy it would be to go down into the cities of the Philistines. There one could make love to the women, and enjoy the many banquets where wine flowed freely and the people teased each other with subtle riddles. The great cultural routes passed through these cities. Vice was always close at hand, but it could lead to drastic consequences.

[177]

The Heroic Age

We are still in the dark about two events in Samson's life. No one has pinpointed the cave where he is supposed to have hidden after burning the fields. But it is not hard to picture it as some cave hidden in the crevices of the mountains nearby.

It is more difficult to imagine a lion roaming around in this region among the olive groves. Perhaps Samson's lion was an unwonted visitor even in his day.

SAMSON'S TOMB

Samson's first tomb was the house which he toppled over on himself and his enemies. Painters have pictured it as a huge palace with majestic columns, being toppled by a human cyclone. The actual building would have been something on a much smaller scale. Grant at Beit-shemesh and Albright at Beit Mirsim found supports or columns which justified the theory that it was a two-story house.

Using imagination more than fact, we can picture a second-floor balcony looking out on a central courtyard. The Philistines had drunk heavily. When they were feeling gay, they chanted for Samson. He is brought out, to the amusement of those sitting around the courtyard and the balcony. Samson rests against two of the supporting columns. Then suddenly he lunges against the column and brings the balcony toppling down on the people below. "Those he killed at his death were more than those he had killed during his lifetime" (Jgs 16:30).

I don't know if the people in Gaza still point out the ruins of the house toppled by Samson to tourists. We have encountered stranger tourist attractions along the way. We would head straight for Gaza, but the frontier limits prevent us. Gaza is the last region within the Egyptian border menacing the territory and the tranquility of the Israelis. The Egyptian threat today bears some resemblance to the ancient Philistine menace.

In Gaza they would have shown us Samson's tomb, which is also venerated by Moslems. It is true, of course, that the Bible pinpoints Samson's homeland as his final resting place: "All his family . . . went down and bore him up for burial in the grave of his father Manoah between Zorah and Eshtaol" (Jgs 16:31). But these details have little impact on popular traditions.

30. ON THE NORTHERN FRONTIER

Our trip to Dan left us with pleasant memories. From the shore of Lake Gennesaret we climbed the rising highway. Soon we reached sea level and then continued upward, 300 feet, 600 feet, 900 feet. Now we could breathe deeply once again; our heads were clear and our reflexes sharp. The lake, lying 1600 feet below (650 feet below sea level), was no longer a depressing nightmare, but a bright patch of blue countryside. Beyond it to the north the Jordan threaded its way toward a small lake about three miles in diameter. North of Lake Huleh the river divides into strands of water fingering their way through the swampy land. It is a pleasure to look down on the thick vegetation below; reeds and rushes covering the landscape, a panorama of green in countless shades. But in the days of antiquity this region was not too healthful. Only the energetic sanitation campaign of recent years has led to the virtual extinction of malaria.

Perhaps the poor climate, or even more, its unsuitability for human habitation, was the reason why this region was not settled by the explorers who came seeking a new homestead.

There is good reason for recalling the ancient story. It has played a decisive role in the recent history of this region. If Dan is the northern limits of Israel today, it is so because it was the northern limits of David's kingdom twenty-nine centuries ago. And it was the northern limits of his kingdom, because one of the Israelite tribes, dissatisfied with the area bequeathed to it, emigrated northward in search of a more peaceful region.

The tribe of Dan had been given the *shephelah,* the area between Judea and the coastal plain occupied by the Philistines. It was not a bad spot. The soil was not as fertile as that of the Philistines, but it was better than the arid mountain stretches of Judea. The big problem was the neighboring Philistines, who refused to live in peace. Even during Samson's lifetime, his fellow

[179]

Danites suffered much; and after his death the situation became intolerable. So the Danites sent "five valiant men" to reconnoiter the land and find a more suitable spot. They set out through the center of the country, as we would have done if the country were not partitioned. But the last stage of their journey followed the same route we have taken. The nearby mountains were already occupied by the tribe of Ephraim; farther north lay the territory of Manasseh. The attractive plain of Esdraelon belonged to Issachar. (At this point the scouts headed up the Jordan.) The region near Lake Gennesaret was good, but it belonged to Naphtali; so they continued northward, unwittingly expanding the territorial frontiers of their people. They passed near Lake Huleh, skirted the marshes, and came out on a magnificent plain and a city named Laish.

LAISH — DAN

We turn off the highway into a road lined by cultivated farm land; well-irrigated fields dotted with green groves, a stream of running water channeled through pipes to every corner of the area. There is even a football field in one section. Just before we come to our destination, we see a group of large pools set aside as trout fisheries. The Israeli farmers, using the most modern techniques, are cultivating this fine fertile region.

The Danites scouting this region found that "the people dwelling there lived securely after the manner of the Sidonians, quiet and trusting, with no lack of any natural resources."

It is true that today's colonists have improved the wealth of this area. But what those ancient scouts saw must have been quite appealing to them. The land was rich, the people were ingenuous, and, best of all, there was an air of peace and quiet which contrasted sharply with the atmosphere in their present home.

Our bus stops at the foot of a low hill. Our guide gives us a few words of caution, because we are near the border. A narrow road slopes upward between dense thickets and shrubbery. To the left we can hear the bubbling water of some stream. In a few moments we find ourselves in a grove of oak trees. Between them runs a shallow stream of clear water. To the right of this stream stands a huge oak tree of venerable, almost sacred, appearance.

[180]

We feel the urge to keep silent, to listen to the running water and the rustling leaves, and to collect our thoughts in this chapel of nature.

We take a wooden gangplank across the stream, cross a trail, and find ourselves before another branch of the river. The view is quite different. In front of us are mountains and parched earth. The river bed has been channeled and has, therefore, lost its air of pristine freshness. What is worse, it is spanned by barbed-wire fencing. We are at the Syrian border. It would not be too difficult to cross over. The water is not deep, even though the current is swift. In a matter of minutes we would be outside Israel, in Arab territory.

If you look carefully at the map, you will notice that Dan juts up from Israel like a bird's beak. It is situated at the southern end of Beqa' (i.e., the valley, between the mountain fasts of Lebanon and Anti-Lebanon). On the left stand the spurs of Mount Lebanon, and beyond them the territory of Lebanon leading to the sea, to Tyre and Sidon. On the right stand the peaks of Anti-Lebanon, and beyond them the territory of Syria leading to the desert, to Damascus. From the hill we are standing on, we can only go in one direction — toward the Jordan valley. The great commercial and military routes were located much farther to the south. The Phoenician trade routes cut down near the coast and twisted around Carmel. The Syrian routes crossed below Lake Gennesaret. On the outer rim of these routes stood "a rich and peaceful city . . . distant from the Sidonians and having no contact with Syria."

When the scouts returned home, they brought good news. "Come let us attack them, for we have seen the land and it is very good. Are you going to hesitate? Do not be slothful about beginning your expedition to possess the land. Those against whom you go are a trusting people, and the land is ample. God has indeed given it into your power: a place where no natural resource is lacking."

The hill is called Tell-el-Qadi, that is "hill of judgment" (= Spanish *alcalde*) which in Hebrew is *dan*. And the stream which bubbles up on this hill is called *Leddan*. The present Arab name apparently is a translation of the ancient Hebrew name. But the Hebrew name supplanted the more ancient Canaanite name,

The Heroic Age

Laish. And such a change does not come about through peaceful means.

The Danites dispatched 600 armed men and "they attacked Laish, a quiet and trusting people; they put them to the sword and destroyed their city by fire. No one came to their aid, since the city was far from Sidon and they had no contact with other people. The Danites then rebuilt the city . . . and lived there. They named it Dan after their ancestor Dan, son of Israel. However, the name of the city was formerly Laish" (Jgs 18).

THE SANCTUARY OF DAN

Even with today's modern means of communication Dan still seems to be isolated and remote, as it was long ago. It would seem to be the ideal spot for a religious sanctuary. The stream bubbling up almost miraculously and the tall oak trees tempt one to establish a ritual cult.

I am not speaking anachronistically. In the days of old there were many trees also, because we are in the foothills of Lebanon. And trees, springs, and hillsides always tempted the Israelites to commit idolatry.

In the time of the Judges there was another factor at work. As yet there was no temple, no centralized cult restricted to one place; nor was there a king. "Everyone did what he thought best" (Jgs 21:25). In their emigration to the north the Danites had to supply themselves with the necessary religious accouterments: a priest and some cultic objects. And so, in the shade of the venerable oak tree, we must read the episode recounted in the Book of Judges (Chaps. 17–18).

In the mountain region of Ephraim lived a man named Micah who had stolen money from his mother. One day he repented and returned the money to her. She, in turn, decided to use a part of the money to build an idol. "She took two hundred shekels of silver and gave them to the silversmith, who made of them a carved idol overlaid with silver." Micah also made some other sacred objects, and consecrated one of his sons who became his priest. A young levite (one of the priestly tribe) from Bethlehem happened to pass through this region, and Micah asked him to be his priest. "I will give you ten silver shekels a year, a set of garments, and your food." The young levite accept his offer.

Then came the Danite scouts, who recognized the levite's accent and asked him what he was doing there. He explained the situation. Then they said: "Consult God, that we may know whether the undertaking we are engaged in will succeed." The priest replied: "Go and prosper: the Lord is favorable to the undertaking you are engaged in." And indeed He was.

Next came the 600 Danite warriors. The five scouts told them about the treasure in Micah's house and said: "Now decide what you must do." Micah was not in the house at the time. The 600 men remained at the door, chatting with the levite. The five scouts stole inside and took the idol and the cultic objects. As they were coming out, the levite stopped them. "What are you doing?" They answered, " 'Be still: put your hand over your mouth. Come with us and be our father and priest. Is it better for you to be priest for the family of one man or to be priest for a tribe and a clan in Israel?' The priest, agreeing, took the ephod, household idols, and carved idol and went off in the midst of the band."

While they were running off, Micah returned to the house and saw what had taken place. He rounded up some neighbors and set out after the Danites. When they got near, they called out. The Danites turned around: " 'What do you want, that you have taken up arms?' 'You have taken my god, which I made, and have gone off with my priest as well,' he answered. 'What is left for me? How, then, can you ask me what I want?' The Danites said to him, 'Let us hear no further sound from you, lest fierce men fall upon you and you and your family lose your lives.' The Danites then went on their way, and Micah, seeing that they were stronger than he, returned home."

The Danites thus went on to acquire a new territory, and a new city with its own sanctuary and priest. The sanctuary was to last many years. When Jeroboam started an independent kingdom in the north, he realized the necessity of establishing a new sanctuary also. So he erected a golden calf in Dan, and it became a center of pilgrimage for people in the north.

It is an ideal site for religious pilgrimages. Today it is a real tourist attraction. The Israeli colonists, who do such a fine job of tilling the land, have little time for religion and little interest in it. This is the normal situation in these colonies. The sabbath is not even kept, because the farm work is too important. They marry before a rabbi and circumcise their children; and that is the extent of their formal religious practice. There are only a few colonies in Israel set up along strictly religious lines.

The shadows of history have not fallen on this region very often. Today the Israeli inhabitants live here in peace, just as the ancient Sidonians did before they were surprised by the conquering Danites.

THE NEW ARRIVALS

On the return trip I sat on the right side of the bus and looked at the other side of the highway. A sparse hillside sloped gradually upward, dotted with huts and barracks. These buildings are constructed of wooden planks overlaid with corrugated zinc plates. The roofs also are made of zinc or uralite. The heat must be terrible inside these barracks. There are clinging vines at the front of some of them. A short distance away a pipeline stretches along the ground, bends upward, and terminates in a faucet. It is the public fountain. (Today, 1964, the barracks have disappeared, and new villages, fresh and vigorous, have taken their place.)

In such installations as these the new immigrants are housed upon their arrival in Israel. Life is hard and uncomfortable. Often they offer their services to nearby colonies which are better established. But in the meantime they wait. They do not send out scouts to find better land, for that is the state's job. It must try to integrate all the immigrants into the full life of the nation: agriculture, industry, the professions, and urban life. And sometimes the state also looks after the religious needs of the people, building synagogues and sending rabbis to care for them.

Today the state is playing the part of Joshua, distributing the tribes throughout Israel. But the determining factor is not ancestry, but rather previous homeland: Holland, Morocco, Bulgaria, Argentina. . . . But sometimes this criterion is inapplicable and the colonies turn out to be a potpourri of languages and other cultural traits. The hope is that the colonists will be united by their mutual goals and their common tasks.

[184]

V. SAMUEL AND THE UNITED KINGDOM: SAUL, DAVID, SOLOMON

Beloved of his people, dear to his Maker, dedicated from his mother's womb, consecrated to the Lord as a prophet, was Samuel, the judge and priest. At God's word he established the kingdom and anointed princes to rule the people. . . . As a trustworthy prophet he was sought out and his words proved him true as a seer. He too, called upon God. . . . He testified before the Lord and his anointed prince, "No bribe or secret gifts have I taken from any man!" And no one dared gainsay him. Even when he lay buried, his guidance was sought; he made known to the king his fate, and from the grave he raised his voice as a prophet, to put an end to wickedness.

After him came Nathan who served in the presence of David. Like the choice fat of the sacred offering, so was David in Israel. . . . As a youth he slew the giant and wiped out the people's disgrace, when his hand let fly the slingstone that crushed the pride of Goliath. . . . When he assumed the royal crown, he battled the enemy on every side. He destroyed the hostile Philistines and shattered their power till our own day. With his every deed he offered thanks to God Most High, in words of praise. With his whole being he loved his Maker and daily had his praises sung. Therefore, the Lord forgave him his sins and exalted his strength forever; he conferred on him the rights of royalty and established his throne in Israel.

Because of his merits he had as his successor a wise son, who lived in security: Solomon reigned during an era of peace, for God made tranquil all his borders. He built a house to the name of God, and established a lasting sanctuary. . . .

How wise you were when you were young, overflowing with instruction, like the Nile in flood. . . . Your fame reached distant coasts, and their peoples came to hear you. . . . Gold you gathered like so much iron, you heaped up silver as though it were lead.   (Sirach 46–47)

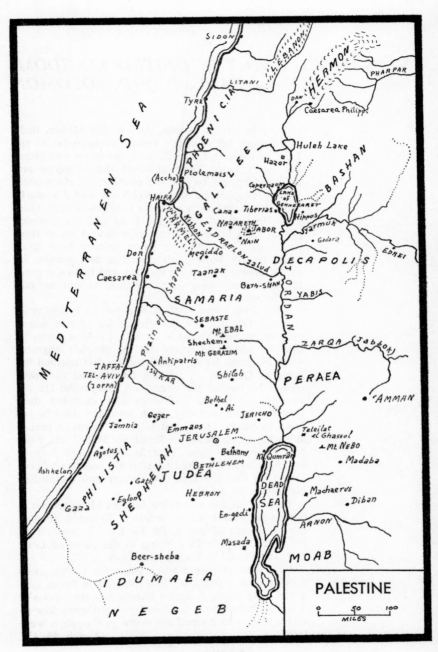

31. *THE SANCTUARY OF SHILOH*

"You may go to Silo, which I made the dwelling place of my name in the beginning. See what I did to it because of the wickedness of my people Israel" (Jer 7:12).

The suggestion was made by Jeremiah, quoting "the Lord's words." So we must go to this formerly great national sanctuary and see what has become of it.

We leave Jerusalem by bus in the morning. First we take the highway of Nablus; then we turn off into a neighboring road full of dust and gravel. The bus can only go a certain distance on it; we walk the rest of the way. This has been an oft-repeated ritual during our journey: the bus stops and our guide tells us to get off. Some take their canteens with them. The water is still fresh if we have only been traveling an hour or so. But if it is more than two hours, the water is already lukewarm. Others prefer to leave their canteens in the relative shade of the bus and to save the water for the return trip. However, no one forgets to take his helmet, the best companion on these tours. Without it I think the sun could melt our brain matter. My helmet has preserved my head in another respect also. Not all the doorways or arches we step through are high enough for a six footer. The helmet prevents an awful lot of nasty bumps on the head. It saved me more than twenty times during our trip. And the worst bump could have been at Shiloh, as I was walking through the entrance of the walls erected by the archaeologists to preserve the digs. The area had nothing special to show us; the remains of a few Corinthian columns and some mosaics, and a patch of shade to shelter us while we were being told about the excavations.

A SHRINE OF PILGRIMAGE

When our guide told us that in its heyday this place was similar to Lourdes, we found it hard to believe. It is situated in a secluded countryside of rolling hills and uneven valleys. The land is arid, and there are no trees or traces of green. We must use our imagination.

On more than one occasion I have helped to arrange a Christmas crib. Sackcloth soaked in lime was always the basic element, used to represent the rolling countryside in a picturesque way. At first you can see the coarse threads, the uneven folds, and the patchwork of gray and white colors. But then you cover this "geological" setting with moss and palms, flocks and shepherds; and it becomes a delightful scene for young and old.

We must try to do the same thing here. The natural substrate is already laid out for us. We must lay a grass carpet over the sloping meadows, and dot them with fig and olive trees. On one of the hillsides we add a vineyard, and we put some stone dwellings and some flocks on the far hills. As a finishing touch we picture the central hill with a sanctuary and a small village. Now the landscape is really charming, and we can believe the words of our guide. And there is every reason to believe that it looked something like that in the days of Samuel.

STORIES — HAPPY AND SAD

After visting the reconstructed edifice and a tiny mosque in the middle of the grotto (where there is an enticing shade), we headed for the main hill and climbed halfway up, stepping over the rocks and walls which testify to the ancient city. The excavators dug them up twenty-five years ago, but the weeds have begun to crop up once again.

Although it is not the most charming spot in the area, it is the proper setting for the stories we wish to recall — the dance of the young virgins, the child who had dreams, and the recollections of an old-timer. All these fit perfectly into our imaginary scene.

The Dance of the Virgins (Judges 21). Every year there was a great festival in Shiloh at which the young virgins of the town performed a dance. Israelites used to come from all over the Promised Land to watch the girls swirl around.

Now a heinous crime had been committed against a levite by the Benjaminites. It fanned the spark of civil war, and all the tribes united to teach the Benjaminites a lesson. Only a few Benjaminites escaped death in the terrible battle which ensued. These survivors had no wives, and the other tribes vowed not to give them any of their women.

Gradually the rancor wore off. It seemed a pity that one of the Israelite tribes should die off; but, on the other hand, a vow was a vow. It was a neat problem, and they worked out a neat solution. They asked whether any Israelite tribe had refused to come to the general assembly and to take the vow. Sure enough, they found that the men of Jabesh-gilead had not joined them. So they decided that they and their wives should be put to death; and the unmarried virgins were to be given as wives to the Benjaminite survivors. This they did, but there were still some Benjaminites without wives. So they formulated another plan, more clever than the first.

The day came for the annual celebration in Shiloh. The Benjaminites hid in the vineyards, while the maidens performed the traditional dance. Suddenly the young men jumped out of hiding; each one grabbed a girl and ran off with her. The inhabitants of the town protested, of course, and their fathers and brothers demanded their return. But the other Israelites soothed their feelings and explained the situation. If the townspeople had given the girls to the young men, they would have violated the oath; but as it turned out, the Benjaminites just took them, so no one was guilty! "The Benjaminites went back to their own territory, where they rebuilt and occupied the cities."

The Child Who Had Dreams (1 Samuel). We do not have to recount this story in detail because it is well known. We need only allude to it in general terms. In the sanctuary of Shiloh a young child named Samuel, who had been consecrated to God, grew up. God came to him in dreams and told him about the future punishment of Eli the priest. There Samuel grew into manhood, and God continued to appear to him. From Shiloh he ruled all Israel, and was recognized as a true prophet. And there he was forced to see the Ark of the Covenant stolen by the Philistines. Later on, the entire city was razed by the Philistines, and Samuel had to move elsewhere. The reader can review the details himself. All I ask is that he not picture the child Samuel as Reynolds has painted him. That would ruin the whole scene.

Memories of an Old-Timer. He died in 1952. When our guide was here studying, the old man was still alive. He was a Dane, Aage Schmidt by name. Together with Hans Kjaer he directed the excavations in Shiloh from 1926 to 1929. Among other things he found a good deal of pottery which antedated the monarchy. But there was a complete lack of later pieces, and the ruins testified to some sort of conflagration.

When the excavation work was finished, Kjaer went home. But Schmidt chose to stay in Palestine. He took up residence in the *École Biblique* run by the Dominicans, and sometimes made trips to his excavation sites. When he came across a visitor, he would explain everything in detail. And the facts would take on added luster from his account.

Our guide met him here one day while he was visiting Shiloh.

The whole area testifies to the mixture of joy and tragedy which marked the biblical events enacted here. In the early days of Israelite occupation it was a religious center. It survived during the heroic age of conquest and lasted until the time of the monarchy. Then its ruins remained as an object lesson for the faithless in Judah. And thus it stands today.

As a final sad touch, our guide points toward a nearby village, Kerioth. This village was probably the home of a man (= iš) called Judas iš Kerioth.

32. *IN THE TERRITORY OF THE PHILISTINES*

IN GERMANY the word "philistine" once had an interesting connotation. It implied rigid conservatism and strict adherence to traditional norms. Against these norms came a young David representing the forces of progress and vitality. Schumann closed his magnificent *Carnival* with the *March of the Davidites Against the Philistines*. It was not just another march, but a proclamation against the academicians of the music world. When you hear *Carnival* and its final march, you are sure that Schumann was in the right.

But in our travels we are not going to abide by such terms or connotations. We see no hint of rigid conservatism in taking a trip to the territory of the Philistines. The fact that David's pebble felled a brutish Philistine encased in armor does not mean that all the Philistines were boors.

Philistine pottery ware was more exquisite than that of the Israelites. They were equal to the Israelites in the art of war. And in the crafts they had an advantage: "Now there was no smith found throughout all the land of Israel, for the Philistines said, 'Lest the Hebrews make sword or spear.' But all the Israelites went down to the Philistines to sharpen each his plowpoint and his coulter and his ax and his mattock; and the price for the plowpoints and the coulters was a pim and a third of a shekel for the axes and for setting the goads."

ON THE FRONTIER

Note what the text says: "all the Israelites went down to the Philistines"; in other words, they had to come down from the mountainous regions of Judea. In the interior of this region lived Judah, relatively safe from attack. The Philistines dwelt along the coast. And between the two lay a fringe of low hills called Shephelah. There was no neat dividing line between these areas. A series of deep valleys ran from the plains, cut through Shephelah, and pierced into the heart of Judah. They were ideal routes for a surprise attack, for guerrilla raids and espionage work by a bold spy. And there were open areas which were the scenes of strategic battles.

Samson's mighty exploits resounded through these valleys. In one of them David met the challenge of Goliath. And in another Saul fought against the Philistines, who claimed Shephelah as their own and sought to occupy strategic points in the valleys which ran through it. Our first stop is at one of these points, a small hill to the right of the highway, standing amid farmland with mountains in the background nearby. It is strategically located near the frontier and has, therefore, changed hands many times.

When Joshua's forces were spreading through Palestine, they could not take this Philistine fortress. It stood firm as a permanent threat to them. A period of peaceful coexistence followed. The Israelites grew in force, conquered their neighbors, and finally took the fortress. In Solomon's day it was definitely theirs. But several centuries later the Philistines took it once again.

THE SEACOAST

After noting the geographical position of the hill, we head straight for the coast. But we cannot visit all five cities of the Philistine Pentapolis because Gaza lies in Egyptian territory near the frontier. We pass quickly through Ashdod and skirt Ekron. Undoubtedly, the most interesting of all is Ashkelon.

The scene brings back memories of the Spanish Mediterranean coast. Groves of orange trees and verdant green contrast sharply with the sand along the roads. Here and there a banana grove and clusters of palm trees. If we substitute vineyards for the orange groves and tall palm trees for the banana trees, we have a good picture of this countryside in the days of the Philistines: a vast fertile region breathing an atmosphere of peace and tranquillity. The inhabitants came from various European islands and peninsulas. No doubt they bore some resemblance to the people living along the

Mediterranean today. They were people who cultivated the land and practiced various crafts. They were skilled in the plastic arts and had an interest in trade. Their warlike acts seem to have been provoked by the Israelite invasion, and were not a part of their basic character.

We climb a hill covered with a thick coating of sand. Slipping and stumbling, we manage to reach the top and empty the sand out of our shoes. The ruins date from a later period and do not help us too much. But the landscape is perfect. The bright Mediterranean light brings the various colors into sharp focus: the blue of sky and sea framing the green palms and yellow sand, the colors which show up so well on a plate of varnished clay, a glass vessel, or a village skirt.

No examples of Philistine pottery have shown up here at Ashkelon. But in the frontier region which we visited already, Mackenzie found a large quantity of it. The usual decoration is some kind of animal. The figure is stylized in elegant strokes. One of the favorite motifs is a swan with its head bent back, in the act of pluming itself. Another interesting thing about these vases is that they have a strainer at the spout. Scholars deduce that these jugs were used as beer mugs, and the strainer prevented barley husks from coming through. (If the Philistines knew how to brew beer, they couldn't have been too boorish!) At any rate, it was some liquid containing a solid residue. But I doubt that a people who drank so much wine at their banquets would use these jugs for a soft drink.

From the hill we descend to the beach. Once again we are reminded of our Spanish Mediterranean beaches. Sand all along the pathways leading to the beach, but a little coarser than that on our shores. Out of reverence for the Mediterranean we take a dip. But there is a treacherous undertow (a frequent phenomenon on the shores of Israel), so we do not go out too far. I don't know if the sea was this unfriendly in the days of the Philistines. If they liked to bathe in the sea, it would be one more item to add to their historicocultural profile. But the Philistines did not write anything down, and we cannot ascertain all their customs and habits.

THE ROVING ARK

Some writers think that epidemics were not infrequent in these areas during ancient times. Coming up the coast from Egypt, the traveler had to cross a swamp-infested isthmus. Soldiers and merchants, who had picked up some bug in this isthmus, would have spread it along the coast of Palestine where the Philistines dwelt. The theory seems quite sound. We know that in those days there was no preventive medicine, and no one studied the cause of epidemics. In many instances it was simpler to attribute collective ill health to religious impropriety. And at one point this explanation seemed to have more than a little validity.

The Philistines had just defeated the newly arrived invaders who were trying to take over their territory. Their enemy from the mountains used to carry a certain object into battle, and it obviously had no military value. It was a huge wooden ark which probably had some religious significance. So the Philistines carried it off as a victory trophy. As they saw it, the gods of the enemy had been vanquished by their own gods. So they reverently deposited the ark of Yahweh the vanquished in the temple of victorious Dagon.

Strange things began to happen soon after. Next morning, when the first priest took his turn in the temple, he found the statue of Dagon toppled over. Thoroughly frightened he told the other priests, and a bunch of them managed to restore the statue to its pedestal. The next day another priest, or perhaps a group of them, entered the temple and found an even more terrible spectacle. On the threshold of the sanctuary lay the statue, minus head and arms. The threshold of the sanctuary was hallowed ground; so they stopped in front of it, staring at the awesome sight. Its meaning was clear to them. The conquered God, Yahweh, was taking His revenge.

The worst was yet to come. An epidemic of boils spread through the people, and they begged their leaders to take the ark outside the city. A consultation took place, and it was decided to take the statue to the neighboring city of Gath. The epidemic followed the ark to Gath; so it was removed to Ekron, but with the same result. And the Ekronites cried out, saying: "They have brought around the ark of the God of Israel to us, to slay us and our people." So all the rulers of the Philistines were summoned and told to "'send away the ark of the God of Israel, and let it return to its own place and not kill us and our people.' For a deadly panic raged throughout the entire city; the hand of God was very heavy there."

BACK TOWARD THE MOUNTAINS

Our swim is over, and it is time to return to Jerusalem. There are good roads leading to the beach, and squares at the crossroads. A short distance away, on a green esplanade, stands a long low building surrounded by a courtyard. It contains stores for the many people who come down to the beach on weekends.

Our return route is similar to that of the ark. The Philistines assembled all the priests and sorcerers to decide on a *modus operandi*. They would have to send a guilt offering along with the ark. So they decided on five gold rats and five gold boils, one for each city, symbolizing the plagues. Then they said: "Take and make ready a new cart, and two milch cows upon which there has never been a yoke; and hitch the cows to the cart, but keep their calves behind them at home. Take the ark of the Lord and place it in the cart and put in a box at its side the objects of gold which you must surely return to him as a guilt-offering. Then send it off that it may be on its way. But observe, if it goes up on the way to its own territory to Beth-shemesh, it is he who has done us this great harm; but if not, then we shall know that his hand did not touch us; we simply met with an accident."

The men carried out the orders to the letter. "The cows went straight in the direction of Beth-shemesh, keeping to one highway, and lowing as they went along." And the Philistine leaders followed at a distance to see what would happen.

ON THE HILL OF BETH-SHEMESH

The ascent to Beth-shemesh is easy and pleasant, even though the landscape cannot compare with the rich verdure of Ashkelon.

The hill was eyed greedily by excavators: Mackenzie before World War I and Elihu Grant before World War II. But their finds were not sensational: a wall about six and a half feet thick, traces of fire, the handle of a jar bearing a seal, and a great deal of Philistine pottery. The visitor today cannot see any of these finds; so there is more pleasure and profit in studying the lay of the land and reconstructing the biblical scene.

At the foot of the hill lay the ripe stalks of wheat being threshed by the hill dwellers. One of the more keen-eyed inhabitants sees a strange cortege heading toward the hill from the plain. His first reaction is a mixture of surprise and worry, when he sees a group of men behind the cart. Who knows what the Philistines might be up to? He raises a cry of alarm and the people stop threshing. Someone manages to make out the object on the cart and cries out: "It's the ark." The good news spreads quickly, a crowd collects, and someone runs off to tell the priests. Meanwhile, the Philistines stay at a respectable distance, watching the proceedings.

The Ark comes to rest in front of a large boulder, in the field of a man named Joshua. The levites take the ark off the cart, and place it and the offerings on the boulder. They build a fire with the wood from the cart, and immolate the two cows as an offering to Yahweh.

When the spectacle is finished, the Philistines return to their respective cities and report what had happened. And we are not too presumptuous in supposing that the chief of Ekron paid a visit to the owner of the cows, and advised him to get two other cows to satisfy the hunger of the orphaned calves.

33. *NAZARETH: GEOGRAPHY FROM A TERRACE*

CERTAIN cities in any country are "national monuments"; in like manner, Nazareth is a sacred village. Every corner and hillside, every square foot, is hallowed ground for us. Reverently we have visited its various sanctuaries and celebrated Mass in its holy shrines.

But let us remember that we are visiting the land of the Old Testament. We must concern ourselves with the preparatory events which paved the way for the transcendent historical events inscribed here.

So I invite the reader to join me in a visit to the Salesian Academy which stands on the most elevated spot in Nazareth overlooking the whole countryside. It is a tiresome climb. First we make our way through the dirty winding side streets. There are small shops along the street, but some are set back on the sidewalk in Arab fashion. We encounter a variety of colors and odors which are not always pleasant. Then we climb up through a lofty pine grove and find ourselves at the Academy. Off to the right stands a white airy basilica dedicated to the Boy Jesus. It is the devotional center of the Academy, but at the moment I am more interested in the terrace.

The panorama is worth our weary climb, and we enjoy it for a few minutes as we catch our breath. Then we begin to study the situation.

A LIVING MAP

After a few years of study we have come to familiarize ourselves with the relief map of Palestine. At the Biblical Institute in Rome there was a huge map composed of three sections, which used to be carried from class to class. There was another full-scale map hanging in another classroom which was not used too much. In Palestine we have found many similar maps in the houses we visited. Almost all of them are copies of one done by Father Köppel, S.J. And invariably the distance scale was indicated in one of the lower corners, 1 centimeter equals almost 1 kilometer.

But today we are looking at a living relief map. And we soon reach the conclusion that a half hour here is worth many hours of looking at a geography book. We collect on the terrace in small groups. Some concentrate on the Carmel mountain range running toward the sea; others are delighted by the multicolored patches of farmland; and one of our number pinpoints various places through a pair of binoculars: Naim, situated halfway up Mount Hermon; Afula, the site of the Israeli farm colonies, with highways cutting through it.

We concentrate on the eastern portion off to our left, the scene of Saul's last battles.

SAUL AND THE PHILISTINES

We are somewhat surprised to find the Philistines in this area. We would expect to find them along the Mediterranean coast, below Carmel. In all probability they had come through the pass alongside Megiddo. Finally we have them pinpointed in a section a little way off to our right. Now we must explain what they were doing there. If the Philistines had been known as clever strategists, we could say that they had planned to attack Saul's army from the north, after coming through Engannim. But this may be too much of an assumption. Perhaps they just wanted to consolidate their trade route to the east, which crossed the plain and linked up with Beth-shan near the Jordan.

From our terrace we cannot see the actual site of the Philistine encampment, but we know exactly where it is; for just around the edge of Hermon lies Shunem. Facing Shunem are the mountains of Gilboa where Saul was encamped. We can see them perfectly, because they are at the edge of the horizon to our left. From his camp Saul looks down on the Philistine camp and trembles. Perhaps it is a presentiment of his impending doom. He calls on Yahweh, but Yahweh does not answer. So he decides to consult a sorceress. And his lieutenants tell him that there is one nearby at Endor.

Nazareth: Geography From a Terrace

We have trouble locating the site of Endor. Our guide tells us that the ancient village was destroyed and that the present-day one has only a few houses. Using binoculars we finally locate it to the left of Naim on the slopes of Hermon. To reach it Saul had to make a fairly long trek. He probably crossed the mountain on the east to avoid the Philistine encampment. Finally he gets there, wearing a disguise and accompanied by two men. The woman denies that she is a sorceress at first, because Saul has outlawed the profession. But the disguised visitor swears that no harm will come to her and asks her to call up the spirit of Samuel. She begins her incantations and the spirit of Samuel appears. The sorceress realizes at once that her visitor is Saul himself.

"Why have you deceived me, for you are Saul?"
The king replies: "Do not be alarmed. What have you seen?"
"I have seen a divine being coming up out of the earth."
"What was his appearance?"
"An old man is coming up, and he is wrapped in a mantle."
Saul realizes that it is Samuel and prostrates himself on the ground. Samuel speaks to him: "Why have you disturbed me by bringing me up?"
"I am in great distress, for the Philistines are waging war against me, and God has turned from me and answers me no more; either by prophets or by dreams; therefore I have called you to tell me what I should do."
"The Lord has done to you as he spoke by me; for the Lord has wrenched the kingdom from your hand, and given it to your neighbor — to David. . . . Moreover the Lord will give Israel along with you into the hand of the Philistines; and tomorow you and your sons with you will fall. . . ." (1 Sam 28).

And Saul fell to the ground and was thoroughly terrified by Samuel's words.

At first Saul did not want to take the meal offered to him by the woman. But at the insistence of his companions he finally ate. They left Endor that same night.

On the following day the battle took place. The Israelites descended to the plain, near Jezreel. From our terrace we can spot the site. It is a thin patch of land slightly higher than the plain, running toward the mountains of Gilboa.

Samuel and the United Kingdom

The Philistines attacked the Israelites and routed them. The Israelites fled toward the mountains, but many were slaughtered by the pursuing Philistines. Now we cannot follow the action visually, because Gilboa, standing in the southwest, cuts off our view. The Philistines probably drove their war chariots over a section which was not too steep.

Saul's three sons were killed as they retreated. Saul kept going until he was brought down by an arrow which lodged in his side.

"Then Saul said to his armor-bearer: 'Draw your sword, and run me through with it, lest these uncircumcised men come and run me through and make sport of me.' But his armor-bearer would not, for he was terrified. Therefore Saul took his sword and fell upon it. So when his armor-bearer saw that Saul was dead, then he also fell upon his sword and died with him. Thus Saul and his sons and his armor-bearer and all his men died together on the same day.

"Then on the morrow when the Philistines came to strip the slain, they found Saul and his three sons fallen on Mount Gilboa. They cut off his head and stripped off his armor and dispatched them throughout the land of the Philistines to bring good tidings to their idols and to the people" (1 Sam 31).

The remains of Saul and his sons were brought to the nearby city of Beth-shan. From the terrace we cannot see this town, but we can see a valley to the left of Gilboa running toward the Jordan. This was the route taken by the triumphant Philistines.

That is our story. Some other time we will visit Beth-shean to see the place where it ended. But for now, we will close our story, as usual, with a biblical fragment, David's elegy over Saul and Jonathan.

Your beauty, O Israel,
Upon your heights is slain.
How have the heroes fallen!

Tell it not in Gath,
Announce it not in the streets of Ashkelon;
Lest the daughters of the Philistines rejoice,
Lest the daughters of the uncircumcised exult.

Nazareth: Geography From a Terrace

O mountains of Gilboa, let neither dew fall,
Nor rain be upon you, O fields of death!
For there was the shield of the mighty thrown aside,
The shield of Saul, not anointed with oil.

From the blood of the slain,
From the fat of the mighty,
The bow of Jonathan turned not back,
Nor empty returned the sword of Saul.

Saul and Jonathan, beloved and lovely!
In life and in death they were not divided;
Swifter than eagles were they,
They were stronger than lions.

O daughters of Israel, weep over Saul,
Who clothed you in scarlet daintily,
Who adorned your garments with gold and jewels;
How are the mighty fallen in the midst of battle!

O Jonathan! by your death am I mortally wounded,
I am distressed for you, my brother Jonathan!
You were exceedingly dear to me,
Your love was more marvelous to me than the love of women!

How have the mighty fallen,
And the weapons of war perished! (2 Sam 1:18–27.)

IN THE SYNAGOGUE

In our memory the mountains of Gilboa are linked to this tragic story. For in them the first king of the chosen people met his death. He fought valiantly to the very end, and did not allow his enemies the thrill of killing him. But, nevertheless, he died on account of his own sins and dragged his people down in defeat along with himself.

The ways of Divine Providence are strange, indeed; but we learn a little about them in the synagogue at Nazareth where Jesus mounted the pulpit to explain a passage from Isaiah. He made His great pronouncement with utter simplicity. But we must elevate our thoughts to understand it properly.

Saul was an anointed person (a *messiah*) and a savior (a *jesus*)

[201]

of his people for many years. But he was not *the* Messiah. His salvation was not definitive, nor could he obtain the remission of his people's sins. Other saviors — Barak, Deborah, and Gideon — had roamed over this same plain and "there was peace for forty years." But their salvation was not definitive either. The chain of temporary saviors continued down through the ages, until the period of waiting was over and the fullness of time had arrived.

One day the anointed Messiah, the definitive Jesus for all time and all nations, would appear. Isaiah had prophesied His coming ecstatically. At some point in history the time would be ripe and *the* Savior would appear, solemn and triumphant.

Then one afternoon Jesus entered the synagogue at Nazareth, took the scroll of Isaiah in His hand, and read these words.

"The Spirit of the Lord rests upon me, because he has anointed me. He has appointed me a messenger to bring the Good News to the humble; to announce release to captives, and recovery of sight to the blind; to set the oppressed at liberty; to proclaim a year of grace ordained by the Lord."

He rolled up the scroll, handed it to the assistant, and sat down. All eyes were fixed on him. And He said: "Today the scripture text you have just heard has been fulfilled" (Lk 4:21).

The chain was complete, the days of waiting were over, the definitive Messiah and Savior had arrived. In the hour of battle His mother Mary will be at His side, as Deborah was with Barak. He will be strong like Samson and die victoriously. He will be shrewd like Gideon in scattering his enemies. He will be meek like David, and wise like Solomon. He will die like Saul, not because of His own sins but for those of all men; and His death will bring definitive salvation.

Remember that we have come to visit the land of the Old Testament. But the synagogue at Nazareth provides us with a key to the understanding of the Old Testament and the country in which its story unfolded.

The tragic fact is that when Jesus finished His discourse, the Jews rose up in anger and tried to throw Him off a cliff. The representatives of the Old Testament wanted to eliminate the representative of the New Testament. Is it not possible that the same thing may happen all over again?

Nazareth: Geography From a Terrace

The Israelis must try to link themselves with the Old Testament period and to prolong it into the present day. One group would like to eliminate every trace and memory of the New Testament. They do not propose to destroy the many Christian monuments, but to export all Christians. They would like to impede the work of the apostolate in every way. The government itself maintains a liberal attitude but is far from friendly. But if the extremists should ever come to power, there would be good cause for concern. They would try to get rid of the Christian monuments as well. If this should ever happen, their efforts at restoring their tie with the Old Testament would lose all meaning and purpose.

But St. Paul tells us to look forward to the day when the Jews too will come to appreciate the full meaning of their history, Jesus Christ.

34. *BETH-SHAN, GATEWAY ALONG THE JORDAN*

I MUST admit that I was frightened on this tour. We had descended below sea level before of course. It is not so dramatic as breaking the sound barrier, but it always gives me a certain feeling of malaise, headache, and general nausea.

To add to this feeling, we passed a settlement surrounded by barbed wire. It is a penal colony made up of army deserters and AWOL's. They are sent here to till the lowlands in the valley. It is a fertile region and in the days of old was famous for its fine flax. The Israelis want to reclaim this land by using modern cultivation techniques. But the climate is harsh, so they entrust the job to those who are being punished for some crime. Two birds with one stone! I doubt that the prisoners are treated too harshly; the climate alone adds poignancy to the old curse — "by the sweat of your brow."

There is also another colony made up of volunteer workers. They are the pioneering spirits who envision the transformation of Palestine into a beautiful countryside dotted with fertile fields. I don't know if they or their children will be able to adapt to the harsh climate, but for the present they are full of high ideals and work away. This ideal colony is also the custodian of a mosaic depicting an ancient synagogue. Its noteworthy features are its representations of the sun chariot and the signs of the zodiac. From this colony, Beth Alpha, we head toward the hill of Beth-shan.

A STRATEGIC HILL

If the inhabitants of Gilead, east of the Jordan, wanted to attack their neighbors west of the river, they would probably cross the Jordan just south of Lake Gennesaret, come down along the river-bank a short way, and turn right into a valley which leads to the plain of Esdraelon. Beth-shean stands exactly at that cutoff point. If the Syrians wanted to attack Samaria, they would come down from the north, ford the Jordan tributary, Yarmuk, and follow it to the mainstream. Eventually they too would turn into the valley controlled by Beth-shan. If the Philistines, encamped along the Jordan, wanted to secure their commercial route to the north, they would first have to secure the remote fortress of Beth-shan. And if the Egyptians wanted to control Palestine as a defense against attacks from Mesopotamia, they would first take over the fortresses commanding the military routes — Megiddo, Jezreel, Beth-shan.

I do not claim that Beth-shan commands all the military and commercial routes through Palestine. But it does command one of the most important routes.

Our bus comes to a stop a few feet from the bottom of the hill. To our left we can see the rushing waters of the Jalud. We climb a side path toward the ruins of a gateway, a mute witness to antiquity. When we reach the top, we feel that we are standing in a huge watchtower overlooking the Jordan valley and its rough vegetation. From here we could observe any troop movements on the opposite side of the river. And one could dig a huge moat at the foot of this hill, linking it up with the nearby torrent of Jalud.

THE EXCAVATIONS

At the end of the past century an intelligent young geographer named George Adam Smith vainly tried to convince the English Archaeological Society to undertake the systematic excavation of this hill. In the first edition of his book he promised great finds to the first archaeologist who explored it.

The first edition of his book came out in 1894, the twenty-fifth in 1934. Now you can't get hold of a copy, even if you search all the bookstores of Jerusalem and Tel Aviv. Under his penetrating gaze the geography, climate, and countryside of Palestine take on deep meaning. And his pen outlines this meaning in vivid strokes. Historical events become living realities for the reader. This book was one of my best traveling companions and clarified many points which could not be explained in a short visit.

Thirty years went by before his predictions started to come true.

In 1922 the University of Pennsylvania financed the excavation of Beth-shan. The excavators found new strata spanning a period of more than twenty centuries. In the days of antiquity the Egyptians dominated this area, and apparently the Philistines dwelt here as vassals of Egypt.

THE END OF SAUL

There is a strain of tragedy running through the biblical events connected with Beth-shean. The armor of a king hanging in the temple of Astarte; Saul's head exhibited in the temple of Dagon; his body and the bodies of his sons suspended from the walls of the fortress as victory trophies.

When Saul saw that his army was defeated, he chose to die by his own hand and fell on his sword. But he did not die immediately. In his death throes he heard the horses and chariots of the Philistines approaching. An Amalekite stranger happened to be passing by. Saul begged him to finish him off "for confusion has seized me, because my life is still in me." The Amalekite fulfilled his request, took his royal crown and bracelets, and went to tell the news to David.

Night fell over the bloodstained mountains, shielding the corpses from vultures and wild beasts. On the following day the Philistines came to despoil the vanquished. They found the bodies of Saul and his sons. They cut off Saul's head, stripped off his armor, and spread the good news through all their cities. That same day the corpses were hung on the ramparts of Beth-shan.

The news also reached the Israelites living on the opposite shore of the Jordan, just south of Beth-shan. They assembled their most valiant men, set out that same night, crossed the Jordan, and stole up to the city as dawn was breaking. The unsuspecting Philistines had been celebrating their victory, and were probably sleeping it off. The bold Israelites "took the bodies of Saul and his sons from the wall of Beth-shan; and they came to Jabesh and burned them there. Then they took their bones and buried them under the tamarisk tree at Jabesh, and they fasted seven days" (1 Sam 31:12–13).

Beth-shan, Gateway Along the Jordan

THE TEMPLE

It would be something to come face to face with those same ramparts, and those temples dedicated to Dagon and Astarte. The excavators found the ruins of four temples dating from the period of the Egyptian domination, but they could not pinpoint the exact dynasty in which they were built. However, the ruins are still very interesting. One temple was dedicated to the goddess Astarte, a double temple was dedicated to the twin deity Anath-Reseph (Reseph was the thundering storm god). They also found an image of the god Teshup (the Horite equivalent of Reseph). The excavators assume that they have found the ruins on which the Philistines hung their trophies, because many believe that the Philistine god Dagon is equivalent to Reseph.

The arguments are not wholly convincing. But the biblical narrative is quite explicit, and no other ruins have been found which could be identified as the temple mentioned in the Bible. And, furthermore, we know that the ancients used to take over existing temples and rededicate them, or build on the ruins of another temple. The site was considered hallowed ground, and its sacred character was respected. Let us not forget that many archaeological finds would go unexplained, if it were not for the biblical testimony.

LINGUISTICS AND BETH-SHAN

We do not have time for philological riddles. But some linguistic considerations will relieve the tedium of the bus ride.

Place names can have a pleasant ring, especially when we know what they mean. Traveling through Palestine we are not too impressed by such names as *wadi Muleija, wadi Sunt, wadi Jundi,* or *nahar Ruben, nahar Auja, nahar Muqatta.* But the names seem pleasant when we learn their meaning — *the salty torrent, the terebinth torrent, the soldier's torrent;* and *the Captain's River, the Winding River, the Choppy River.*

Beth-shan, as a name, has caused much linguistic speculation. It is a fine example of the complexities involved in analyzing place names. In the days of antiquity only the consonants of a word were noted. So in this case (shan), we have only three — s, h, n. If we

[207]

take them in that order, the word means "repose" or "rest"; and Beth-shan would mean "house of repose" (in contrast with the fierce countryside, perhaps). The modern Arab name is Tell El Husn. Again we have s, h, n, but in a different order; and the word means "fortified hill" or "fortress" — alluding to the strategic value of the site. Finally we can reverse the letters to form the word *nahas* which means "serpent." In this case it would refer to the city dedicated to the serpent goddess. Phonetically all three arrangements are possible, so there is no solution on these grounds. And the archaeological data do not tell us the proper position of these consonants. The traveler can take his choice. "House of repose" does not seem appropriate to me. The traveler could be eclectic and accept all three interpretations. For the earliest inhabitants it was a sanctuary, "the house of the serpent"; for the Israelites it was "the house of repose"; and for the Arabs it was "the hill fortress." Though this compromise may not be accurate, it helps us to remember the history of this city.

35. THE CONQUEST OF JERUSALEM

THE city which was to become the capital of the united kingdom, the symbol of heaven itself, and a disputed site for centuries to come, was not conquered at once by the Israelites. Joshua began his campaign of conquest against Jericho and then gradually moved northward. During the two centuries when the kingdom was loosely organized under the judges, the city was not coveted by the Israelites, or else it was considered too impregnable. The first Israelite king, Saul, set up court near Jerusalem, but he had no plans of conquering this fort lying in his kingdom. David was the first to undertake this project. According to the Bible it was his first undertaking after the Israelites proclaimed him king at Hebron. When he had conquered the fortress, he felt that it would be the ideal spot from which to govern all the tribes in the north and the south.

To the modern-day visitor the hill scarcely seems impregnable. He must fill in certain details to appreciate the situation fully. The hill takes up a fairly large area and extends from north to south. On the right lies the brook of Kidron cutting off any access from that direction. On the left that is a gradual incline which was once about thirty-eight feet deeper. It would have been hard to reach it, and impossible to scale it. Down below three valleys ran together — Hinnon, Tyropoeon, and Kidron. No attack could be launched from there. Up above, the hill joins up with other high spots — the present-day temple area and that of St. Ann's Basilica. It seems to be an easy access route today. But it may have been well fortified in ancient times.

The Jebusites had built stout defense walls around the city, and from these walls they taunted the invaders below. "You shall not come in here, but the blind and the lame shall prevent you" (2 Sam 5:6). David had demonstrated his strong-willed determination and resourcefulness on many previous occasions; but he realized the truth of the Jebusites' taunts. The fortress could not be taken in a direct assault. So he tried to devise a stratagem which would get him inside the city.

We have examined the hill from above and from below. The most noteworthy items at the bottom are the well and the tunnel — we shall come back to them shortly. On the top there are ruins of defense walls which cannot be dated exactly. Some have concluded that these are the remains of the Jebusite walls, or that at least the lower levels of rock date from this period. But the hypothesis has not been proven.

While David is working out his stratagem, we shall discuss the defense systems used by ancient cities and consider one example.

WATER AND WALLS

Without a water supply a city cannot exist. Without defense fortifications it cannot persist. These two simple facts of life caused acute problems for the ancient inhabitants of Palestine. A city sequestered high on a hill and ringed with a fine defense wall was secure from attack. But if its water supply lay outside the fortress, the defense wall was useless. And if the wall had to descend to the valley to encircle the water holes, then it would be an easy prey to enemy attack.

The Book of Judith describes the tragic plight of the city of Bethulia. The city's defenders had secluded themselves inside the ramparts. At night a circle of bonfires rings the wall, lighting up the outlines of the fortress and the night watchmen. The enemy army is encamped around the hill.

There is one weak point in Bethulia's defense setup; her water springs are located at the foot of the hill. It is easy for Holofernes to station men at these springs and wait patiently for the city to surrender. Thirty-four days go by and the public cisterns inside the city give out. Water is rationed by the city officials. The rainy season is nowhere in sight. The people begin to weaken and mutiny. The city chief asks the people to be patient for five days. Judith hears the news and decides to save the city on her own. We all know the rest of this beautiful story. The important lesson here is the significance of the location of the city's water supply.

The Conquest of Jerusalem

THE SOLUTION IN MEGIDDO

The two factors involved in the problem are water and defense walls. The solution is simple, in theory at least. Since the walls cannot be extended down to the water supply, bring the water supply up inside the walls. And sixteen centuries before Christ a group of engineers worked out a daring scheme to accomplish this: an underground tunnel. The well was camouflaged on the outside, and the water came up to the city through this underground passageway. But the practical realization of this project involved many intricate problems. However, Megiddo was such an important strategic fortress that they deemed the project worthwhile.

We are going to examine this stupendous project. And we must note in passing that it was almost as difficult for the archaeologists to dig up and clear this tunnel without destroying it as it was for the ancient engineers to construct it.

First, the ancient engineers built an outside channel, three feet wide and six feet high. It had a protective cover on top and was shielded by solid walls. But as time went on, it became obvious that there was too much exposed surface. It may have been some energetic chieftain who ordered them to undertake the more ambitious project. From the data we possess, we have good reason to believe that the inhabitants of Megiddo were aware of the system used in the city of Gezer and in the fortress of Urusalaim. It may have been discovered by spies; or it may have been a system used by some common overlord, such as the pharaohs of Egypt. We have no solid information on this point.

But the fact is that the engineers began work on this project at Megiddo. On one of the slopes of the hill the visitor will find a large, deep well. If he has a guide and enough time, he can inspect the underground passage. But we did not have enough time.

The workers began to dig vertically, shoveling away the earth and reinforcing the opening with retaining walls. Next they hit upon a thick layer of rock. Once the well was opened up, they dug out a rock staircase along the side. Then they changed direction and constructed a ramp with stone steps. So far they had gone down some eighty feet. From this point, or perhaps from the spring, they opened up a horizontal tunnel leading to the bottom of the ramp.

A CHANGE IN PLAN?

The subterranean cavern could be a double-edged weapon. An enemy might use it to sneak into the city, surprising the lookout on duty. Did such a thing happen at Megiddo? We cannot say for sure, because our data are scanty. So we shall simply present the data we have and let our imagination take over from there.

Exhibit I: The Corpse in the Cavern. Next to the underground cavern but somewhat higher up, there is another cavern leading to the outside. It corresponds to the original water level in the well. When the water vein was lowered, the upper cavern was converted into a guard post. In this cavern the archaeologists found mute witnesses to the past: human bones and some charred remains. He may have been a lookout surprised at his post.

Exhibit II: Changes in the Well. At some point the military engineers decided to make some changes in their plan. They decided to eliminate the sloping ramp and extend the tunnel as far as the wall of the well. Then, by lowering the bottom of the well, they could make a small cistern where water would accumulate. The inhabitants could lower a bucket into the well by means of a rope. And the thirty feet of sheer wall below the spiral staircase would prevent any surprise assaults. Was this the reason for the change in plan? It would seem so. Only security reasons could have persuaded them to undertake such a difficult task.

The fate of Megiddo is not known to us. The sentinel has told us only that he was there — nothing more. But we do know that there were similar tunnels in other cities. And there is an interesting hypothesis concerning the tunnel in Jerusalem.

A WELL AND A THEORY

In 1866 the English official Warren was exploring the land around Jerusalem. In the pool of Mary near the brook of Kidron he found a tunnel and began to go through it. He had only gone a short distance when he realized that the roof of the tunnel rose up in the form of a well. Like a true adventurer he headed up the well, and after a difficult climb he came out on the surface of the hill.

The Conquest of Jerusalem

Today the two extremes of the well are plugged up, and I don't think they allow people to climb to the top.

Warren's bold climb suggested an interesting theory. Wouldn't David have used the same method to conquer the city? Strangely enough, the Bible gives no detail about his surprising exploits.

To be more precise, scholars were not certain whether the biblical text mentions the stratagem or not. It reads: "Nevertheless David took the citadel of Zion. . . . David said on that day: 'He who would smite the Jebusites, let him gain (or strike) the *sinnor*, and all will be as lame and blind who hate David's life!' "

The text gave rise to various interpretations because of the key word, *sinnor*. Many scholars interpreted it as meaning some part of the body and translated the passage: "let him strike in the *neck, the joint*, etc." Others interpreted it as some weapon: "let him strike him with ——." Father Vincent chose Birch's explanation and thus it gained a certain prominence.

David promises a reward to the man who climbs the well (the *sinnor*) and penetrates into the city. Joab, with a companion perhaps, makes the climb by night, gets inside the city, and opens the gates for his companions. The impregnable city had fallen and Joab becomes the chief and commander.

It is an appealing theory. But there are serious grammatical difficulties involved and many scholars refuse to accept it. On the other hand others have embraced it wholeheartedly and now use the word *sinnor* to designate this particular type of subterranean connection linking city and water supply.

THE prophet Isaiah pronounced the following threat against Assyria: "His splendid forests and orchards will be consumed, soul and body; and the remnant of the trees in his forest will be so few, like poles set up for signals, that any boy can record them."

The curse seems to have come true in Palestine too. At least that is the impression we got from our ten-day stay in Jerusalem. During that period we visited all the biblical sites in Jordan, west of the Jordan river; from Taanach to Hebron, from Latrun to Jericho. And one of my companions kept repeating: "So this is the land of milk and honey!" I was going to tell him that it would look that way to people who had just come from the desert. But this explanation did not even satisfy me.

The countryside has almost always been arid and dusty. For some strange reason the olive trees don't even seem to add a touch of green to the landscape. There were only a few patches of real greenery: the rolling plain of Jericho with its many palm trees; the secluded area where Solomon's reservoirs are located, and the beautiful gardens of En-gannim near the plain of Esdraelon. In antiquity the situation was somewhat different. When the Promised Land was portioned out among the twelve tribes, Ephraim and Manasseh received mountainous forest land; and Bethel, which is now so parched, once had a dense thicket inhabited by bears.

One day the prophet Elisha started up a hillside. Some children made sport of him, chanting; "Up you go, baldy, up you go." Elisha turned around and gave them a dirty look. Then he uttered a curse in the name of the Lord; and two bears came out of the nearby thicket and mangled the children. I don't know if this was an inspired act on the prophet's part, or if it had some deeper meaning. But I find his angry retaliation a little bit hard to take, even though the children may not have shown proper respect for a prophet.

Trees

Perhaps there was more to their jesting than meets the eye. But even when we found ourselves in a ticklish predicament — the mischievous children at Hebron, the threat of being pelted with stones in Jerusalem — we would never have thought to turn bears on our tormentors. Nor would they have come, because they no longer exist in this region.

FORESTRY AS A NATIONAL POLICY

When we come to the western sector of Jerusalem, the landscape begins to change. There are wooded areas and a district with villas and gardens.

The Book of Deuteronomy has some comments on trees in its military code. "When you are at war with a city and have to lay siege to it for a long time before you capture it, you shall not destroy its trees by putting an ax to them. You may eat their fruit, but you must not cut down the trees. After all, are the trees of the field men, that they should be included in your siege? However, those trees which you know are not fruit trees you may destroy, cutting them down to build siegeworks with which to reduce the city that is resisting you." And when Moses dispatched scouts to reconnoiter the land, one of the things he wanted to know was whether the land had trees or not. After our trip through Palestine we would have to answer "yes." There are the extensive orange plantations along the coast, the rows of eucalyptus trees along the highway, the delightful groves around Lake Gennesaret, the magnificent gardens of Ramath-Gan ringed with cypress trees, and the newly established colony of Beth-Shearim which looks like a public park dotted with houses. Yes, we would have to say that there are many trees; but even more important is the fact that there will be many more.

One of the most habitual sins castigated by the prophets was Israel's idolatry "under every spreading tree." The shady area of a tree was regarded as an ideal spot for cultic worship. Today in Israel there is a real tree cult, but it has no religious element in it. The Israelis are working to transform the mountains and the hillsides into vast woodlands, and the project is moving forward at a rapid pace.

[215]

THE MARTYRS' GROVE

The most notable example of this policy is the "martyrs' grove." In the mountains running from Jerusalem to the coastal plain, the Israelis want to plant a huge pine forest — six million trees — in memory of the six million Jews slaughtered by the Nazis.

This forest monument will not be as spectacular as other well-known monuments to the dead. But it will provide food for thought. Each human life that was uprooted in the war will be represented by a growing tree. The memory of those who died in other lands will be preserved in the new land of Israel. And the growing pine trees will symbolize the people's desire to settle and take root in the soil of Palestine.

About two and a half million trees have been planted so far. Rich Jews who die in other lands now have a new clause in their will: "a grove of 2000 pines," and various sections are named after the different donors — the Chaim Weizmann grove, the Theodore Herzl grove, the Harry Truman grove, etc.

RIDING THROUGH A THICKET

In order to reach one of the famous kibbutzim our bus has turned off the main highway onto a road lined with thick vegetation. Our guide tells us to watch our head and arms because the branches stick out and brush the windows. And, up above, the branches claw at the luggage. One piece of luggage is torn in the encounter.

Now we could appreciate how Absalom died. He rebelled against his father David, and fought against him "in the forest of Ephraim." The rebels were defeated, and "scattered in disorderly fashion. And the forest devoured more people that day than the sword.

"Absalom was riding upon a mule, and the mule went under the thick branches of a great oak and his head caught fast in the oak, and he was left hanging between heaven and earth, while the mule that was under him passed on." Absalom couldn't extricate himself at all. His feet were off the ground, he could not use his hands to free his head. He did not think to cut the branch off with his sword; and he was afraid to cry out lest he attract the

[216]

attention of his enemies. One of David's men saw him hanging there and ran to inform General Joab.

" 'Behold, I saw Absalom hanging in an oak.'

"Then Joab said to the man who had told him, 'You mean to say that you saw him! Why then did you not fell him to the ground at once? Then it would have been my part to have given you ten shekels of silver and a girdle!'

" 'Though I were to feel the pressure of a thousand shekels of silver in my hand,' said the man to Joab, 'I would not put forth my hand against the king's son; for in our hearing the king charged you and Abishai and Ittai, saying: "Spare for my sake the young man Absalom!" Or if I had treacherously made away with him, nothing would have been hidden from the king, and you yourself would have stood aloof!'

" 'Not so,' said Joab; 'I would have assuaged his wrath.' Then he took three weapons in his hand, and thrust them into Absalom's vitals, while he was still alive in the midst of the oak; and ten men who bore Joab's armor gathered around and smote Absalom until he was dead.

"Then Joab blew the trumpet, and the people returned from pursuing Israel; for Joab held back the people. Thereupon they took Absalom and cast him into a great pit in the forest, and raised over him a great heap of stones."

When the king heard the news, he was greatly troubled; and he wept for his dead son. "Thus, he said, as he wept: 'My son Absalom, my son, my son Absalom! O that I, even I, had died instead of you, Absalom, my son, my son!'

"And the victory that day was turned to mourning for all the people. . . . Therefore the people stole away furtively into the city, as people who are put to shame when they have fled in battle steal away" (2 Sam 19).

37. THE STORY OF TWO FOUNTAINS
(1 Kings 1)

SUCH would be the title of a classical drama. If it were a comedy, it might be entitled "Everything Happens at Two Fountains." And if it were an adventure story — "The Fountains of Intrigue."

The hill which David captured from the Jebusites and made his capital lies outside the walls of present-day Jerusalem. It extends from north to south, parallel to the brook of Kidron and facing Mount Olivet. At the extreme southern end of the hill the valley of Hinnom runs into the brook of Kidron at a right angle.

We visited this whole area one afternoon while we were in Jerusalem. It contains important archaeological remains — royal tombs and defense walls which cannot be dated accurately. The accepted opinion is that this hill is Ophel, David's official residence.

So this is the picture. The king, old and failing, is living in his palace at the top of the hill — about 150 feet from the bottom. Although his servants wrap him in blankets, he still feels cold and spends the night shivering. Meanwhile his court officials are thinking about his successor.

Don't forget that there are two fountains at the bottom of the hill. Gihon lies in the north; and beyond the confluence of Kidron and Hinnom lies Rogel. From the city you can reach either one in a matter of minutes, even though Rogel is a bit farther away. And to complete the picture, you cannot see one from the other, but they are within calling distance.

Just as there are two fountains, so there are two factions in the palace. The king has two wives, and each one wants her son to become the next king. Haggith is plugging for her son Adonijah, the younger brother of Absalom; Bathsheba is campaigning for Solomon, who was born after the treacherous assassination of Uriah.

There are also two generals: Benaiah for Solomon and Joab

[218]

The Story of Two Fountains (1 Kings 1)

for Adonijah; and two priests: Zadok for Solomon and Abiathar for Adonijah. In short the three most influential elements around the king — the army, the priests, and the queens — are divided up into two opposing factions. And the old king, attended by a beautiful Shunamite maiden, is unaware of all these intrigues.

ACT 1

Adonijah makes the first move and is the central character in the first act of our story. ". . . He provided for himself a chariot and horsemen and fifty men as runners to go before him. Now his father had never in his life restrained him by saying: 'Why do you do thus and so?' He was besides a very handsome man, and he was born next after Absalom. Accordingly he negotiated with Joab, the son of Zeruiah, and with Abiathar the priest, so that they became Adonijah's helpers." But he did not reckon with one personage who was to play the decisive role in the drama.

Adonijah decided to present the court with a *fait accompli*, by having himself proclaimed king at a solemn banquet. He sent out invitations to the most important royal personages, carefully screening out his opponents — Zadok, Benaiah, the trained warriors, Solomon (presumably), and the prophet Nathan.

He chose the fountain of Rogel as the site of the banquet. It was a good spot for a get-together, located a short distance away from the heart of the city. There he sacrificed sheep and oxen and fat cattle by the Serpent's Stone. The preliminary stages of the banquet took some time. The animals had to be quartered and skewered; the fire had to be started and kept going.

Today the fountain is called Bir Ayub, not Rogel. If the name was of Hebrew origin it would mean "the traveler's fountain." Even today it is frequented by many people. Its location at the junction of two valleys and its fine water make it a favorite spot. Travelers starting out from this area get water from it. Passersby refill their canteens here. And those heading for the city stop to take a drink before climbing up the hill. A fine water hole lying near the city, but not too near, it is no wonder that Adonijah chose it as the setting for his *coup d'etat*.

PALACE INTRIGUE

The prophet Nathan is the first to discover the plot. He meets Bathsheba and outlines their counteroffensive to the last detail.

Bathsheba enters the throne room, and David asks her what she wants. She replies:

"My Lord . . . you yourself swore to your maidservant by the Lord your God: 'Solomon your son shall be king after me and he shall sit on my throne.' Now, behold, Adonijah is king and you, my lord, O king, do not know it. He has sacrificed oxen and fat cattle and sheep in abundance, and has invited all the sons of the king, and Abiathar the priest, and Joab, the commander of the army; but he has not invited Solomon your servant. Now, my lord, O king, the eyes of all Israel are upon you, that you should tell them who shall sit on the throne of my lord the king after him. As it stands, the result will be that when my lord the king shall sleep with his fathers, I and my son Solomon will be regarded as rebels."

While she is speaking, Nathan *just happens* to seek an audience with the king. He brings a similar report to the king. "They are eating and drinking before him, and have said: 'Long live King Adonijah!' . . . Has this thing been brought about by my lord the king?"

David could still react quickly. First he calls Bathsheba and reiterates his promise. Then he summons Zadok, Nathan, and Benaiah. "Take with you the servants of your lord and cause Solomon my son to ride upon my own mule, and bring him down to Gihon." Then he completed the arrangements for his succession (1 Kgs 1).

AT THE FOUNTAIN OF GIHON

The royal party sets out in silence for the fountain of Gihon. The name refers to a fountain which gushes over impetuously. Its water is reported to be somewhat salty. None of us tried it when we saw women washing their feet in it. Instead we waded in barefoot for an adventure underground, which we shall report later (Chap. 54).

Right now the important point is the fact that it takes only five minutes to get to the fountain from the city. Even though the royal cortege may have taken somewhat longer, it reached its destination quickly.

"Then Zadok the priest took a horn of oil from the tent and anointed Solomon. Whereupon they blew the trumpet and all the people said: 'Long live King Solomon!' Then all the people went up after him playing upon flutes and rejoicing with such great outburst that the earth was rent with their voice." But one member of the cortege heads off for the other fountain, where there are also shouts of "Long live the king" (1 Kgs 1).

AT THE FOUNTAIN OF ROGEL

General Joab is the first to hear the trumpets and he wonders: "Why this noise of the town in uproar?" Jonathan, the son of Abiathar, arrives to tell him what he has seen. It had only taken him ten minutes to get from one fountain to the other. Adonijah speaks: " 'Enter, for you are a valiant man and bring good news.'

" 'No, rather our lord King David has made Solomon king . . . they have caused him to ride on the king's mule. Zadok the priest and Nathan the prophet have anointed him king in Gihon, and they have gone up from there rejoicing, so that the town is in uproar.' So Solomon has actually taken his seat on the throne of the kingdom. . . . Furthermore, thus the king has said: 'Blessed be the Lord, the God of Israel, who has today granted one of my offspring to sit on my throne, my own eyes beholding it.'

". . . Then all the guests whom Adonijah had were terrified and arose and each went his way. But Adonijah was in such fear of Solomon that he arose and went and caught hold of the horns of the altar" (1 Kgs 1).

The biblical story comes to life in its historical setting. It is rather difficult for us to understand why there should have been so much debate about the exact location of these fountains. Father Vincent blamed it on those scholars who love arguments but know little about the actual lay of the land around here. After surveying the area, we are inclined to agree with Father Vincent.

It is like reading a novel where the action takes place in a well-known city whose name has been changed. We follow the action perfectly, because we have lived in the city for a long time. And we know each spot being described by the author, even though he has changed the names. Today the two fountains have different names: Ain Umm ed-Daradj (Gihon) and Bir Ayub (Rogel). But the change of names is unimportant, because we are quite familiar with the scene of the biblical events.

Once again we realize that an on-the-spot visit can provide a fine lesson in exegesis.

38. A MODEL EXCAVATION — MEGIDDO

THE greatest builder and organizer in Hebrew history was King Solomon. His tyrannical policies greatly enhanced the material splendor of the kingdom, but they also fomented internal discontent. After his death the northern tribes seceded, and the united kingdom was no more.

We could look for Solomon's imprint in many parts of Palestine. We could even go down as far as the gulf of Aqaba, where he worked the mines, established foundries, and built a harbor with its own dockyards. But this distant spot is not on our itinerary; and, besides, the excavations of Glueck at this site were on a small scale. We are going to select arbitrarily the hill of Megiddo, where the most extensive excavation work in Palestine was carried out. The excavation efforts of the archaeologists at this site could be likened to Solomon's mania for building. And, furthermore, Megiddo represents one of Solomon's great projects.

THE LAYOUT OF MEGIDDO

There is much truth in Vásquez de Mella's statement that "geography often determines the course of history." In the case of Tell el-Mutesellim (Megiddo) it is absolutely true. In the year 1852 the tireless traveler, Edward Robinson, stopped here. The hill was in a fine location, situated just outside a narrow pass and overlooking the plain of Esdraelon. Merchant caravans and the conquering armies of Egypt and Mesopotamia would have had to come through this pass, right by the hill. Robinson looked over the countryside and saw the wheat fields ripening on the hillside. And he thought to himself: What a perfect spot for the ancient city of Megiddo! But there was no visible trace of an ancient city; only the wheat fields ripening for the harvest.

But Robinson's intuitions had been correct, and his sense impressions, based on superficial evidence, were wrong. Under his feet lay twenty strata of ruins, ancient cities piled one atop the other. Undoubtedly, for many centuries the inhabitants of this hillside had monitored the flow of commerce through the pass, and had watched the battles between contending armies.

THE NARROW PASS

Looking at a map of Palestine, the reader will see a mountain chain running up parallel to the coast. Somewhere around the middle of Palestine it cuts to the left (Mount Carmel) and runs toward the sea, separating the north of Palestine from the south. To bypass this obstacle a traveler can take one of three routes; and we have tried all three in our travels. First, there is a route which slopes down from the mountains of Judah and Samaria into the plain of Esdraelon. But to take this route the traveler would have to have free access to the mountain region. Practically speaking, this route is not usable.

The second route curves around Mount Carmel along the sea-coast. We used it on a trip from Jerusalem to Haifa. It is safe and quick for someone using a modern highway and having no enemies on the buttes of Carmel. But it would have been quite different for the ancient armies and the merchants riding on camels.

The third route is wadi Arah, a narrow pass which cuts through the mountain. This is the route we took to visit Megiddo, and thus we came to realize the strategic value of the fortress. We leave Jaffa (Joppa) and head toward Beth-shan, following the *via maris*. The narrow pass is not at all imposing. I suddenly realize that it would be easier to blockade the pass and dominate its two walls than to wait calmly at the end for an approaching enemy. I am not the first to realize this. In 1479 B.C. Thothmes was marching toward the north. When he reached the foot of Mount Carmel he summoned his army staff. They suggested that he go around the mountain at some less expected point. But Thothmes decided upon a more daring stroke. Those who wished to follow him would have to follow him through the pass. Meanwhile, the enemy had ruled out this approach and had left it undefended. Thothmēs came through unmolested and routed them. As we come out of the pass, the picturesque hillside comes into view. The bus starts up a causeway, passes through a wire gate supported by wooden planks, and stops before a house with a walk in front. A few leafy trees are growing nearby.

ON THE HILL

From the house we go up a steep path. One member of our group is wearing slippery shoes and must be helped up. I follow the driver along a side trail. Although it winds around the hill, it is still a shortcut. This driver is an interesting character. He does not just quote the guidebook; he has a real interest in these excavations. Perhaps it is a mixture of interest and national pride. Perhaps he feels the blood of these ancient settlers pulsing in his veins. We cannot exclude the possibility that one of his ancestors belonged to a garrison at Megiddo. This bus driver may be the descendant of some charioteer in Solomon's day.

On reaching the top I leave the driver to go over and listen to our guide.

At the beginning of this century (1903–1905) the *Deutscher Palästina Verein* put Schumacher an (engineer named "shoemaker"!) in charge of the excavations at Tell el-Mutesellim. By that time Petrie had already discovered the fundamental principle of pottery-dating. But the industrious engineer, who laid out beautiful plans and drawings of the hill, was guilty of two weaknesses typical of that era. First, he was anxious to make sensational finds which would attract the attention of museums; so he neglected to fill in the data of ancient history. This mania for finding museum pieces was quite common at that time; and it is quite legitimate to seek recognition for one's work. But it had unfortunate consequences for the progress of Palestinian scholarship. Second, Schumacher was not very interested in pottery-dating, and his ignorance of the ceramic index to chronology vitiated his stratigraphy. If we add to this the contemporary tendency, especially in the German school of archaeology, to interpret everything in cultic terms, we can see the major flaws in Schumacher's work.

His best find was a seal made of jasper and bearing the inscription: "Shema, officer of Jeroboam." The name was quite well known and belonged to an historical figure who lived around 800 B.C. Schumacher collected the tidy sum of ten thousand dollars for it, quite a respectable amount in those days. The other finds could not be moved or sold: a surrounding wall and two large forts; a large open area with stone columns placed at regular intervals. These stone columns could only be *masseboths* (i.e., cultic stelae), thought Schumacher.

The work published by Schumacher provides an excellent topographical analysis of the hill; but the stratigraphy is quite untrustworthy. At the time it was an interesting scientific contribution, but its relative merit declined as time went on. And the famous hill of Megiddo was still almost completely intact. The German excavator had only inflicted light wounds on it. It carried an academic scar, and no more.

At that time they used the trenching method. They dug long narrow ditches about eighteen feet wide, cutting through the various strata. Luck was with them because all the finds lay in the limited area of one trench, like a prize in a fortune cookie.

"THE IDEAL EXCAVATION"

In 1924 the Chicago Oriental Institute was planning to perform a model excavation in Palestine. It was to be a perfect example of scientific excavatory work. Breasted, the director of the Institute, planned the project with great care.

But what did he mean by a perfect excavation? Perhaps an analogy may clarify this point. There are times when a chef wants to outdo himself. So he decides to make a special layer cake with many tiers on it. He starts off with simple unadorned layers of cake, then covers them with chocolate icing, cookies, whipped cream, burnt almonds, cream puffs, and egg whites. We are tempted to take a gleaming knife and cut ourselves a nice slice of the tempting pastry. But our purpose is to analyze the masterpiece from a culinary point of view, so we carefully lift off the top layer and let the proper experts begin their analysis. When we are through with the first layer, we take off the second layer and do the same thing. And so, level by level, we work our way down to the platter itself.

[226]

A Model Excavation — Megiddo

I can picture Breasted smacking his lips in Chicago, as he planned his perfect excavation. He would have a corps of experts in his equipage: photographers, chemists, pottery experts, architects, engineers, an epigraphist, a doctor, and a foreman.

The site chosen for this ideal excavation was Megiddo. The hill would be stripped layer by layer until it was completely leveled. However the ideal excavation still lacked one thing — an ideal endowment. In other words, they would have to interest some magnate like Rockefeller in the project. They finally succeeded and the work began. Between 1925 and 1929 the work on Megiddo cost a million dollars.

Two items will indicate how much attention was paid to detail. First of all, the field headquarters had its own tennis court. Second, the photographers eventually got their own balloon so that they could get aerial photographs.

It took a few years for the excavators to realize that the ideal does not exist in reality. But American realism finally won out. First they got an attack of scruples, or something like it. They realized that they wanted to level the whole cake by themselves, leaving nothing for future excavators who would probably come better prepared. So they decided to limit their work to two specific zones on the hill. The second consideration was monetary. Not even a Rockefeller could bear the endless costs involved. But, all in all, the excavation work, directed in turn by Fischer, Guy, and Loud, was perfect as far as it went, and made definite contributions to every branch of archaeology.

SOME OF THE FINDS

The view from the top of the hill is extensive, because of the large quantity of ruins scattered over a wide area. Some of these ruins are typical: stone walls about two hands high, the remains of houses. In some spots the width and depth of the digs is very impressive, especially when you look at them from the bottom of the hill. And when you realize that each stratum had to be dug up, removed with great care, and carefully annotated, then you must admit that it was an enormous task.

To summarize the most important finds, we would have to leaf

[227]

through the various levels one by one. Standing at the site, one finds it hard to pick out the most interesting objects; one is more impressed by the overall picture. But the official publications, done up in magnificent style, give a detailed account of every item.

At the lowest level the troglodytes lived in the virgin rock some 6000 years ago. In the first half of the third millennium the native inhabitants constructed a wall of huge rocks thirty feet thick. Around 2300 B.C. the inhabitants built a temple with an altar of unhewn stones (as Yahweh had commanded the Israelites), five feet high and twenty-nine feet in diameter. It is still easily recognizable today. Around 1250 the people built three ivory rooms in Egyptian decor.

The fourth strata from the top dates from the time of Solomon (965–926 B.C.).

We must focus on this stratum, because we have come in search of Solomon. Now would be the time to examine the stone pillars which were dubbed as cultic stelae by Schumacher. But this topic requires a chapter all to itself. And before treating it, we must briefly explain how the archaeologists managed to date its levels and the finds encased in them.

39. *POTTERY AS A CALENDAR*

By THIS time we have already visited a score of museums, not counting the one in Cairo which is in a class by itself. We have scrutinized the objects in such museums as the one at the American University in Beirut, the Lebanon museum, the Damascus museum, the Amman museum, the magnificent museum in Arab Jerusalem, and the new one in Israeli Jerusalem. And we have also visited smaller museums such as the one in Beer-sheba and the one at the Biblical Institute in Jerusalem.

And in every single case we have encountered a large collection of pottery on display.

In Byblos we watched Dunand's assistant working in a small room, oblivious to the Mediterranean panorama outside. He was arranging the pieces of a vase and gluing them together with the patience of an Oriental. One of the curators in the Amman museum brought us into his workshop and showed us the chemicals used in treating pieces of pottery.

This pottery business must be pretty important. However at times the name seems to be misapplied. It seems appropriate when you are talking about a finished piece which has come down to us intact or has been fully restored. But very often it is applied to a collection of bits and pieces which might be more appropriately called "shards." Judging by the amount of space reserved for pottery in the museums, the layman would think that the Israelites were a race of potters or ceramic specialists.

But this would be an exaggeration, even though the Israelites and other ancient peoples have left behind a beautiful collection of pottery objects — vases, pots, kettles, earthen jars, pitchers, jugs, bowls, cups, cruets, bottles, vials, etc.

JEREMIAH'S INTEREST IN POTTERY

Jeremiah was the prophet most interested in this business. On three occasions he uses imagery drawn from pottery-making as the basis of an oracle. One day he goes to the potter's workshop and finds him working at his wheel. "Whenever the object of clay which he was making turned out badly in his hand, he tried again, making of the clay another object of whatever sort he pleased. Then the word of the Lord came to me: 'Can I not do to you, house of Israel, as this potter has done?' says the Lord. 'Indeed, like clay in the hand of the potter, so are you in my hand, house of Israel' " (Jer 18:4–6). On another occasion Jeremiah goes into a shop stocked with wine flasks. The prophet meets a group of people and points out: " 'Every wine flask is meant to be filled with wine.' — 'Do we not know that every wine flask is meant to be filled with wine?' And Jeremia answers: 'Thus says the Lord: "Beware! I am filling with drunkenness all the inhabitants of this land. . . . I will dash them against each other . . ."' " (Jer 13:12–14).

The third time Jeremiah puts on a more solemn display. First he buys an earthen flask. (If the Hebrew word *baqbuq* is meant to be onomatopoetic, mimicking the sound of the water as it comes out of the flask, then it would be a deep flask with a narrow neck.) Then he assembles some of the elders of the people and of the priests and heads for the Potsherd Gate. (So picture the strange cortege led by a man with a flask in his hand.) When they reach the gate, the prophet stops and the cortege assembles around him. Without uttering a word he dashes the flask against the rocks. The spectators look on wonderingly and Jeremiah explains the significance of his act. "Thus says the Lord of hosts: 'Thus will I smash this people and this city, as one smashes a clay pot so that it cannot be repaired' " (Jer 19:11).

Jeremiah added to the prestige of the pottery business, because he usually performed symbolic acts when he delivered an oracle. But images referring to pottery-making crop up in the words of other prophets and inspired writers — Isaiah, Job, St. Paul, St. John, the Psalms, the Book of Wisdom, etc.

A NEW USE FOR POTTERY

But these allusions to pottery which crop up throughout the Bible do not justify the archaeologist's interest in the most insignificant shards and the countless museum exhibitions. The fine arts might be interested in certain pieces which have an exceptionally beautiful shape, or design, or glaze. And the cultural historian might be interested in other pieces which are less artistic but are indicative of technical or industrial progress. But there must be a deeper reason for this almost obsessive interest in pottery on the part of the archaeologist.

We shall get an explanation from the bearded patriarch of Palestinian archaeology; for he discovered the real value of those objects which were cast off by the ancients. In our trip to Beersheba we passed near the hill of Tell el-Hesi. We did not stop to visit it because there is nothing special to see on it. But from a distance we paid our silent respects to the venerable figure who began the excavation of Palestine on this hill — Sir William Flinders Petrie.

He was born in England in 1853. In his lifetime he published seventy-five books and gave countless lectures. It was his good fortune to live at a time when a pioneering individual had great leeway. At his death almost ninety years later his name was associated not so much with the fantastic adventures of his younger days (e.g., living in a tomb), or his finds at El Amarna, or his many books, but rather with his discovery of the ceramic index to chronology. It is quite likely that the basic idea came to him in a flash of intuition. We must proceed more slowly and lead up to it.

THE CHARACTERISTICS OF POTTERY

To begin with, pottery was a common household object in the days of old. It was cheap, lightweight, and easy to make. It could be used by Gideon's soldiers to hide their lamps and by the Philistines to hold beer. It could serve as a vessel to multiply the widow's oil in the years of scarcity, to light the way for a bridal party, or to preserve the perfumes of noble ladies. Pottery was everywhere and had a thousand uses.

The second point is that pottery could come in many different shapes and designs. The introduction of the potter's wheel revolutionized the industry. And when the oven was perfected, the quality

[231]

of the earthenware improved at once. The processes of glazing, varnishing, and enameling gave added elegance and purity. Even more important than these improvements in technique was the human factor — taste. This ever changing element was to be the key clue.

And the third characteristic of pottery was its fragility. When St. Paul wishes to describe man's weakness he tells us that we carry the treasure of grace in vessels of clay. Once the vessel is broken, it is of no further use; unless one wanted to write a message on it, when a battle was going against him (cf. Chap. 55).

And finally it is important to note that pottery fragments are very durable. A silver vessel melts in a fire, a wooden pot rots away in water. But crockery has an indestructible quality. The shards resist the ravages of fire and time.

POTTERY-DATING

So all the pieces of the puzzle are there. Wherever we excavate we will find pottery, if human beings dwelt there in ancient times. And we can date the area on the basis of this pottery — its quality, shape, type of decoration, glaze, style, etc. It is just as if we were given a pile of undated magazines and told to arrange them in chronological order, year by year. It might be a good idea to turn to the fashion pages. Styles change each year; and a close comparative study might give us our chronology: half-sleeve, short skirt = year x. Now if we did the same thing with the pottery, we would have solved the great archaeological riddle — when?

This was Petrie's great discovery. It is true that he did not apply his new-found weapon with complete accuracy and that his conclusions were not definitive. But one can't expect an inventor to work out all the kinks. His idea was ingenious and opened up a whole new range of possibilities. Later workers began to catalog their finds systematically and thus laid the basis for typological dating (sequence-dating). Pottery pieces could now be dated with great accuracy and assigned to their proper epoch.

Now you can understand why pottery is of such great interest to archaeologists and curators of museums. This would be the time to visit the model exhibit of pottery from different epochs in the museum of the American University at Beirut. But we do not have enough time; and except for their archaeological value, the pieces are not worth the trip.

If you want to see ancient pottery of real artistic merit, you should visit the museum at Nicosia where there is a fine collection of Cypriot pottery. Then go to the museum at Candia in Crete and look at its collection of Cretan pottery. Apart from the Greek and Roman vases with their red surface and black decorations, I have never seen decorated vases which match those of Cyprus and Crete.

After seeing these pieces we would have to rate Philistine pottery much lower. (The Philistines were one of the sea peoples who invaded the coast of Palestine around the twelfth or thirteenth century B.C.) The remaining pieces of Palestinian pottery have little or no artistic value. Even though they purport to have artistic and aesthetic merit, the gap is too great. When the Israelites entered Palestine, the artistic and technical quality of pottery declined notably. The Israelites were not, in fact, skilled in the plastic arts; their artistic merit lay in the field of literature.

LATER DEVELOPMENTS

Petrie's discovery did not win immediate acceptance. It was too radical and too imperfect at first. The basic principle had been formulated; but only a slow inductive process would lead to a complete and accurate chronological index. In the beginning, different investigators using Petrie's theory showed discrepancies of 500 or even 700 years. A theory which allowed such a wide margin of error would hardly appeal to scholars. Petrie formulated the principle in 1891. In 1907 the noted Clermont-Ganneau made fun of the no less noted Sellin because the latter tried to use this elastic chronological index. In 1925 the debunkers were not so well known: Conder in England, Nowack in Germany. Handcock's attempt at a synthesis in 1916 may have hurt the cause, because it was too premature. Twenty-five years is not enough time to gather a corpus of certain results.

The next generation of students was less original in ideas, but more thorough in its work and more cautious in its conclusions. By the time Petrie's "grandchildren" in the field of archaeology took over, his principle had matured noticeably. Archaeologists working independently now reach the same conclusions. Monographs are written on chronological typology. And Miss Kenyon is preparing a systematic work on the subject. But the door must always be left open for future revisions. However, even if revisions must be made, the data carefully written up in the official publications will always remain valid. Only the interpretation of the data will have to be reviewed.

40. *KING SOLOMON'S CAVALRY*

ONE OF the areas we visited at Megiddo was the famous temple (discovered by Schumacher) and its "cultic stelae" (!). We had difficulty getting to it because the top of the hill is a broad flatland with many rough spots. We had to make our way around deep trenches and follow the narrow trails of gravel and cactus which cut through the piles of excavated boulders. At one point we thought we had reached the right spot, because we came across a stele. But it was the bus driver who finally got us there. The sight which greeted us was a disorderly heap of rocks lying on a rough stretch of ground. Long periods of neglect, during which the remains were prey to all sorts of disturbances, have destroyed any possibility of reconstructing the original edifice. In my mind's eye I had a sketch of the archaeologists' reconstruction, but I found it hard to correlate it with the scene before me.

The American excavators had carefully examined the stone markings without any predispositions toward "cultic" interpretations. The stone pillars were about six feet high and had a hole in one corner about a foot from the top. Near the pillars, they found long narrow receptacles of hollowed-out rock standing high off the ground. They were too small to be bathtubs but would have made fine mangers. The biblical data were to shed light on the exact nature of these finds.

THE DOMESTICATED HORSE

It seems ridiculous to call the horse "the noble beast" nowadays. Without denying his noble ancestry we must point out that man has done a good job of training him and that the animal has responded very well. The horse, along with the dog, has become the favorite of civilized man. I suspect that these two banded together and were instrumental in the creation of the S.P.C.A.

We have so much respect and love for the horse today that we forget he was once a wild animal (like the dog and the camel). We all know that horses were introduced into America from Europe and adapted marvelously to their new home. But it is not so well known that domesticated horses first appeared in India during the second millennium before Christ, as far as we can tell from the archaeological evidence.

The most probable date is somewhere around the eighteenth century B.C. A few centuries later we find two interesting items. In the great Mitanni kingdom, formed by the union of the Horite principalities, appears a series of kings or influential chiefs with Indo-European names. For example, Bardaswa ("owner of magnificent horses") and Tusrata ("owner of a magnificent chariot"). This Indo-European predominance in such a diversified kingdom is a curious thing. It could very well have been due to their character as cavalry-men. Owning a horse and a swift chariot was a great privilege enjoyed by the *mariannu*. The proper lumber was imported from the Caucasian mountains; the horses were tamed on the plains of India. In peacetime the chariots were the best messenger service; in war they produced a new concept in strategy, based on mobility.

Now we move northward to a spot in Turkey near the present-day city of Ankara. It was once the capital city of the Hittite kingdom, Hattushash. Among the palace records an interesting treatise was found, entitled *The Arts of Caring for Horses*. It is a translation of a Horite original, made by a man named Kilkuli. And it contains a series of Indo-European terms; for example, *wartana* ("turn"), *tera wartana* ("three turns"), *sata-wartana* ("seven turns"), *navartanna* ("nine turns").

The translation was made in the thirteenth century B.C. By that time the horse had learned to live in stables and to pull a war chariot. Mounted riders do not appear on the battlefield until later. Until recently the victories of the Hyksos had been attributed to their war chariots. But now it seems that this theory must be revised.

WAR CHARIOTS AND THE ISRAELITES

When the Israelites entered the Promised Land, the northern plain dwellers had war chariots in their military equipage. A coalition came out against Joshua, "an army numerous as the sands on the seashore, and with a multitude of horses and chariots" (Jos 11:4). The leaders of the coalition joined forces and encamped by the waters of Merom. Joshua and the Israelites launched a surprise attack and slew every single one of the enemy. As Yahweh had ordered, Joshua hamstrung the horses and burned the chariots.

Tactically, it might have been better for the Israelites to take advantage of this military weapon. But such was not God's plan. The words of Deborah apply to this period: "Then the hoofs of the horses pounded, with the dashing, dashing of his steads" (Jgs 5:22).

SOLOMON'S POLICY

Solomon initiated a new policy. He decided to extend and consolidate his empire, like other rulers did. And in those days (the tenth century before Christ) this could only be done with a standing army. But foot soldiers alone could not resist the assaults of swift chariots. So Solomon added a fleet of chariots to his army and portioned them out among various strategic cities.

"Moreover Solomon gathered together chariots and horsemen; and he had fourteen hundred chariots and twelve thousand horsemen, that he stationed in the chariot cities and with the king in Jerusalem. . . . Solomon's transport of horses was between Egypt and Kuë; the king's traders received them from Kuë at a price, and a chariot could be imported from Egypt for six hundred shekels of silver and a horse for a hundred and fifty" (1 Kgs 10:26–29). "Now Solomon had forty thousand stalls of horses for his chariots, and twelve thousand horsemen" (1 Kgs 4:26).

As we stood in that graveyard of boulders, rocks, and broken pillars and heard our guide say that it was the site of Solomon's stables, some of us smiled skeptically.

The archaeologists reason this way. Megiddo was an important military fortress rebuilt by Solomon. And we know that he had horses for the chariots, and stables for the horses. So it should be easy to find traces of these items in the excavated city. So what do we find but these stone pillars capable of supporting a roof and having a hole to which one could tether a horse. And near the pillars we find hollowed-out rocks which look like mangers. Correlating the biblical data with the archaeological evidence many concluded that "these are the stables of Solomon." This line of reasoning is not overpowering, of course; but neither is it outlandish or ridiculous. Remember that many archaeological finds would be inexplicable if we did not have written documents dating from the same period. Our document happens to be the Bible.

One of the architects on the staff has reconstructed a model of the stables. There was a central corridor lined with stalls on both sides. The mangers are located between stalls. The horses faced the corridor to make it easier for the grooms. The stalls were sectioned off in groups of five. In an outside patio there was a huge water container which served as a trough. In Megiddo there was room for a total of 450 horses. "Also barley and straw for the horses and the swift steeds they brought to the place where it should be, each according to his assignment" (1 Kgs 4:28).

From the data we possess, it seems that in Solomon's day the Israelites did not use cavalry as an independent force; although there were probably some swift horses reserved for the king's messengers.

SOLOMON'S SUCCESSORS

Solomon set the example for his successors and organized the basic system. They continued to maintain a fleet of war chariots. From that time until the days of the Maccabees, the horse is a familiar figure in the Bible.

Job chants the epic saga of the horse:

Do you give the horse his strength and endow his neck with splendor? Do you make the steed to quiver while his thunderous snorting spreads terror? He jubilantly paws the plain and rushes in his might against the weapons. He laughs at fear and cannot be deterred; he turns not back from the sword. Around him rattles the quiver, flashes the spear and the javelin. Frenzied and trembling he devours the ground; he holds not back at the sound of the trumpet, but at each blast he cries, "Aha!" Even from afar he scents the battle, the roar of the chiefs and the shouting (Job 39:19–25).

And, in a different vein, the lyric beauty of the horse inspires the author of the Canticle of Canticles to compare his beloved to "the steeds of Pharao's chariots" (Ct 1:9).

ENTER "THE CAVALRY"

Horses had been used for a long time to pull chariots. (We have seen examples of these fine chariots in the Cairo Museum.) Then one day the Assyrians got the idea of putting men on horseback. The idea apparently originated during Tiglath-pileser's reign. And with this innovation the Assyrian empire began to grow and expand "under the hoofs of its horses." Magnificent relief works depict her archers charging into battle under such leaders as Shalmaneser, Esarhaddon, and Sennacherib.

One of Alexander's successors relegated horses to a minor role, making them the cover escort of the elephants.

Israel and Judah adopted the military tactics of each era, even though the chariots could not maneuver in mountainous regions and the horses could be stampeded by infantry.

The prophet Isaiah railed against the military alliances signed against the will of Yahweh:

> Woe to those who go down to Egypt for help, who depend upon horses; who put their trust in chariots because of their number, and in horsemen because of their combined power, but look not to the Holy One of Israel nor seek the Lord! . . . The Egyptians are men, not God, their horses are flesh, not spirit (Is 31:1–3).

THE HORSE AS A SYMBOL

The horse also appears in the Bible as a symbolic animal. In the fantastic visions which are a characteristic feature of the apocalyptic genre, future events and transcendental realities are expressed by mysterious symbols. War and horses are two symbols which crop up frequently in these visions. Artists have accepted this symbolism, and thus the horse has come to possess an air of mystery and profundity. Even though we may not understand the full meaning of the symbol in all its depth, we are still impressed and startled by it.

[239]

In the Old Testament the visions of the fifth-century prophet Zechariah are noteworthy. At one point he sees horsemen as the messengers of the good news (the office of messenger was one of the oldest functions learned by the horse) : "I had a vision during the night. There appeared the driver of a red horse, standing among myrtle trees in a shady place, and behind him were red, sorrel, and white horses. Then I asked: 'What are these, my lord?' and the angel who spoke with me answered me: 'I will show you what these are.' The man who was standing among the myrtle trees spoke up and said: 'These are they whom the Lord has sent to patrol the earth.' And they answered the angel of the Lord who was standing among the myrtle trees and said: 'We have patrolled the earth, see, the whole earth is tranquil and at rest!' " (Zech 1:8–11.)

We usually depict angels as having wings so that they can fly from heaven to earth with divine messages. In their role as messengers they could just as well be depicted as horsemen. In the Second Book of Maccabees the sacred author continues this well-known tradition. He shows us the heavenly riders intervening in the course of history; the dreadful rider whose horse kicks Heliodorus (2 Mc 3:25) ; the five resplendent riders mounted on horses with gold bridles, who rout the enemy (10:29) ; and the other rider clothed in white, wearing golden armour and brandishing his lance, who appears before the battle (11:8).

THE FINAL BATTLE

The hill of Megiddo has seen many battles in its day. Thothmes, Barak against Sisera, Josiah against Necho, the Maccabees, the Roman legions, the Moslems and the Crusaders, Napoleon, Allenby against the Axis forces.

In the Apocalypse, the last book in the Bible, St. John stages the last battle of all on the hill of Megiddo. The evil spirits go forth to the kings of the earth to gather them for the great battle, on the great day of God Almighty. And they gather in a place called in Hebrew Armageddon ("hill of Megiddo").

"I saw heaven opened. I saw a white horse, and its rider is called Faithful and True. He judges and wages war justly. His eyes are like a flame of fire, and on his head are many diadems. He has a name inscribed that no one but he knows. He is clothed in a garment sprinkled with blood, and his name is 'The Word of God.' The armies of heaven, clothed in fine linen, white and clean, were following him on white horses. From his mouth comes a sharp sword with which to strike the nations. He will rule them with an iron rod, and he treads the wine press of the fierce anger of God Almighty. He has on his garment and on his thigh a name inscribed, 'King of Kings and Lord of Lords.'

"I saw an angel standing on the sun. He cried in a loud voice to all the birds that fly in mid heaven, 'Come, assemble for the great supper God had prepared, in order to eat the flesh of kings, of captains; of mighty men, of horses and of their riders, the flesh of all men, free and slave, small and great.'

"I saw the beast and the kings of the earth and their armies assembled to wage war against him who was riding the horse and against his army. The beast was captured and with it the false prophet who worked wonders in its presence, and thus deceived those who accepted the mark of the beast and worshiped its statue. Those two were hurled alive into the lake of fire that burns with brimstone. The rest were killed with the sword of the rider of the horse, the sword that came from his mouth. All the birds were glutted with their flesh" (Ap 19:11–21).

This world of symbols stirs us with its deep shadows and dark meanings. As the birds of prey circle over the corpses, we conclude our visit to the hill where Solomon housed his horses and war chariots. The past and the future are assembled here, summoned by the prophets and the apocalyptic writers. We take our leave with a feeling of awe lodged in our hearts. The horses of King Solomon have carried us very far indeed!

VI. THE DIVIDED KINGDOM: THE NORTHERN KINGDOM BETWEEN PHOENICIA AND SYRIA

Solomon finally slept with his fathers, and left behind him one of his sons, expansive in folly, limited in sense, Roboam, who by his policy made the people rebel; until one arose who should not be remembered, the sinner who led Israel into sin, who brought ruin to Ephraim and caused them to be exiled from their land. (Sirach 47)

So they sent and called Jeroboam, and he, with all the assembly of Israel, came; and they spoke to Rehoboam, saying; "Your father made our yoke galling. Now then lighten the galling service of your father and his heavy yoke which he laid upon us, and we will serve you." . . .

Then King Rehoboam took counsel with the old men who had stood before Solomon his father. . . . They spoke to him, saying: "If you will be a servant to this people today and will serve them, and when you answer them, speak kindly to them, then they will be your servants forever." But he rejected the counsel of the old men . . . and took counsel with the young men, who had grown up with him and who were his companions. . . .

Then the young men who had grown up with him spoke to him, saying: ". . . thus shall you say to them: My little finger is thicker than my father's loins! And now, whereas my father loaded you with a heavy yoke, I will add to your yoke; my father chastised you with whips, but I will chastise you with scorpions!" . . . So he spoke to them according to the counsel of the young men. . . .

Now when all Israel (the northern tribes) saw that the king had not listened to them, the people replied to the king, saying: "What portion have we in David? Yea, we have no heritage in the son of Jesse. To your tents, O Israel! See now to your own house, O David!" . . .

But Rehoboam reigned over the Israelites who dwelt in the cities of Judah (the southern tribes). (1 Kings 12)

[243]

The Divided Kingdom

(Henceforth the northern kingdom was called "the kingdom of Israel" or "Israel"; and the southern kingdom was called "the kingdom of Judah" or "Judah.")

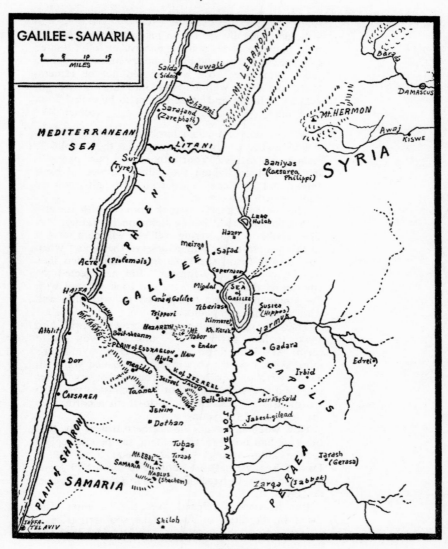

41. THE EXCAVATOR AT HIS DIGS

THE main character in the long, hard, monotonous endeavor known as an excavation campaign is the director. And there is a special delight in listening to him tell of his campaigns and their results.

With this in mind we leave Nablus one morning and head northeast on a small highway. The hill on our itinerary is less than twelve miles away. To reach the top we must climb a steep slope. The summit is a wide piece of flatland, 1900 feet by 950 feet. By Palestinian standards this is quite a large area. It could have been the site of a pretty large city in the days of antiquity. Furthermore the hill has a fine location, overlooking the valley which runs from the Jordan to the center of Samaria. Travelers coming from the east who cross the Jordan in the north must come through Bethshan; those who came through central Palestine must pass Tell el-Far'ah.

We finally arrive at the makeshift house where provisions, equipment, and all the finds are stored. There we are told that Father de Vaux is at the excavation site. We are in luck!

The illustrious Dominican meets us at the gate of "his" excavated city. If the reader pictures him in his fine religious habit, he is mistaken. The noted excavator is wearing his work clothes: dark boots, socks, khaki pants, a short-sleeved shirt — unbuttoned. He is bareheaded, sporting a fine tan and an unkempt beard.

First he orientates us in his domain, recalling the memory of the first illustrious guest in this region — Abraham. But then he cautiously adds that Abraham was a guest here, if he crossed the Jordan in the central part of the country.

He goes on to give us a clear and simple explanation of the various aspects of the excavation work. It is a real pleasure to meet an excavator of this type. The pure archaeologist, who is not a biblical exegete or historian, is interested only in the details of

[245]

excavation work. And we, who are not pure archaeologists, are bored by the repetition of uninteresting details. But Father de Vaux is also an authority on exegetical questions; and he knows how to select those elements of the data which clarify, illustrate, or confirm different biblical passages.

His finds included the city gate, and under it the sewer newly covered with smooth stones; an enclosure near the gate where official business and law cases were handled; a couple of houses whose similar design is attested to by the four-feet walls so carefully dug up; other houses of smaller size — for more average families, perhaps. Father de Vaux's explanation is interrupted by a young boy whom we noticed meandering through the work area and inspecting something. He calls Father de Vaux aside and whispers something to him. When he has gone, Father de Vaux tells us the news. The workers have just found a hole. Don't laugh! A hole can be important for an excavator. It could be the storehouse of valuable objects, or a tomb, or the chimney of a stove. In short it is a positive quantity for an archaeologist.

He tells us about one trench which caused great confusion at first. The ceramic index was no help to them because the trench contained a mixture of all kinds of pottery. It took some time to solve the mystery. Apparently it was a dumping ground, where at a later time work had been done.

BIBLICAL MEMORIES (1 KINGS 16)

We whiled away an hour listening to these interesting comments, scarcely noticing the heat. In a matter of minutes we passed through the different archaeological strata, and also through the corridors of history.

Even though Jeroboam may not have reigned in Tirzah, he had some connection with it because his son Abijah died there. Another son, Nadab, succeeded him and reigned for two years. In the third year of his reign he was assassinated by Baasha who went on to kill all the members of Jeroboam's family. Baasha reigned for twenty-four years, doing evil in God's sight, and was buried at Tirzah. His son, Elah, succeeded him and reigned for two years. In the third year of his reign Zimri assassinated him and proclaimed

[246]

himself king. Zimri reigned seven days and was succeeded by Omri (cf. 1 Kings 16).

In a matter of verses we have seen six kings belonging to four distinct families. Such are the fleeting memories of Far'ah, presuming it is the site of ancient Tirzah. At first this seemed to be a definite identification. According to the pottery remains the site was unoccupied during the period of Omri's reign — as the Bible indicates. And the topography supported a positive identification. But two problems cropped up. In the first place there were no remains of a palace. And even though Elah was slain by Zimri while he lay drunk in the house of his steward, he undoubtedly had his own palace.

The new king quickly eliminated the family of the preceding king. We might almost say that it was the one official act of his reign. His time came seven days later. The army of Israel was encamped against a Philistine city when the news came. " 'Zimri has conspired and also slain the king,' then all Israel made Omri . . . king . . . and they beseiged Tirzah. . . . But as soon as Zimri saw that the city was taken, he went into the castle of the king's house, and burned the kings's house over him, and so died . . ." (1 Kgs 16–18). One faction wanted to make Tibni king, but a civil war ensued and Omri emerged victorious.

Omri initiated a new dynasty and established a new capital. Tirzah was abandoned for the six years of his reign. This is the root of our second problem. The authentic testimony of the pottery indicates continued life in Tirzah after Omri's departure. One would expect a period of decadence (cf. 1 Kgs 17).

So now we find ourselves in a state of uncertainty after Father de Vaux's explanation. Here we are, with a fine city in an ideal location — and no name. There are good reasons for calling it Tirzah, and the opposing arguments are not convincing. And that is all the excavator can tell us.

If the reader prefers absolute certainties, he should switch to mathematics which is an exact science. In archaeology we must be content with degrees of probability and leave room for future revisions.

We can console ourselves by visiting the beautiful fountain about a mile from the tell. However we cannot take snapshots because this is prohibited. The reason seems to be the fact that fugitives encamp around here and come to fill their canteens at the fountain. It is a real shame because it is a very picturesque site. The tourist agency should include this site in its prospectus.

Till like a fire there appeared the prophet whose words were as a flaming furnace. Their staff of bread he shattered, in his zeal he reduced them to straits; by God's word he shut up the heavens and three times brought down fire. How awesome are you, Elias! Whose glory is equal to yours? You brought a dead man back to life from the nether world, by the will of the Lord. You sent kings down to destruction, and nobles, from their beds of sickness. You heard threats at Sinai, at Horeb avenging judgments. You anointed kings who should inflict vengeance, and a prophet as your successor. You were taken aloft in a whirlwind, in a chariot with fiery horses.

(Sirach 48)

42. IN PHOENICIAN TERRITORY

OUR ship was moving slowly into the harbor at Beirut. A passenger next to me queried in French: "Your first venture on Asian soil?" — "Yes, first time in the Near East." — "Asia, nevertheless." — "True, it is my first time on Asian soil."

And I felt no special thrill then, just as I had not when I stepped on African soil for the first time. Being a Spaniard, I was more excited by the fact that this was Phoenician territory. Standing on the deck as the boat turned toward the dock, I found the view quite enchanting. A fine looking city surrounded by a pleasant countryside with a backdrop of high mountains. The inhabitants would almost be compelled to look toward the sea. It was their only escape route. Already I felt myself in contact with the Phoenicians.

The second impression was somewhat jarring. In some of Madrid's subway stations you hear a loud voice saying: "Let 'em out first, let 'em out!" And then the train comes rumbling in. Well, in Beirut it is just the opposite. The passengers are crowded near the gangplank loaded down with baggage. All of a sudden a voice shouts: "Let 'em on first, let 'em on!" And a mob of visitors pile on to welcome their friends, and plow through the mob of passengers. The cellist in the ship's orchestra knew what was going to happen, so he went into the ballroom and waited until the coast was clear. Perhaps this mad rush onto the ship is a trait inherited from their seafaring ancestors. But the experience was too "corporeal" for me to consider it another contact with the ancient Phoenicians.

The third impression was much better. The customhouse is in a huge hangar. There are benches along the walls, a small tourist office, and a long table for the customs inspection. Two whirlybird fans are suspended from the roof. The atmosphere is quite European and reminds us that the Phoenicians acted like Europeans in many of their endeavors.

The Divided Kingdom

VISITING BYBLOS

A morning trip along the coast proves to be delightful. Time and again I am reminded of the Basque coast. A grotesquely shaped boulder juts out toward the sea, blocking the road. But we cut through a tunnel underneath, unperturbed. Near the Nahr el-Kelb river stands a hill covered with rocks testifying to its strategic value. The river empties slowly into the sea forming a beach on the left bank. In the shelter of a grove nearby stands a diner. Atop a high hill there is a statue of the Blessed Virgin, the Queen of Lebanon. We cross another small river which rises somewhere in the mountains nearby. On our right we see the remains of an ancient bridge. Then we pass vineyards, fig trees, villages, and some more beaches.

Finally, we reach Byblos. It is mentioned a few times in the Bible, but the name alone is enough to set us thinking; Byblos — Bible, hmm! But we are not going to investigate this problem right now. Instead we leave the modern town and head southward to the site of the ancient city. When excavation work was started almost thirty years ago, it was a broad flatland sloping down to the sea; on it stood the ruins of a medieval castle erected by the Crusaders. The excavating has been going on ever since, with only a few breaks; the flatland has dropped lower and lower and the medieval ruins have become more prominent. We pass a high fence through an entrance-way and find the medieval castle on our left. It is a perfect spot for childhood dreams and adventure stories: a stone staircase hidden between thick walls, a prison chamber; a door which leads nowhere, a mutilated row of wall, a spacious parlor with a high ceiling, a tower surrounded by a terrace.

From the terrace we get a fine panoramic view of the area, and the excavations seem to shrink in scale. Our guide, who spent some time in these excavations, points out the interesting finds. That area was the site of an ancient sanctuary built by the Egyptians in the third millennium B.C. You can't even see traces of the fire anymore; all you can see are the remains of a later sanctuary. There stood a Roman theater, which was moved closer to the sea so that the excavation work could continue. I myself worked in that section, he tells us.

And thus we continue to look around, as the workers climb up the slopes to dump their loads of earth. Then we descend from the tower to examine the terrain. It is quite level because the excavator has carefully stripped it, layer by layer.

Our path is strewn with broken vases and human bones. We walk in Indian file between the rail tracks, taking care not to step on the remains of wall almost at ground level. The road leads down to the sea. This is probably the ancient port of Byblos, where Egyptian ships docked to take on cedarwood, where Solomon's ships were loaded with Hiram's cedar and cypress trees. "The king made of the sandalwood pilasters for the house of the Lord and for the king's house, and harps and lyres for the singers. There never had come such sandalwood, nor has it been seen to this day" (1 Kgs 10:12).

At last M. Dunand, the excavator, appeared. He has devoted his entire scholarly life to this city and can't seem to pull himself away. As the picks and shovels cut through the different strata, the years piled up on him. Dunand is already past seventy, but he is still in good shape.

He accompanies us and comments on various sites; the Greek theater, Hiram's tomb. We climb down a steep staircase and examine the spot where they found Hiram's sarcophagus.

"Now Hiram, king of Tyre, had sent his servants to Solomon when he heard that they had anointed him king in place of his father; for Hiram had always been fond of David" (1 Kgs 5:1). Solomon asks him to supply timber for the temple he is planning to build. "When Hiram heard the words of Solomon, he was very greatly pleased. . . . So Hiram sent to Solomon, saying: '. . . I stand ready to perform all your pleasure in the matter of cedar and cypress timbers. My servants shall bring them down to the sea from Lebanon, and I will make them into rafts to go by sea to the place that you shall direct me, and I will have them broken up there, and you shall take them up. You shall also accomplish my desire by providing food for my household.' . . . And there was peace between Hiram and Solomon, and the two of them ratified a treaty" (1 Kgs 5).

In the Beirut Museum we had admired the sarcophagus, noted for its lions, its reliefs, and, especially, its Phoenician inscription.

Dunand accompanies us to the entrance of his domain and shows us the formidable outer walls of the ancient cities. They are between nine and twelve feet high and twelve feet thick.

The Divided Kingdom

Our trip to the ancient city is finished. Back at the modern city the most interesting sight is a medieval church built by the Crusaders.

Once again the bus passes various bright, picturesque villages. King Solomon gave Hiram twenty cities in Galilee as payment for the timber and gold. "But when Hiram came out from Tyre to see the cities . . . they were not acceptable. . . . Therefore he said: 'What are these cities which you have given me, my brother?' . . . However, Hiram sent to the king one hundred and twenty talents of gold" (1 Kgs 9:12–14).

43. A "MUST" VISIT

No PARK in the world, not even the Bois de Boulogne in Paris nor London's Hyde Park, is so famous as the Cedars of Lebanon. Not to visit them while in Palestine would be a real *faux pas,* a breach of tourist etiquette. We would be spurning many important biblical memories. So after touring Byblos, we leave the coastal highway and head inland, climbing almost a mile upward.

It is a beautiful climb, the kind which tests the driver's skill and offers a wonderful panorama to the passenger. About fifteen hundred feet up is a village nestled on the side of a mountain; on the opposite slope stands a monastery ideally located for a life of solitude. There our bus stops, and we get out to eat our provisions in a kind of inn. On a table with circular holes rest several earthen jars sporting a drinking spout and a collar handle. The Spaniards in our group give a demonstration, lifting the spout way up. Our hosts marvel at our surprising skill. Did the Phoenicians teach us this also? Well, the ceramic remains found on Mediterranean islands include vessels of this type, but we cannot be certain that the Phoenicians invented this drinking technique.

The next stage of our journey runs through the wondrous valley of Qadicha. It is almost impossible to describe the scenery. You can only appreciate it if you yourself have taken a similar excursion. The bus winding up the steep highway; patches of asphalt road above and below you; the chugging motor, the intent gaze of the driver, the wide-eyed looks of the passengers. Then the bus runs parallel to a river which gathers momentum down below, and ahead we can see our crossing point. But first we must descend into the valley ahead to reach the proper slope for the crossing. We pass by the villages we had seen from a distance and watch them recede into the background. The air becomes cooler and more rarified. Suddenly to the right of the highway there is a waterfall, a stream of water which must jump down to continue on its way.

The last villages are summer vacation spots with plenty of boarding houses and modest hotels. The highest village is Becherra, and it has a beautiful hotel, a convent belonging to Italian Carmelites. The view overlooking the deep gorge of Qadicha is restful and impressive. We enjoy the scenery while the bus rests its motor for a short while. Then we continue on along the steep road and find ourselves at the entrance of a large hotel, a few feet away from the hallowed grove.

This is all that remains of the countless ancient groves. A few cedars encircled by a wall, and a ticket entrance. The forest does not prevent one from seeing the trees at all. Each cedar is a creature with its own distinct beauty. These are the stoutest trees which have seen their countless companions fall one by one, from age or the ax.

Solomon was not the first, but certainly the most famous of the despoilers. The temple and the palace in Jerusalem were proud displays of cedarwood. "So he built the house and finished it; and he covered the house with cedar. He also built the enclosed galleries against the whole house . . . and they were joined to the house with timbers of cedar. . . . He built the walls of the house on the inside with boards of cedar; from the floor of the house to the rafters of the ceiling. . . . He also made an altar of cedar in front of the inner room and covered it with gold. . . . And he built the inner court with three courses of hewn stone, and a course of hewn cedar beams" (1 Kgs 6:9–36).

But this was nothing compared to his palace, which was called the Forest of Lebanon House. It had three rows of cedar columns, with fifteen columns in each row. "Above it was covered with cedar. . . . And he made the porch of the throne where he might pronounce judgment, even the Porch of Judgment; and it was covered with cedar from floor to rafters. . . . His own house . . . was of like workmanship. He also made a house for Pharaoh's daughter (whom Solomon had taken to wife) like this porch. . . . Also the great encircling court had three courses of hewn stone and a course of cedar beams . . ." (1 Kgs 7:3–12).

The inspired author sums it up with an hyperbole. "The king made silver in Jerusalem as common as stone, and he made cedars as plentiful as the sycamore trees that are in the lowland" (1 Kgs 10:27).

To accomplish all this he had a veritable army of craftsmen: lumberjacks, porters, seamen, carpenters, cabinetmakers, and architects.

Most likely Solomon's workers did not come up this far to cut down cedar trees; if they had, the few remaining trees probably would not be here. They would have chosen the lower slopes lying closer to the sea and its harbor. Perhaps they shipped the trunks downstream on a river, then lashed them together on rafts and sent them along the coast to Jaffa, about ninety-two miles away.

Archaeologists are excavating Tell Qasila which lies just north of Tel Aviv, near the mouth of the Yarkon river. The excavator told us that they found the remains of a harbor near the sea. He thinks that the cedar rafts were shipped up the southern branch of the Yarkon to Jerusalem. (Every excavator likes to have famous visitors in his excavated city.) But looking at a map, it seems that there was a better choice. The Rubin river cuts through the valley of Soreok and comes within a few miles of the capital. The only problems would be to choose a mild season for the trip along the coast and a rainy season for the trip to Jerusalem. But the other theory would fit also. The king may have had no regard for the welfare of his servants and driven them to the utmost. But it seems certain that Hiram would not endanger his expert seamen.

Before we leave the grove, I want to take one final look and imprint the scene on my memory. I have not taken any snapshots. Dusk is falling. The slope mounts upward to the summit, a glistening ochre streaked with patches of snow. The aroma of the cedars scents the air and the clear evening light shines above and between the branches. But not enough comes through to let me take pictures.

We come down by another road, keeping the mountain wall on our right and the gorge on our left. Our driver takes certain curves in two runs.

On a good stretch of road, where the bus could make up some time, we are halted by a procession. The villagers move along singing a monotonous strain and reciting some prayers. In front a coffin is being carried on the shoulders of a few men. But the cortege does not seem sad or mournful in these environs. These people are

The Divided Kingdom

Maronites, who have preserved their Christianity intact in this mountain area. The procession turns left into a cemetery and the highway is clear once again.

The secluded sanctuaries, convents, churches, and chapels fall behind. The highway curves repeatedly to ease us down the slope. In fifty miles of traveling we have descended almost a mile and find ourselves at Tripoli. The lights of the city begin to glow because night is falling. We pass by without stopping, leaving behind the gasoline stations which give any city an international atmosphere. From the highway we can see minarets here and there, because it is a Moslem city; and we are reminded briefly of Tarablus, the Crusaders' city with its three caravan routes.

It is already night when we reach Beirut, carrying with us the memories of one of our most beautiful tours.

44. *TYRE AND SIDON*

ONCE again we start out early and travel along the coast, never tiring of the blue of Mediterranean sea and sky. Small beaches, little villages, and miniature ports.

We are only going to stop at two places along our route. After riding some twenty miles we get our first distant glimpse of Saida; a high white mass jutting out into the sea. It approaches rapidly and splits up into houses, walls, and streets. The details become sharper, and a castle detaches itself from the city and takes up its position a little way out in the sea. It is the perfect site for a panoramic snapshot; so the photographers get off the bus. The rest of us wait in the bus and contemplate the view.

When we get to Saida itself (ancient Sidon) we head for an ancient *khan* which has been converted into a convent. From the terrace we have an excellent view of the harbor installations. The most picturesque sight is a small islet nearby linked to the shore by a wharf. On the islet stands a castle dating from the Crusades. Farther away a larger island interrupts the smooth flow of rolling waves and the water ripples toward the shore. Directly in front of us lies the present-day harbor defended by a natural wall of rock and an artificial row of boulders. The seaside picture is completed by a few small boats. If we exclude the castle from our range of vision, we have a real water-color scene before us. Yet, in the days of antiquity, this was one of the most important ports along the Mediterranean. At first the Bible mentions only Sidon; but later Tyre and Sidon are mentioned together. Two sister cities, experienced in the art of trade and navigation. When Solomon decided to build a fleet and a harbor on the gulf of Aqaba at Ezion-geber, Hiram's experts came to organize the project: shipbuilders, harbor masters, and pilots. Their navigators boldly launched out for the "far country," the remote shores of Tharsis (Spain or Italy?). Their homeland was little more than an island port; and they were always ready to weigh anchor for a round-trip excursion or a new venture in colonizing. And all the while they ran a thriving business in international commerce.

The present-day inhabitants retain something of this wanderlust. Interestingly enough, Argentinians distinguish two kinds of immigrants, among others: the *gallegos* — Spanish peoples, and the *turcos* — usually meaning the Lebanese.

In the sixth century before Christ Ezekiel sang of Lebanon's exploits:

> Citizens of Sidon and Arad served as your oarsmen; skilled men of Samar were in you to be your mariners; the elders and experts of Gebal were in you to caulk your seams.
>
> Every ship and sailor on the sea came to you to carry trade. Persia and Lud and Phut were in your army as warriors; shield and helmet they hung upon you, increasing your splendor. The men of Arad were all about your walls, and the Gammadites were in your towers; they hung their bucklers all around on your walls, and made perfect your beauty. Tharsis traded with you, so great was your wealth, exchanging slaves and articles of bronze for your goods. . . . From Beth-Thogorma horses, steeds, and mules were exchanged for your wares. The Rodanites trafficked with you; many coastlands traded with you; ivory tusks and ebony wood they gave you for payment. Edom traded with you, so many were your products, exchanging garnets, purple, embroidered cloth, fine linen, coral, and rubies for your wares. Juda and the land of Israel trafficked with you, exchanging Mennith wheat, figs, honey, oil, and balm for your goods. Damascus traded with you, so great was your wealth, exchanging Helbon wine and Sahar wool. Javan exchanged wrought iron, cassia, and aromatic cane from Uzal for your wares. Dedan traded with you for riding gear. The trade of Arabia and of all the sheikhs of Cedar belonged to you; they dealt in lambs, rams, and goats. The merchants of Saba and Regma also traded with you, exchanging for your wares the very choicest spices, all kinds of precious stones, and gold. Haran, Chene, and Eden, the merchants of Saba, Assur, and Chelmad traded with you, marketing with you rich garments, violet mantles, embroidered cloth, varicolored carpets, and firmly woven cords. Ships of Tharsis journeyed for you in your merchandising. You were full and heavily laden in the heart of the sea (Ezek 27:8-25).

Tyre and Sidon

Not even the bazaars of Damascus can give us an adequate idea of this thriving ancient port. The camel caravans of the former could not match the ship caravans of the latter in size or range of activity.

Our commentary has run ahead of our trip, because we are not yet in Tyre. We quit the terrace, walk through the narrow streets with their unattractive bazaars, and get on the bus. It is our ship and camel, all in one.

We make one more stop to photograph the site of ancient Zarephath — where the Sidonians made their precious glassware, where Elijah generously repaid a widow's hospitality. He made her a pot of meal which was never exhausted and a cruse of oil which was never spent. Thus they survived the days of want. And then he raised her son from the dead.

We are not interested in the present-day city of Tyre. We skirt it from below, cutting between orchards to reach the ancient Phoenician port to the south. Standing on a promontory we try to get our bearings. We are on the southwestern tip of the island. On the left the sand has been piling up over the centuries, converting the island into a peninsula.

And what about the ancient port? Those reefs scarcely floating on the surface are the only visible remains; the rest of it lies under water and sand. Father Poidebard directed a study of the ancient port, using aerial photography to ascertain the rough outline, and diving equipment to fill in the details. The initial foundation for the project was a line of sand banks and reefs parallel to the coast. Other series were used to form a discontinuous breakwater outside. The reefs were adjusted to sea level. Then they dug a deep, wide crevice into which they poured the cement walls. The southwest corner facing the dominant wind currents was rounded out so that the surf would not hit it head on, but instead lose force rounding the curve. The works were spread out over a mile in the cove. The most spectacular of these works seem to date from the period of Roman domination; but it seems likely that the Phoenicians used the same principles on a smaller scale.

Father Poidebard wrote an interesting book in which he describes these constructions. We are satisfied to gaze vacantly at the reefs, which seem to have little significance. But they are a remnant of the glorious ancient port. I am not going to recite an elegy over these ruins, because Ezekiel and Isaiah did this many centuries ago:

As for you, son of man, utter a lament over Tyre, and say to Tyre that is situated at the approaches of the sea, that brought the trade of the peoples to many a coastland: Thus says the Lord God: Tyre, you said, "I am a ship, perfect in beauty."

In the midst of the sea your builders placed you, perfected your beauty. With cypress from Sanir they built for you all of your decks; cedar from Lebanon they took to make you a mast; from the highest oaks of Basan they make your oars; your bridges they made of cypress wood from the isles of Chetthim. Fine embroidered linen from Egypt became your sail (to serve you as a banner). Purple and scarlet from the isles of Elisa covered your cabin. . . .

Through the deep waters your oarsmen brought you home, but the east wind smashed you in the heart of the sea.

Your wealth, your goods, your wares, your sailors, and your crew . . . sank into the heart of the sea on the day of your shipwreck. Hearing the shouts of your mariners, the shores begin to quake. Down from their ships come all who ply the oar; the sailors, all the mariners of the sea, stand on the shore, making their voice heard on your behalf, shouting bitter cries, strewing dust on their heads, rolling in the ashes. For you they shave their heads and put on sackcloth, for you they weep in anguish, with bitter lament. In their mourning they utter a lament over you; thus they wail over you; Who was ever destroyed like Tyre in the midst of the sea? With your goods which you drew from the seas you filled many peoples; with your great wealth and merchandise you enriched the kings of the earth.

Now you are wrecked in the sea, in the watery depths; your wares and all your crew have gone down with you. All who dwell on the coastlands are aghast over you, their kings are terrified, their faces convulsed. The traders among the peoples now hiss at you; you have become a horror, and you shall be no more (Ezek 27).

Isaiah's elegy is just as beautiful: "Wail, O ships of Tharsis, for your port is destroyed; from the land of the Chetthim the news reached them. Silence! you who dwell on the coast, you merchants of Sidon, whose messengers crossed the sea over the deep waters. The grain of Sihor, the harvest of the Nile, was her revenue, and she the merchant among nations. . . . Pass over to

Tyre and Sidon

Tharsis, wailing, you who dwell on the coast! Is this your wanton city, whose origin is from of old, whose feet have taken her to dwell in distant lands? Who has planned such a thing against Tyre, the bestower of crowns, whose merchants are princes, whose traders are the earth's honored men? The Lord of hosts has planned it, to disgrace all pride of majesty, to degrade all the earth's honored men. Cross to your own land, O ship of Tharsis; the harbor is no more. His hand he stretches out over the sea, he shakes kingdoms; the Lord has ordered the destruction of Chanaan's strongholds. . . . Lament, O ships of Tharsis, for your haven is destroyed" (Is 23:1–11, 14).

This is the island which successfully resisted the ten-year siege of Sargon and Shalmaneser, which Nebuchadnezzar could not conquer in ten years, which withstood Alexander for seven months. Already weakened, it resisted Antigonus for fourteen months; and the Crusaders for five and a half months. Twice it mocked the assaults of Saladin.

But it could not resist the silent onslaught of the sands, nor the prophetic elegies of the prophets. The waves echo the refrain: "Your haven is destroyed."

45. THE BEIRUT NATIONAL MUSEUM

THE building has an air of newness about it. It is designed specifi-
cally as a museum, with large rooms, good overhead lighting, and
felicitous placement of the displays. The most valuable piece in
the museum is King Hiram's sarcophagus bearing the inscription
of his son: "Itobaal, son of Hiram, king of Byblos, made this coffin
for his father Ahiram, as an eternal resting place. . . ." The name
Itobaal reminds us of another biblical figure, his daughter Jezebel.
(We try to put her out of our mind, but her memory haunts us
during the tour.)

Over here there is a fine wall map of the entire Orient in ancient
times. These wall maps have two arbitrary features which mold our
outlook to some extent. They depict the earth as a flat surface and
mark the top as north. Thus the east is on our right and the west on
our left. The Semites faced the sun, putting the north on their left
and the south on their right. They called the former *semaal* and
the latter *yamin*. Thus the people in the south were called *bin-
yaminu* and southern Arabia was called Yemen.

On this particular map each country is designated by a colored
drawing. Below it there is another map depicting the country in
relief. The two mountain ranges, Lebanon and Anti-Lebanon, are
marked clearly; and circled areas represent points of particular
archaeological interest.

A beautiful Roman sarcophagus catches my eye. It depicts a
sailboat with a stern shaped like a swan's head. The relief work
is a visual epitaph, recalling some naval boast.

In a glass display case there are some rough bronze figurines
of soldiers. In an ivory case a raging bull is attacked by a griffin
and a lion. A vulture stands atop a corpse. There are some clay
figurines and panoramic scenes in relief and some magnificent Greco-
Roman mosaics.

The museum is not too rich, but it has an interesting selection of Phoenician artwork. However, I am still haunted by the memory of Hiram's granddaughter.

PORTRAIT OF A LADY

Does our subject cut a gracious figure? No, even though she is a woman. She was a power-hungry ruler, a creature with predatory instincts. In terms of our previous display she was the griffin and her husband Ahab was the lion. And the raging bull was Jehu, mounted on his invincible chariot.

We are going to draw her portrait, in words. The Hebrews did not distinguish themselves in the plastic arts. When Solomon decided to construct a grandiose palace and temple, he had to bring in Phoenician craftsmen and artists. A man named Hiram, born of an Israelite mother and a Phoenician father, was put in charge of the bronze works.

But the Israelites surpassed all their neighbors in literary skill. Their verbal images are superior to those sculpted by their neighbors. The Phoenicians made relief works and precious objects for the Hebrews. The most valuable art treasures found in Palestine are of Phoenician vintage. In return, the Israelites used their literary skill to draw us a magnificent portrait of a Phoenician woman. No member of that race is so clearly imprinted in our memory as she is — thanks to the vivid portrait drawn by the inspired author.

We might do well to divide this portrait into several panels, each one depicting some trait of this woman's personality.

1. *Her Religious Fanaticism.* Once she was married to Ahab, Jezebel zealously propagated her own religion and persecuted the Israelite prophets, and she persuaded Ahab to do the same. "When Jezebel ordered the prophets of the Lord exterminated, Obadiah had taken a hundred prophets and hidden them by fifties in a cave and supplied them with bread and water." Elijah was the first hardy soul to challenge Jezebel. In a solemn scene on Mount Carmel he vindicated the name of Yahweh and had fifty of Jezebel's prophets slain. When the queen heard the news, she sent a message to Elijah: "As surely as you are Elijah and I am Jezebel, so may God requite me and worse, if I do not make your life as the life of one of them

by tomorrow about this time." So Elijah fled to Mount Sinai (cf. 1 Kgs 19).

2. *Her Unscrupulous Methods.* Ahab wanted to buy Naboth's vineyard to round out his palace garden. But Naboth refused to sell. "The Lord forbids that I should give you the inheritance of my fathers." Ahab returned to the castle disconsolate, went to bed, and refused to eat. Jezebel came to him and asked him what was the matter. " 'Why is your spirit so vexed that you eat no food?' Accordingly he spoke to her: 'Because I spoke to Naboth . . . but he said: I will not give you my vineyard.' Then Jezebel his wife said to him: 'Do you now hold sway in Israel? Arise, eat bread, and let your heart be of good cheer. I will get the vineyard of Naboth the Jezreelite for you.'

"So she wrote letters in Ahab's name and sealed them with his seal, and sent them to the elders and to the nobles who were in his city, who presided with Naboth. . . . 'Proclaim a fast and seat Naboth in a conspicuous place among the people. Then seat two unscrupulous men before him and let them bear witness, saying: "You have cursed God and the king." Then take him out and stone him to death.'

"So the men of his city . . . did as Jezebel had sent to them. . . . Then they sent to Jezebel, saying: 'Naboth has been stoned and is dead.' Accordingly, as soon as Jezebel heard . . . Jezebel said to Ahab: 'Arise, take possession of the vineyard of Naboth the Jezreelite, which he refused to sell for money; for Naboth is not alive but dead.' Now as soon as Ahab heard that Naboth was dead, Ahab arose to go down to the vineyard of Naboth the Jezreelite to take possession of it" (1 Kgs 21).

Then Elijah was instructed by God to go to the king and announce the destruction of his whole house. And concerning Jezebel he told him: "The dogs shall eat Jezebel in the district of Jezreel."

3. *Her Violent Death.* Jehu assassinated the two kings of Israel and Judah. He shot Joram with an arrow; and his cohorts dealt Ahaziah a fatal wound.

"When Jehu came to Jezreel, Jezebel heard of it, and she painted her eyelashes and adorned her head and peered out at the window. As Jehu was entering the gate, she said: 'Is it well, you Zimri, your master's murderer?' But he raised his eyes to the window and said:

[264]

The Beirut National Museum

'Who is on my side? Who?' At that two or three eunuchs peered out at him. 'Let her drop,' he said. So they let her drop, so that some of her blood spattered on the wall and on the horses, and he drove over her. Then he went in and ate and drank.

"'Take charge now of this cursed woman, and bury her; for she is a king's daughter,' he said. But when they went to bury her, they found no more of her than the skull, the feet, and the palms of the hands. When, therefore, they returned and told him, he said: 'This is the word of the Lord, which he spoke by his servant, Elijah the Tishbite, saying: In the territory of Jezreel shall the dogs eat the flesh of Jezebel. And the corpse of Jezebel shall be as dung on the face of the field in the territory of Jezreel, so that they cannot say: "This is Jezebel"'" (2 Kgs 9:30–37).

Yes, dear reader, this is Jezebel, her portrait etched in relief in the pages of the Bible.

46. MOUNT CARMEL

PICTURE a long train stretched along the tracks with a highway and the sea directly on its left. A car in the middle of the train is out of line. It slants leftward, almost touching the sea. So there is a blank space in the row of cars, an obstruction on the highway, and a spattering of sea spray on the front bumper of the detached car.

Something like this happened to a Palestinian mountain range in the Miocene Age. Its general direction was from north to south. But some disturbance in the interior of the earth erupted to the surface. The mountain chain broke around Nazareth and one section swerved leftward to the seashore. The chain of mountains was interrupted by a blank space, the plain of Esdraelon; the coastal traveling route was blocked off, and the maverick mountain found sea spray at its feet.

So Mount Carmel has stood for centuries, looking out at the sea and blocking off the north from the south. It has channeled all the travel routes through a strategic gorge. There it stands, tall and proud. Yahweh predicts a future event thus: "It will come, as surely as Carmel stands." And the beauty of its lofty groves inspires the bridegroom to tell his beloved: "Your head is like Carmel."

We climbed Carmel on a day when part of our group was leaving for home. Trees and houses are cropping up along the slopes. On the top there is an international monastery belonging to the Carmelite Fathers. In the chapel, dominated by a large statue of our Lady of Carmel, we celebrate a Mass of thanksgiving. Then in the refectory we eat our parting meal amid farewell speeches and songs.

Looking northward we can see the port of Haifa, where units of the nascent Israeli navy are docked. Directly in front of us lies the sea and it truly seems to be *Mare Nostrum*. It is almost as if there were an invisible bridge stretching from here across the Mediterranean to Avila. Our thoughts cross the bridge to seek the noble

Spanish saint (Teresa). But perhaps our thoughts were responsible for the bridge in the first place.

This view overlooking the sea is the first noteworthy feature of Carmel.

ELIJAH AND AHAB (1 Kings 17 ff.)

St. Teresa's name is linked mystically to Mount Carmel; and St. John of the Cross wrote a book — *The Ascent of Mount Carmel* — which describes the mystic's ascent to perfection in blazing poetic imagery.

But the saint who is most closely connected to Carmel, by his deeds and his physical presence, is the prophet Elijah.

"Now Elijah [= Elias] the Tishbite, of Tishbe in Gilead, said to Ahab: 'As the Lord, the God of Israel, lives, before whom I stand, there shall be neither dew nor rain these years, except by my word.'" And the fields and streams dried up. Then Elijah went to Phoenicia. Three years later he returned because Yahweh gave him the order: "Go, show yourself to Ahab; and I will bring rain upon the face of the ground."

"The famine was severe in Samaria; and Ahab had called Obadiah who was in charge of the household . . . and Ahab said to Obadiah: 'Come, let us go through the land to all the springs of water and to all the brooks; perhaps we shall find grass and so save the horses and mules alive, that we may not lose the beasts.' So they divided the land between them to pass through it: Ahab went in one direction by himself, and Obadiah went in another direction by himself."

Then the great contest (which we shall narrate later) took place. When it was over, Elijah said to Ahab: "'Go up, eat and drink; for there is the rushing sound of rain.' So Ahab went up to eat and drink but Elijah went up to the top of Carmel, and crouched down upon the earth, with his face between his knees; and he said to his servant: 'Go up now, look toward the sea.' So he went up, and looked and said: 'There is nothing.' 'Go back seven times,' he said. So the servant went back seven times. However, the seventh time he said: 'There is a cloud, the size of a man's hand, rising out of the sea.' 'Go up,' he said, 'say to Ahab: Harness your steeds and go down, so that the rain may not stop you.' Moreover, in a very short time the heavens grew black with clouds and wind, and there was a great downpour."

When the inhabitants were scouring the land in search of water, their deliverance came from the sea. And Carmel is the alert lookout who first sights a trace of cloud in the sky.

ELIJAH AND THE FALSE PROPHETS (1 KINGS 18)

In another situation, where men were vacillating between Yahweh and Baal, the deciding factor came from heaven. And again Mount Carmel was the setting for God's dramatic action.

This is the second noteworthy feature of Carmel: it is a proving ground. The kingdom of Israel straddles Mount Carmel. On the northern slope it links up with Phoenicia; on the southern slope, with Judah. Its inhabitants wander from one side to the other, leaning now toward the Phoenician god, Baal, and now toward Israel's God, Yahweh. The northern influence began to take over. Even though the king paid token acknowledgment to Yahweh, his wife the queen was a Phoenician who strove diligently to promote her native religion. And Jezebel dominated her husband Ahab completely.

Again Mount Carmel was to play its part in the final outcome. "So Ahab sent to all the Israelites and gathered the prophets together to Mount Carmel. Then Elijah came near to all the people and said: 'How long are you going to limp upon two diverse opinions? If the Lord be God, follow him, but if the Baal, follow him.' But the people gave him no answer." The decision on Carmel must come from heaven. The slopes of the mountain face in different directions; but its summit looks to heaven.

"Then Elijah said to the people: 'I, even I only, am left as a prophet of the Lord, but the prophets of the Baal are four hundred and fifty men. Let them therefore give us two bulls, and let them choose one bull for themselves and cut it in pieces and lay it on the wood but make no fire, and I will prepare the other bull and place it on the wood, but I will make no fire. Then call on the name of your god and I will call on the name of the Lord; and the god who answers by fire, he is God.' Thereupon all the people answered and said: 'It is a fair test!'"

[268]

Everything was arranged as Elijah had said. The prophets of Baal spent all morning calling on the name of Baal. "O Baal, answer us." But no matter how much they danced around the altar, nothing happened. Around noon Elijah mocked them and said: "Cry with a loud voice, for he is a god; either he is meditating, or he has gone aside, or he is on a journey, or perhaps he is asleep and needs to be awakened!" So they shouted louder and slashed each other with swords and lances to draw blood. "And when midday had passed they worked themselves into a prophetic frenzy until the offering of the oblation; but there was no voice nor answer, and none regarded."

Then Elijah readied his altar. He built a trench around it, laid the chunks of the quartered bull on the wood, and had water poured over it three times. The trench also was filled with water.

"Then when it was time to offer the oblation, Elijah the prophet came near and said: 'O Lord, God of Abraham, Isaac, and Israel, let it be known today that thou art God in Israel and that I am thy servant, and that at thy command I have done all these things. Answer me, O Lord, answer me, that this people may know that thou, O Lord, art God, and that thou hast turned their heart back again.'

"Then the fire of the Lord fell and consumed the burnt-offering and the wood, the stones and the dust, and licked up the water that was in the trench. So when all the people saw it, they fell upon their faces and said: 'The Lord, he is God; the Lord, he is God!' But Elijah said to them: 'Seize the prophets of the Baal; let not a man of them escape.' So they seized them, and Elijah brought them down to the Brook of Kishon and slew them there" (1 Kgs 18).

Elijah thus made use of water on one occasion. But fire was his foremost weapon. When Ahaziah sent out men to seize Elijah, the prophet called down fire from heaven to devour them. In the contest on Mount Carmel the fire from heaven proved to be more powerful than the sea water sprinkled on the altar. And a fiery chariot carried Elijah off to heaven. He himself was a firebrand burning with zeal for the glory of God.

All this was nothing more than a preparation and a type for the spiritual fire about which Jesus spoke; the fire He wished to see enkindled on the earth.

The Divided Kingdom

What a perfect spot for contemplation and sacrifice! Perhaps that is the reason why it was chosen by the hermits of East and West in ancient days, by the Carmelites in the days of the Crusades, and by the Reformed Carmelites of later times. Carmel was the ideal site for contemplation and the ideal retreat for the grueling practice of daily virtue; and sometimes for the bloody sacrifice of their own lives. The Saracens sacrificed all the monks on one occasion. In the eighteenth century the Moslems returned to slay all the Carmelites and raze the monastery. The present-day monastery was built in the nineteenth century along the lines of a fortress.

Under the main altar of the church lies a crypt commemorating the fiery prophet Elijah. And at the same time I was reminded of another Carmelite, no less ardent in spirit, who sang of "the flame of living love."

> Then Eliseus, filled with a twofold portion of his spirit, wrought many marvels by his mere word. During his lifetime he feared no one, nor was any man able to intimidate his will. Nothing was beyond his power; beneath him flesh was brought back into life. In life he performed wonders, and after death, marvelous deeds.
>
> (Sirach 48)

47. *THE ROAD TO DAMASCUS*

THE fact that our journey took place in midsummer had one advantage. We would see Damascus at just the right time of year. We leave Beirut, cross the Lebanon mountain range, and head for Anti-Lebanon across the Beqa' valley. As we mount the slopes of Anti-Lebanon and slowly approach the Syrian border, we gradually forget the colorful panorama behind us. The blue Mediterranean, the snow and cedar trees of Lebanon, and the bright green countryside have faded away in the distance.

Erasing the memory of this bright scenery is the best way to prepare for the sight of Damascus. And by the time we reached the border, I had almost succeeded. The highway had threaded its way across the barren mountains: an austere panorama of uniform colors and shapes, one color repeated in different shades along the snake-like road.

At the Syrian border we were detained almost two hours by the usual formalities of protocol. It gave us time to forget the meal we had eaten in a diner near one of the Jordan's springs. It was a beautiful spot, dotted with trees and fed by a plentiful supply of fresh water. But now this scene too had faded from our memory.

From the border the highway wound down through arid countryside to the plain below. Then suddenly we got our first hint of what was to come from a small oasis. And in another few moments the green countryside exploded into view.

THE MAGIC OF WATER

Fireworks exploding in the darkness of night and spraying colors across the sky! I can think of no other way to describe the approach to Damascus.

The Barada (or Abana) river rises in the heights of Anti-Lebanon. Fed by rain and snow it rushes down toward the plain. It knows

[271]

that its strength lies in water, so it zealously tries to preserve its precious force. Once its water supply is diminished it will be as weak as Samson without his hair. It keeps the water burrowed in the riverbed so it cannot escape. And it cuts through a sheltered gorge so that the sun cannot dry it up from above. Then, when it reaches the plain, it bursts into the open with all its power and explodes into trees, gardens, orchards, hedges, pools, reservoirs, canals, and brightly colored diners — a unique and extraordinary city. And it is really an explosion because all this greenery pops up suddenly in the midst of a desert region.

After this explosion of bright greenery the landscape is reduced to frail scorched reeds once again. And the river, its force spent, heads meekly for the desert to become the breeding ground for mosquitoes and the hapless prey of the sun. But this fate befalls it about four miles away from the city which it has created.

THE JORDAN OR THE ABANA?

Which river is better? The commander of the Syrian army was very proud of his river. He was a brave and robust man, but he had contracted leprosy. One of his wife's servants was a young Israelite girl who spoke frankly to her master and mistress. "Would that my master were with the prophet who is in Samaria! Then he would cure him of his leprosy." It may have been only a sentimental outburst on the girl's part, but the commander decided to give it a try. Loaded with gifts he "came with his horses and his chariots and halted at the door of Elisha's house. Whereupon Elisha sent a messenger to him, saying: 'Go and wash in the Jordan seven times, and your flesh shall be restored and you shall be clean.' But Naaman was enraged and left, and he said: 'Here I have been saying to myself; He will surely come out and stand and call on the name of the Lord his God, and wave his hand toward the place and cure the leper. Are not Amana (= Abana) and Pharpar, the rivers of Damascus, better than all the waters of Israel? Could I not wash in them and be clean?' " (2 Kgs 5.)

That was the opinion of the Syrian commander. And to tell the truth, the Jordan was not able to create one good city. It managed to form a small lake, Huleh, and a large one, Gennesaret; and in the spring their banks are pleasant enough. But then it sinks down into a bed which descends 600, 900, 1200 feet below sea level, and creates an almost intolerable atmosphere around it. And it finally empties into a barren lake of salt, sulphur, and asphalt bypassed by fish and sea gulls. The only two cities located near it, Jericho and Beth-shan, were not built too close. So Naaman's preference seems quite justified.

The Israelis have great plans to utilize the waters of the Jordan. We saw these plans outlined on one of those huge wall maps. By 1970 all of Palestine, as far down as Beer-sheba, will be irrigated by water veins coursing from the Jordan for the most part. Then this river will be able to compete with the Abana and its reputation. But it won't be quite the same, because there will be no great city rising up unexpectedly in the midst of the desert.

The answer to our question lies elsewhere. Naaman's servants came to him and said: " 'My father, if the prophet had demanded of you some great thing, would you not have done it? How much, rather then, when he has said to you: "Wash and be clean?" ' So finally he went down and dipped himself seven times in the Jordan, according to the word of the man of God, and his flesh was restored like the flesh of a little child, and he was clean." In short Jordan's value did not derive from the natural quality of its waters, but from a mysterious invisible force. And it was only a symbol and portent of what was to come. When the waters of the Jordan touched the body of the Messiah, they acquired a vital power which was to spread to every bit of water on earth — the power to cleanse those baptized in the name of the Trinity. The Abana too acquired this mysterious power. It cleansed the soul of a man named Saul, who was baptized in Damascus by Ananias and renamed Paul.

ENTERING DAMASCUS

The sudden explosion of greenery was so breathtaking that we failed to drink in the passing view bit by bit. Before you hit the city itself you travel several miles through a charming countryside. George Adam Smith has given us a vivid description:

> It is best to enter Damascus in summer, because then everything predisposes you for her charms. You come down off the most

barren flanks of Anti-Lebanon. You cross the plateau of Sahra-ed-Dimas, six shadeless miles that stretch themselves, with the elasticity of all Syrian plains in haze, till you almost fancy you are upon some enchanted ground rolling out with you as you travel. But at last the road begins to sink, and you come with it into a deep rut, into which all the heat and glare of the broad miles behind seems to be compressed. The air is still, the rocks blistered, the road deep in dust, when suddenly a bank of foliage bursts into view, with a white verandah above it. The road turns a corner; you are in shadow, on a bridge, in a breeze. Another turn and you have streams on both sides, a burn gurgling through bushes on the left, on the right not one stream but one banked over the other, and the wind in the poplars above. You break into the richer valley of the Abana itself. You pass between orchards of figs and orchards of apricots. For hedges there are the briar rose, and for a canopy the walnut. Pomegranate blossoms glow through the shade; vine-boughs trail across the briar; a little waterfall breaks on the edge of the road. To the left the river, thirty feet of dark green water with white curls upon it, shoots down a steep, smooth bed. And all this water and leafage are so lavish that the broken mud-walls and slovenly houses have no power to vex the eye, exulting in the contrast of the valley with the bare brown hills that shut it in. For two miles more you ride between trees, through a village, over a bridge, between high banks of gardens — road and river together, flecked with light. You come between two streams, one washing the roots of aged fig-trees, past a quarry where the desert sinks in cliff upon the road, beside an old aqueduct whose Roman masonry trails with brambles. The gorge narrows, there is room only for the aqueduct and river, with the road between, but just as the cliff comes near enough to overhang the road the hills turn sharply away, and the relieved river slackens and sprawls between islands. We are out on the plain; there are gardens and meadows; men and boys, horses, asses and geese loaf upon the grass and the shingle; great orchards, with many busy people gathering apricots, stretch on either side. Still, there is no city visible. A mile more of orchards, then through the walnuts a crescent gleams, and the minaret it crowns. You come out on a grassy level, cut by the river into two parks. There is a five-arched bridge across it, and over the bridge minarets and low white domes. You pass some public gardens, cross the river, ride between it and another garden with lofty trees, and halt in a great square, with the serai, the courts of justice, the prison, and the barracks of the principal garrison of Syria. The river has disappeared under the square by three tunnels, from which it passes in lesser conduits and pipes to every house and court in the city. By the northern walls a branch breaks again into the open; here the chiefest gardens are spread beneath walnuts and poplars, and the water rushes by them swift and cold from its confinement.

Fifty years later I can confirm the accuracy of his description and supply a few new details. The people sitting in the parks and diners, the multicolored lights glistening through the foliage; the trunks of the young trees clustered together like a crowd in a ball park; the beautiful main street leading into the center of the city; the glistening modern buildings reflecting the classical Arabic style in their own unique way.

48. DAMASCUS IN THE BIBLE

THE entire foreign policy of the Northern Kingdom was dominated by the fact that Damascus lay to the northeast. As you know, the ancient inhabitants did not leave enduring traces in the city. There are no excavated ruins to tell us about them. We must seek their memory in the atmosphere of the city and glimpse their shadows in the passing wind. Our inner eye must be alert to catch the invisible clues which will summon up the outlines of the ancient city.

The variety of racial types encountered on the streets and in the bazaars is significant. I got the whole picture when we climbed to the highest part of the city and surveyed the scene below. A small island of houses clustered amid a lake of greenery; and around this lake the vast reaches of the desert.

The desert is the homeland of the Bedouins. For miles around there is no other patch of oasis. The coastal plain of the Phoenicians is crouched behind a double wall of mountains, and the less enticing coast of Palestine is defended by the Jordan river. But the Abana river, faithful to the desert, penetrates its sandy wastes and opens up an oasis in its midst; a port of call for the caravans crossing the great commercial trade routes. The abundant waters of this oasis do not dry up in summer like the springs, or run short like the wells. It is no wonder that a city soon sprouted here. The very first book of the Bible, Genesis, mentions Damascus as a commercial and military throughway. And Abraham's servant was from Damascus.

But the city acquired historical importance much later on. Moortgat has given us a clear outline of the situation. In the thirteenth century B.C. the international balance of power is represented by a triangle: Babylon near the Persian Gulf, Egypt along the Nile and extending into Palestine, the Hittites sprawled across Asia Minor and extending down into Syria. The triangle was broken by the great migrations which followed. From the north the "sea

[276]

peoples" descended upon the Hittite empire and the frontier domain of the Egyptians. From the south waves of nomads, the Arameans, swept over the countryside and succeeded in establishing separate political states. One of the principal Aramean states was Damascus. At one point in history it was the capital of their confederation. And it is mentioned throughout the Bible.

During our stay in Damascus we resided in the Christian sector of the city. In the Orient it is not rare to find different sectors of a city inhabited by a particular race or creed. Today's political circumstances have eliminated the Jewish sector. But even on fairly recent maps you will find an outline of the Christian sector, the Kurdish sector, the immigrant sector, and the Jewish sector. This proliferation of distinct sectors, prompted by political, commercial, or religious considerations, might inspire us to devote our attention to the "biblical" sector of Damascus.

THE NORTHERN KINGDOM IN DAMASCUS

Rezon, the founder of an independent Aramean kingdom with its capital at Damascus, was hostile to Solomon. But the first serious encounter took place between Ahab, the son of Omri, and Ben-hadad, king of Syria. The conflict had many picturesque details and reveals a mentality quite different from ours.

First came the boastful challenge. Ben-hadad assembled his army of thirty-two vassal kings, besieged Samaria, and sent messengers to Ahab. "Your silver and your gold are mine; your wives also and your children are mine." The king of Israel sent his reply. "According to your statement, my lord, O King, I am yours, together with all that I possess." The messengers returned with an order from Ben-hadad. "About this time tomorrow, I shall send my servants to you and they shall ransack your house and the houses of your servants; and whatever pleases them they shall take in their hands and carry it away." Ahab consulted the elders and then sent his reply. "All that you demanded of your servant at the first I was ready to do, but this thing I cannot do." Ben-hadad sent another threat. "May the gods requite me and worse, if the dust of Samaria suffice for handfuls for all the people who follow me." Ahab retorted: "Let not him who is girding on his weapon boast himself

[277]

as he who is ungirding." Then Ben-hadad said to his servants: "Form in line" (1 Kgs 20).

(Even today we hear this kind of interchange between warring powers, in an updated version, of course.)

While the Syrian army was encamped outside the city, the Israelites made a sortie. The Syrian lookouts informed their king, and Ben-hadad, beaming with confidence, gave his order: "Whether they have come out for peace, take them alive; or whether they have come out for war, take them alive." But in the ensuing battle the Syrians lost many horsemen and chariots, and had to retreat to Damascus. The servants of Ben-hadad knew he was a vain man, and were able to explain the defeat away. "Their gods are mountain gods, therefore they were too strong for us; but let us fight against them in the plain, and surely we shall be stronger than they." They spent one year preparing for the new campaign. When the proper season arrived, they encamped on the plain and taunted Israel. For six days the two armies stood facing each other; on the seventh day the battle began. Again the Syrians were routed. Apparently their retreat route was cut off, because Ben-hadad had to hide in a nearby city. His servants then said to him: "Behold, now, we have heard that the kings of the house of Israel are merciful kings; let us therefore, I pray you, put sackcloth on our loins, and ropes about our heads, and go out to the king of Israel; perhaps he will spare your life."

When Ben-hadad was taken prisoner, Ahab "took him up into his chariot." Ben-hadad said: "The cities which my father took from your father I will restore . . . and you may maintain bazaars of your own in Damascus as my father did in Samaria." "And I," said Ahab, "will let you go with this understanding."

To have a foothold in this important commercial city was a great advantage. And the system has lasted down to our own day. Foreign powers are granted commercial bases, or concessions, in some sector or city of a country. We might say that Ahab acquired the first Jewish sector in Damascus.

The first prophet to see this sector was probably Elisha the wonder-worker. The route of his journey was probably quite similar to the one taken many centuries later by Saul of Tarsus. The prophet may have wanted to visit the Jewish community living in

Damascus. At any rate Ben-hadad was sick when he arrived. The king heard the news of his arrival and sent Hazael with a present to consult him about his illness. The trusted messenger came to Elisha and said: "'Your son Ben-hadad, king of Syria, has sent me to you, saying: "Shall I recover from this sickness?"' Then Elisha said to him: 'Go, say to him, "You shall surely recover," but the Lord has shown me that he shall certainly die.'

"And he fixed his gaze and stared at him until he was ashamed; but the man of God wept. 'Why does my lord weep?' said Hazael. 'Because,' he said, 'I know the evil you will do to the Israelites: Their fortresses you will set on fire, their choice young men you will slay with the sword, their little children you will dash in pieces, and their women with child you will disembowel.' 'But what is your servant — a dead dog — that he should do this great thing?' said Hazael. 'The Lord has shown me that you are to be king over Syria,' said Elisha. When he left Elisha and came to his master, he said to him: 'What did Elisha say to you?' Then he said: 'He said to me that you would certainly live.' But on the morrow he took the coverlet and dipped it in water and spread it over his face, so that he died. And Hazael became king in his stead" (1 Kgs 8).

Perhaps it is because I am in Damascus that the fixed gaze of Elisha, peering into the future of Hazael, reminds me of another judgment, both divine and human. In the instance cited above the king relied on the report of his courier, but the prophet saw the truth: "the evil that you will do to the Israelites." In this other instance it is the man of God who relies on the reports of others. "Lord, I have heard from many a person about this man, how much evil he has done to your saints at Jerusalem. Even here he has authority from the high priest to arrest all who invoke your name." "Go," the Lord commanded him, "for this man is my chosen instrument to carry my name among nations and their kings and among the children of Israel as well" (Acts 9:13–15).

DAMASCUS AS AN ALLY

If we stop to consider the significance of Damascus during the reign of the Omayades, when Mohammedanism held sway from Persia to the Atlantic, we begin to appreciate the value of this desert city. And when we recall its persecution of Christians in the early centuries A.D. and the days after the Crusades, and its persecution of the rebellious Druses in recent times, it seems that Elisha foresaw the future of Damascus for a long time to come and wept over its persecution of the new chosen people. Did he also foresee the growth of the extremist sect, the Moslem Brotherhood? It makes us somewhat fearful even though we cannot foresee the future.

Even today the strategic position of Damascus makes it a welcome ally. But then, today, any place seems to be strategic in the interplay of alliances. In the days of old, Damascus was a key spot in the full sense of the term.

Picture the triangle once again. In the southeast corner stands Babylonia; in the northern corner Assyria is devouring the fragments of the disintegrating Hittite empire; in the southwest corner lies Egypt. And along the western side of the triangle lie three kingdoms, one below the other — Damascus, Israel, Judah.

The two separated sister kingdoms, Israel and Judah, hardly ever got along well with each other. In their many disputes each tried to make alliances with the neighboring powers and often had recourse to Damascus. In other words, the odds had to be two to one. Looking at the game from a safe distance, it seems more like a political comedy. Basa, king of Israel, attacks Asa, king of Juda. Asa sends presents to Ben-hadad of Damascus and asks him to attack Israel. Damascus takes advantage of the offer, Baasha withdraws from Judah, and Asa breathes easier. Ahab of Israel joins Jehosaphat of Judah in an attack against the king of Syria. But Yahweh is against it, and their armies are defeated. On another occasion Ahaziah of Judah joined Joram of Israel against Hazael of Damascus; and Joram was wounded in the battle. Then Phaces of Israel joins Rasin of Damascus in an attack on Ahaz of Judah (it was on this occasion that Isaiah told Ahaz: "the virgin shall be with child, and bear a son, and shall name him Emmanuel"). But Ahaz breaks the rules of the game by asking Assyria to intervene on his side. Tiglath-pileser agrees to his request, invades Damascus, and leads its inhabitants into captivity. The entrance of a fourth party, a powerful kingdom, ruined the playful aspect of the game and inaugurated an epoch of transcendent historical importance. But it is not yet time to discuss this matter.

Damascus in the Bible

THE BAZAARS OF DAMASCUS

This is another must visit for the tourist. The sight alone will delight anyone with an eye for color, beauty, fine craftsmanship, and the eccentricities of popular taste. The sales techniques of the merchants will interest anyone with a commercial bent. And anyone with money in his pockets is sure to spend some of it along the half-mile strip of bazaars.

Damascus has sported precious items from the remotest days of antiquity. Being an oasis for the desert caravans, it was only natural that it should. Not only did treasures pass through Damascus, they accumulated here while business transactions were pending. And plenty was left over for the native inhabitants. When Naaman the Syrian was cured of leprosy, he offered Elisha ten talents of silver, six thousand shekels of gold, and ten festal garments. The prophet did not want the riches of Damascus and rejected the present. But Gehazi, his servant, ran after Naaman and asked for a present. Naaman gave him two talents of silver and two festal garments. When Elisha found out, he gave Naaman's leprosy to Gehazi as well (2 Kgs 5).

When Hazael went to consult Elisha about his king's health, he brought him "all kinds of goods of Damascus, forty camel loads."

The items most attractive to the tourist are the rich brocades and damasks, the inlaid woodworks, the copper kettles with their fantastic engravings, and the well-wrought pieces of gold and silver. All this, of course, testifies to the Arab influence which can also be found in the shops of Toledo and Granada. But the display of varied colors which brightens up the bazaar is a typical Oriental phenomenon.

ST. PAUL

For the Catholic visitor in Damascus the most important places of pilgrimage are the Straight Street (Acts 9:11), the house of Ananias, and the gate of St. Paul. They are all located in the Christian sector of the city and can be visited in a single morning. The Straight Street is quite ordinary: narrow, hot, and unpaved; a pack mule, small windows, etc. In view of all the historical events which

[281]

have left their imprint on this city, it is difficult to say how much is an authentic replica of St. Paul's day. At least a certain atmosphere remains, or else we have created it ourselves. The house of Ananias is an underground chapel. The gate of St. Paul is a fine stretch of wall flanked by two towers and sporting a high window. It is a modern piece of construction intended to mark the approximate spot where St. Paul was lowered in a basket to escape the Jewish lookouts.

In recalling the memory of St. Paul I am not going against my intention to visit the land of the Old Testament. Much of the Old Testament would be difficult to understand, if it were not for him. It seems hard to believe that St. Paul, whom many commentators still regard as the one who gave Christianity its distinctive orientation, is the one who is most concerned to show the connections between the Old Testament and the New.

He did this not so much for apologetic purposes — to win over the Jews — as for theological reasons — to instruct the Gentiles. And thanks to this lifetime preoccupation of his, he restored a forgotten dimension to the Old Testament — the concept of fulfillment. The enduring truths of the Old Testament find their fulfillment in the New. There the various strands are woven together and preserved as a unified whole.

If there were a bright ray of light, but it did not focus on any object, it would be invisible and lost to us. And that is what the Old Testament by itself is to many people. But let us watch St. Paul at work and learn from his example. Let us watch the mysterious light of the Old Testament as it is reflected in the New Testament. Suddenly the object is lit up and the light itself acquires real meaning.

As a case in point, take one of St. Paul's most important Epistles, the one which presents the theology of grace, the Epistle to the Romans. Turn to Chapter 9 and start counting the references, allusions, and arguments drawn from the Old Testament. The history of Abraham and Rebecca's two sons, the vision of Moses and the warning to Pharaoh, an allusion from Isaiah, a text of Hosea, two texts from Isaiah.

St. Paul was a man reared in the intellectual and religious milieu of the Old Testament. He had scrutinized every page of the Greek

[282]

Septuagint translation and had stored the traditions of Hebrew literature in his mind, his heart, and even his subconscious. When St. Paul formulates his theology and writes it down in Greek, he is using words, concepts, and themes rooted in the Old Testament.

Yes, without this trip to Damascus, our visit to the land of the Old Testament would be quite incomplete. And without exceeding the limits of the chapter heading, I have been able to leave Damascus with a tribute to the Apostle of the Gentiles.

49. WATERS, SALTY AND FRESH

A swim in the Dead Sea is already a tourist ritual. Even the non-swimmers are fearless, because anyone will float in these waters.

To get there you descend from Jerusalem to Jericho, and then head for the mouth of the Jordan river. There you take a side road until you reach a police station. The police stop the car and tell you that you can go no farther. You show them a permit and are allowed to continue. Soon the road ends and you find yourselves on a beaten trail winding up and down and from side to side, following the configurations of the bumpy terrain.

Our driver is a real expert, a huge hulk of a man who takes up more than his share of room on the seat. We watch him in the mirror as if it were a television program. He keeps his eyes fixed on the road, and when he reaches a rough stretch, his tongue protrudes like that of a reptile guarding the entrance of his cave. It seems to have a magic hold over the car. When it moves to the right, the car follows dutifully; when it moves to the left, the car rears slightly and straightens out once again.

At one point the procedure was more involved. The incline narrowed because of a stretch of rocks on the left side of the road. The wheels grazed the rocks and had difficulty getting by. Our driver's tongue came way out. When the danger was past and the tongue had gone back in, we clapped our approval. But he disowned the tribute with a shake of his head and kept his magic wand in action.

I hope you will not consider it disrespectful if I quote a biblical verse which occurred to me during this spectacle. In his Epistle St. James says: "Consider ships also. Large as they are and driven by strong winds, yet by means of a very small rudder they are steered wherever the will of the pilot determines. So too the tongue is a small member, yet it can boast of great achievements" (Jas 3:4–5).

Of course he is really referring to the power of speech, as the reader can see.

AIN FESHKAH

The bus comes to a stop about three hundred feet from a miniature oasis. No palms or trees, just grass. It is a circular pond with water gushing out of the ground. Nearby is a field of reeds which accompanies the rivulet some three hundred feet toward the sea. And around the pond there is a large flock of black sheep huddled together and waiting to take a drink. The shepherds turn to look at the visitors.

They try to dissuade us from taking a drink, telling us that it tastes bitter and has laxative effects. But we want to give it a try anyway. The taste is indeed salty and bitter, reminding us of those infamous purgatives forced down our throats as children. But the water is quite fresh and its clarity refreshes our eyes. I don't know whether it is the salts in the water or the reeds which cause the sheep's wool to be black. It seems that Jacob put stripped bark in the troughs to give his sheep a distinctively colored coat.

A little path between the reeds brings us to a bank of sand and rocks — the beach. In the twinkling of an eye we are in the water. It is warm and we scarcely feel a change in temperature. But we do feel a smarting sensation in every patch of raw skin on our legs. The dip is amusing because it is impossible to straighten one's legs vertically. And you float high atop the water like a ship without cargo or ballast. The taste of the water is intensely disagreeable. In one area, where a rivulet pours into the lake, the water is fresher and swimming comes easier.

After the swim we just have to take a shower; otherwise our bodies would stay coated with a thick film of salt. There are no overhead showers, so we have to stretch out in the running waters of the rivulet and hold on to the reeds. Thus we return the icing of salt to the sea once again. Thanks to us the Dead Sea will preserve its high salt solution. The horizontal shower is so pleasant that we spend ten minutes at it. And when we come out, the sun takes over the job of giving us a quick-dry.

The Divided Kingdom

That same afternoon, after visiting the ruins of Jericho under a blazing sun, we went for another swim — in the Jordan. Tradition pinpoints this section near the mouth as the site of Jesus' baptism. We were willing to accept this tradition until we took a swim. Unless the river conditions have changed radically, this could not be the place. The state of Jordan has just finished a new stretch of highway which brings you right to it. You cut through a low stone fence and pass in front of a small chapel which commemorates the gospel event. It is well proportioned; and the glass windows give off a nice color display.

This part of the Jordan is not a very good swimming hole. If it were not for the heat, we would not bother to go in. The riverbed is not very wide and the current is strong; so it is very difficult to cross it in a straight line. The opposite shore drops rather abruptly, but it has some shrubbery which you can grab. The beach side has a thick muddy bottom, and the muck makes it rather uninviting. Even the Dead Sea has more to recommend it.

How different it is at the point where the Jordan leaves Lake Gennesaret! The river bed is wide and the waters are clean and crystal clear. There are smooth stones on the bottom, and the minnows tickle your feet as they flit by. And all around the parks provide a delicious shade.

I am reminded of still another swim in Lake Gennesaret, the longest one we took. Along the shore stood thick groves of eucalyptus trees, and you eased your way into the water over smooth flat slabs of stone. Once in the water you had a fine view of the surrounding shoreline. You could see the imposing rock where Christ confirmed the primacy of Peter, and the little shrine which commemorates the event. Higher up seven streams of water cascaded down into the sea through the dense shrubbery. And farther on stood a small bridge, its ancient stones casting a thick shadow.

I then joined two of my companions who were swimming up and down parallel to the beach. We started doing a slow crawl stroke, trying to keep time with one another; and thus we enjoyed a bit of leisurely exercise. Isaiah has described it perfectly: "He will stretch forth his hands in Moab as a swimmer extends his hands to swim; he will bring low their pride as his hands sweep over them" (Is 25:11).

Just across the highway from the ruins of Jericho lies a beautiful spring. As we come down from the mound of rock and sand with parched throats, people line up along the conduit with their water containers: a few goatskin flasks, many tin cans, and, here and there, a pitcher. Some of the women are dressed in black, some wear bright dresses in the 110-degree heat. But snapshots are prohibited because some of the women belong to the colony of 20.000 refugees living near Jericho.

We make our way to the head of the conduit, since the fountain is covered by houses and is inaccessible. I have long arms so I am deputed to fill our containers. I am anxious to finish quickly because I too want to try the water; not only because it is a hot day but also because the water here ranks with the best in Palestine.

The taste of Ain Feshkah is still fresh in our mind, so it is easy to make a comparison. They say that the water of Ain Sultan was once like that of Ain Feshkah, and that Elisha was the one who made it drinkable.

After Moses, Elisha is the greatest wonder-worker in the Old Testament. The Second Book of Kings devotes various chapters to his exploits, just as the classical hagiographers devote certain chapters to "the miracles worked by this servant of God."

The first miracle takes place right after his master Elijah is carried off to heaven in a fiery chariot. Elisha struck the waters of the Jordan with Elijah's mantle and opened up a passageway (at the spot where I had to fight the current to swim across). "And when the members of the prophetic order who were at Jericho opposite him saw him, they said: 'The spirit of Elijah is upon Elisha.' . . . Then the men of the city said to Elisha: 'See now, the site of the city is pleasant as my lord sees; but the water is bad, and the land is unfruitful.' 'Bring me a new jar,' he said, 'and put salt in it.' So they brought it to him. Then he went out to the spring of the water supply and cast salt in it and said: 'Thus say the Lord: I have rendered these waters pure; neither death nor untimely birth shall

[287]

be due to them any more.' So the waters have continued pure down to this day, in accordance with the word of Elisha which he spoke" (2 Kgs 2:12–22).

It seems that Elisha specialized in water miracles. He opened a passageway in the Jordan, purified the waters of a fountain, cured Naaman's leprosy with the waters of the Jordan, and created pools of water in the valley of Moab (2 Kgs 2–4). But we will close our account with another miracle.

"Now the members of the prophetic order said to Elisha: 'See now, the place before you where we dwell is too limited for us. Let us go now to the Jordan and each take from there a beam and let us make a place for us there, where we may dwell.' 'Go,' he said. Then a certain one said: 'Be pleased, now, to go with your servants.' 'I will go,' he said. So he went with them, and when they came to the Jordan, they cut down the trees, but as one was felling a beam his iron ax fell into the water. At that he cried out, and said: 'Alas, my master! for it was borrowed.' 'Where did it fall?' said the man of God. When he showed him the place, he cut off a stick and threw it in there, and made the iron float. 'Take it up,' he said. So he reached out his hand and took it."

We might sum up our excursion in this way. The prophet converted the waters of Ain Feshkah into the waters of Ain Sultan: and he made the Jordan support an ax, even as the Dead Sea supported our bodies.

50. OUR BUS TRIPS

So the young man (the servant of the prophet) went to Ramoth-gilead; and just as he came, the commanders of the army were in session.

"I have a word for you, O commander," he said.

"For which one of us all?" said Jehu.

"For you, O commander," he said. Then he arose and went into the house; and the servant poured the oil on his head and said to him: "Thus says the Lord, the God of Israel: I have anointed you king over the people of the Lord, even over Israel. And you shall cut off the house of Ahab, your master, that I may avenge the blood of my servants, the prophets, and the blood of all the servants of the Lord at the hands of Jezebel. . . ." Then he opened the door and fled.

Now when Jehu came out to the servants of his master, they said to him: "Is all well? Why did this mad man come to you?"

"You know the man and his talk," he said to them.

"It is false! Tell us now," they said.

So he said: "Thus and thus he said to me, saying: 'Thus says the Lord: I have anointed you king over Israel.' "

Then they quickly took each his garment, and put it under him on the stairway, and blew the trumpet and said: "Jehu is king!". . .

So Jehu said: "If it be your mind, let no one make his escape from the city to go and tell it in Jezreel."

(2 Kgs 9)

[289]

The Tunnel of Hezekiah

How many were the hours we spent cramped in the narrow confines of a bus! We covered almost 2000 miles without even being able to stretch our legs. And I have not yet said a word about these hours. When you travel sixty or seventy miles to visit some place, the hours spent in the bus pass quickly enough. But when you travel a thousand miles or more inside a bus, this becomes a way of life in itself and a source of anecdotes. So allow me to tell you something about these trips.

Our buses were not the up-to-date kind with soft reclining seats, air brakes, and a microphone system; they were more like transport trucks. They were not too comfortable but they could get us over the roughest kinds of road. The front seats were the usual kind, while the back ones were more like saddles and transmitted every bump of the wheels. Sitting in the back of the bus was like riding a bucking bronco. But our buses held up very well. In the thousands of miles traveled there was not one flat, crash, or mishap; although on our trip to see the cedars of Lebanon the bus did stall once.

Our activities aboard the bus did not show too much variety. At times we recited the rosary in common; four strong voices in the rear would start the prayers and twenty-eight others would murmur their response. But sometimes the bus would be climbing a hill in first gear and the motor would drown out our most spirited responses. Sometimes we sang songs. There were songs familiar to all of us — in Latin, German, and Italian — which were devotional in content or told about student life and the hazards of travel.

Other songs were of national origin. Our American companions had Negro spirituals and such songs as "God Bless America" in their repertoire. We Spaniards had a smaller common repertoire because we came from different parts of Spain.

In the dreary moments of travel (for example, on the train ride from Damascus to Amman) our lightly satirical songs were able to brighten the atmosphere. We even sang a couple of numbers which went on interminably. We kept on harmonizing until our audience called for a record change. Then a distinguished seminary rector taught us a humorous ditty with a simple air to it.

One day, when the trip was more trying than usual, we vowed to stay in good humor no matter what. This meant singing when the going got rough. And we kept our vow admirably!

[290]

Our Bus Trips

When we were not engaged in some group activity, each person distracted himself as best he could or gave way to boredom. A yawning mouth was the giveaway sign. The yawn might be half-hearted or it might be a full-bodied one. Usually they grew in proportions as time went on. The trick was to cover the yawn as it started, and each individual had his own cover technique. A German tourist used the detailed maps he was studying so diligently; one Italian used the window through which he was surveying the dull countryside. Two of the Spaniards talked the yawns away and a Hollander conscientiously smoked his pipe. One American had wisely provided himself with a pocketbook and another diligently read *Time* magazine. Another passenger sniffed the odor of burnt gasoline to pass the time away and ended up with a slight case of nausea. As for myself, I whiled away the time by snoozing or letting my thoughts ramble.

On many a hot night I found myself admiring the speed with which my companions managed to drop off to sleep. I, on the other hand, was tormented by the heat and had to go out on the terrace for a breath of air. There I provided a fine meal to the hungry mosquitoes. But on the bus rides I won the prize for sleeping.

One of the strange things which came over me time and again on these bus trips was a feeling of envy for the camels. I was not envious of their dull eyes, or their elastic neck, or their hump — but of their double-jointed legs. What a blessing! Every time I stepped on a bus, I tried to find a comfortable seat where I could stretch my legs. But I often ended up with aching joints in a cramped seat. Double-jointed legs would have been a big help!

I also thought about the advantage of wearing white in hot weather — and dark glasses, of course; about the usefulness of matches and shorts, and about the abolition of passports and such things. I marveled at the photometer, which registers the mystery of light on a scale of numbers. And I weighed the advantages of growing a beard; it would enhance my self-esteem and raise a few eyebrows. These were the kind of unbiblical thoughts which ran through my mind during our travels. But such diversionary ramblings are necessary now and then, if we are going to concentrate properly at the sites we visit.

However, I also spent a fair amount of traveling time in reading

The Divided Kingdom

appropriate biblical passages. I have one passage which is quite appropriate for bus rides. But before I mention it, let me finish my ramblings.

Very often a pedestrian would try to flag our bus down along the road. Some just wanted to save time and shoe leather; others thought it was the regular bus service, because our bus was the ordinary type. Almost always we had to disregard the plea.

Hitchhiking is a very common practice in Israel, utilized by the young kid returning to or from his *kibbutzim*, the penniless wayfarer, the soldier on a pass, and the young girl going home from work. The buses of the Egged Company — to which our bus belonged — have fixed stopping points where they pick up passengers. Our bus heartlessly sped by these stops; but now and then it would pick up a few strays, mostly soldiers, at other points.

In Lebanon we encountered many fancy cars; in Syria, transport trucks. In Jordan there were regular bus lines and taxis which carried several persons to their different destinations. In Israel we encountered simpler cars belonging to businessmen, tractors, and agricultural machinery.

Now, having duly paid tribute to the many hours of dull confinement, I feel that I must say something which will benefit the reader. Perhaps a word about the ancient means of transportation would be in order.

A bus, no matter how fast it travels, does not convey a feeling of real speed. Even though it is faster than a horse-drawn chariot, the sensation is quite different. A technicolor movie by Warner Brothers or Twentieth Century Fox would devote many feet of film to a chariot race or chase. But it would never use a bus for such a scene. A steam engine or a locomotive can do the trick; but not our poor friend, the bus.

I can think of no better way to end this commentary on bus travel than to evoke the memory of Jehu.

Jehu, the usurper, the impetuous army chief, is the great charioteer in biblical history. When he charges forward, the ground falls back under his wheels, the enemy sentinels spot him at once, and kings flee before him.

He was the commander who was secretly anointed by one of Elisha's helpers as Yahweh's anointed. After being anointed Jehu did not tarry one day. "Then Jehu mounted his chariot and went to Jezreel, for Joram was lying there; and Ahaziah, king of Judah, had gone down to see Joram. Now as the watchman was standing on the tower in Jezreel, he saw the dust cloud raised by Jehu, as he came on, and he said: 'I see a dust cloud.' 'Take a horseman and send him to meet them that he may say: "Is it peace?" ' said Joram. Accordingly the rider of the horse went to meet him and said: 'Thus says the king: "Is it peace?" ' 'What have you to do with peace?' said Jehu. 'Rein in behind me.' So the watchman reported saying: 'The messenger came to them, but he does not return.'

"Then he sent out a second horseman who came to them and said: 'Thus says the king: "Is it peace?" ' 'What have you to do with peace?' said Jehu. 'Rein in behind me.' Again the watchman reported, saying: 'He came to them, but he does not return; also the driving is like the driving of Jehu, the son of Nimshi, for he is accustomed to drive furiously.' 'Make ready,' said Joram.

"As soon as they had made ready his chariot, Joram, king of Israel, and Ahaziah, king of Judah, set out each in his chariot. Thus they went to meet Jehu, and they reached him in the field of Naboth the Jezreelite; and when Joram saw Jehu he said: 'Is it peace, Jehu?' 'How can there be peace,' he said, 'as long as the harlotries of Jezebel your mother and her witchcrafts are so many?' Then Joram reined about and fled, and said to Ahaziah: 'Treachery, Ahaziah!' But Jehu drew his bow and shot Joram between his shoulders, so that the arrow went clear through his body; and he collapsed in his chariot. . . .

"Now when Ahaziah, king of Judah, saw this, he fled in the direction of Beth-haggan. But Jehu pursued him, and said: 'Him also! Pin him to the chariot.' So they wounded him at the ascent of Gur, which is by Ibleam. Nevertheless he kept on to Megiddo where he died. Then his servants took him by chariot to Jerusalem, and buried him in his own sepulcher with his fathers in the city of David" (2 Kgs 9).

The victorious Jehu entered the city on his chariot and had Jezebel thrown out of a window. A few days later, again on his chariot, "he met with Jonadab, the son of Rechab, coming to meet him. He greeted him and said to him: 'Is your heart in

[293]

accord with my heart, as mine is with yours?' 'It is,' said Jonadab. 'If it be, give me your hand,' said Jehu. So he gave him his hand and he took him up to him into the chariot. 'Come with me, and see my zeal for the Lord,' he said. So he induced him to ride in his chariot, and when he came to Samaria, he slew all who remained to Ahab in Samaria, until he had exterminated them according to the word of the Lord which he spoke to Elijah" (2 Kgs 10:15–17).

Jehu eradicated all trace of Phoenician idolatry in his territory, but he did not touch the traditional idolatrous practices of the Israelites. And during his reign another king more impetuous than he, King Hazael of Damascus, began to nibble away at the territory of the Northern Kingdom on the other side of the Jordan.

VII. THE DESTRUCTION OF THE TWO KINGDOMS: ISRAEL AND JUDAH

Then the king of Assyria came up against the whole land, and went up to Samaria and besieged it three years. In the ninth year of Hoshea, the king of Assyria took Samaria and carried Israel away captive to Assyria and settled them in Halah and on the Habor and the river Gozan, and in the cities of the Medes.

Now this came about because the Israelites had sinned against the Lord their God, who had brought them up from the land of Egypt, and had feared other gods, and walked in the statutes of the nations whom the Lord dispossessed before the Israelites. The Israelites uttered things that were not right against the Lord their God and built for themselves high places in all their cities, from the watchtower even to the fortified city, and set up for themselves sacred pillars and sacred poles on every high hill and under every spreading tree, and offered sacrifices there on all the high places, as did all the nations whom the Lord had carried away captive before them, and they did evil things, thus provoking the Lord to jealousy. They also served idols in regard to which the Lord had said to them: "You shall not do this thing."

Yet the Lord warned Israel and Judah by all his prophets and seers, saying: "Turn from your evil ways and keep my commands and my statutes in accordance with all the law which I commanded your fathers and which I sent to you by my servants, the prophets."

However, they would not listen, but were willful, as were their fathers, who did not believe in the Lord their God. Moreover they rejected his statutes and his covenant which he made with their fathers, and his decrees which he decreed for them, and followed vanity and became vain in accordance with the nations who were around them, concerning whom the Lord had commanded them that they should not do as they did. They forsook all the commands of the Lord their God and made for themselves molten images, even two calves, and made a sacred pole, and worshipped all the host of the heavens and served the Baal. They also made their sons and their daughters pass through fire, and used divination and

[295]

sorcery, and sold themselves to do evil in the sight of the Lord, thus provoking him to jealousy. Therefore the Lord was exceedingly angry with Israel and removed them out of his sight; there was nothing left but the tribe of Judah only.

Also Judah did not keep the commands of the Lord their God, but walked in the statutes of Israel. . . .

(2 Kgs 17)

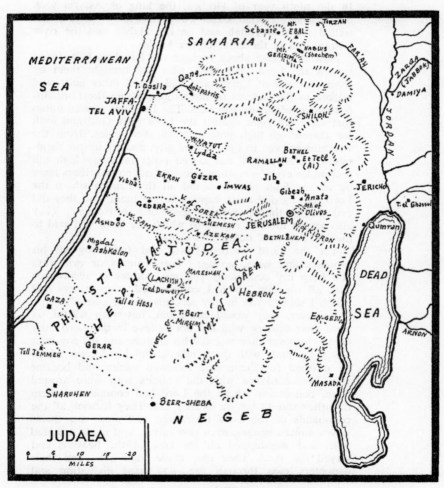

51. *SAMARIA — SEBASTE*

THE ruins of Sebaste gave us an idea of the smallness of ancient Palestinian cities. Sebaste, ancient Samaria (or Shomeron), was the third and most important capital of the Northern Kingdom.

We visited the first capital which Jeroboam established at Shechem. It was a small site nestled on the slopes of Ebal. Then we headed northeast to visit Tirzah, which the excavator regards as the second capital of the Northern Kingdom. It was situated on a rather large shelf atop a hill of medium height. Then we turned north to visit the third capital located northwest of Nablus. It is on a small piece of flatland atop a prominent hill.

The modern village is located in a wide and pleasant valley. It sports an ancient church built by the Crusaders which has been converted into a mosque. And the villagers say that it contains the remains of St. John the Baptist, or did at one time.

You cross the village on a dusty road which leads up to a clear esplanade dominated by a dozen beautiful columns. It is the end of July and the scene before us is a real summer one. The un-threshed grain is strewn over the ground and the threshers turn slowly and monotonously, raising the dust on the threshing floor. Strangely enough, some Arab women are engaged in this form of public activity. Neither the donkeys nor the workers are interested in the columns; European tourists are a more interesting sight. We, on the other hand, are more interested in the columns than in the donkeys and workers. In Samaria the threshing floors are adorned with Herodian columns.

In back of these columns stands another esplanade on a higher level. Amid its magnificent remains stands a fantastic staircase and a stout circular tower dating from the period of Roman occupation. From there we look down into the valley at the ruins of an enormous hippodrome.

The emperor Augustus gave this village to Herod as a gift and he in turn renamed it Sebaste (= Augustus). He embellished it luxuriously without going so far as to erect columns on the threshing floors.

We cross the great stairway to the more ancient sector of the hill, the site of the ancient city. Suddenly the luxurious trappings disappear and everything is reduced to a smaller scale.

Yet this was the great capital of the Northern Kingdom against which the prophet Amos railed.

"Hear and bear witness . . . says the Lord God, the God of hosts: On the day when I punish Israel for his crimes . . . Then will I strike the winter house and the summer house; the ivory apartment shall be ruined, and their many rooms shall be no more . . ." (Am 3:13–15).

"Lying upon beds of ivory, stretched comfortably on their couches, they eat lambs taken from the flock, and calves from the stall! Improvising to the music of the harp, like David, they devise their own accompaniment. They drink wine from bowls and anoint themselves with the best oils . . ." (Am 6:4–6).

This hill has also been a memorable site in the history of Palestinian archaeology. In 1907 a rich American presented $50,000 to Harvard, and the university decided to finance an excavation in Palestine. Fifty thousand dollars could do a lot in those days! The director, G. A. Reisner, brought along his new techniques with him.

Petrie the Englishman had discovered a fundamental principle: pottery dating. The German Burckhardt had introduced new techniques in Egyptian archaeological work. Reisner utilized the principles and techniques of both. And he added the American touch by systematically recording and cataloging every piece of data. This methodological synthesis produced a model excavation and heralded a new epoch in excavation work.

King Omri paid two talents of silver to buy the hill itself. It would cost him and his successors much more to build it up and adorn it. But apparently it cost just as much to disinter the ancient ruins.

In no time at all the excavator reached the layer of virgin rock, the bare site bought by Omri. This is an interesting point because at other sites the virgin rock lies much deeper down in time and space. In Jericho it dates from about 5000 B.C., in Megiddo before 3000 B.C., etc. In Samaria it dates from 800 B.C., solidly supporting the Bible narrative.

The other interesting items mentioned in the Bible are palaces and rich ivory works.

Apparently they also found the remains of palaces. According to the first excavators a quadrangular building with rooms located around a central courtyard and a porch in front was probably Omri's palace. Additional walls which extend from this basic layout probably delimit Ahab's palace. More recent workers at this site would want to revise these conclusions, but as yet there is no clear solution.

They also found some beautiful ivory pieces, but not enough to account for the ivory palace and couches condemned by the prophet Amos. These ivory pieces could have been carried off as war booty. The "house of ivory" may have had removable ivory panels on the walls which were carried away by the looters. At any rate the excavators were not as lucky here as they were at Megiddo, for example. And their only recourse was to fill the gaps with hypotheses.

For purely biblical reasons I especially wanted to see the city gate and the pool. I did not expect to find a huge pond or a stupendous gate. Some remains of moderate size would have been enough to evoke two biblical scenes. But the actual remains are so scanty, and covered with so much earth and rock that I had difficulty in recalling the original scene. Fortunately the imagination can overcome such obstacles, especially when aided by a good narrator like the author of the Book of Kings.

King Ahab, Jezebel's weak husband, had invited Jehosaphat, king of Judah, to come up and plan a joint attack against the Syrians. We must picture them seated on two thrones at the city gate, for that is where official business was conducted. A messenger had assembled all the prophets because the king of Israel wanted to know if the gods favored this expedition against Ramoth-gilead. Four hundred prophets of Baal pronounced favorable auguries; some spoke and some performed ritual acts. One prophet named Zedekiah made horns of iron and said: "With these you shall gore the Syrians until they are destroyed." The king of Israel was quite pleased, but the king of Judah wanted to consult a prophet of

The Destruction of the Two Kingdoms

Yahweh. Micaiah (Micah) was the only one still living in the area. Ahab hated him because he never prophesied good for him. But at Jehoshaphat's request he summoned him. The messenger hurries off and gives Micaiah the order. And he urges Micaiah to give a favorable augury as the others have done. Don't rock the boat! The prophet answers dryly: "What the Lord says to me, that will I speak."

The prophet is greeted with stony silence or sneers by the prophets of Baal. The king begins the conversation.

AHAB: "Micaiah, shall we go to Ramoth-gilead to battle, or shall we forbear?"

MICAIAH: "Go up and prosper, for the Lord will deliver it into the hand of the king!" (*Spoken in an ironic tone.*)

AHAB: "How many times must I adjure you that you speak to me nothing but the truth in the name of the Lord?"

MICAIAH: "I saw all Israel scattered on the mountains, like sheep without a shepherd; and the Lord said: These have no master; let them return back to his home in peace."

AHAB: "Did I not say to you [Jehoshaphat] that he would not prophesy good concerning me, but only evil?"

MICAIAH: "Therefore hear the word of the Lord: I saw the Lord sitting on his throne and all the army of the heavens standing by him on his right hand and on his left; and the Lord said: 'Who will deceive Ahab so that he may go up and fall at Ramoth-gilead?' Then one said one thing and another another, until a spirit came forth and stood before the Lord and said: 'I will deceive him': and the Lord said to him: 'By what means?' He said: 'I will go forth and become a lying spirit in the mouth of all his prophets.' Thereupon he said: 'You shall deceive him and also succeed! Go forth and do so.' Now therefore, behold, the Lord has put a lying spirit in the mouth of all these prophets of yours, since the Lord has spoken evil concerning you."

"Then Zedekiah . . . approached and struck Micaiah upon the cheek . . . The king of Israel said: 'Put this fellow in the prison and feed him with bread and water scantily until I return victorious.' Whereupon Micaiah said: 'If you do indeed return victorious, the Lord has not spoken by me. Hear, all you peoples!' " (1 Kgs 22.)

We have heard accounts of the pond cut out of rock and coated with lime and ash; but we cannot find it at the site itself. All we find is an opening which could have served as a water conduit. And the pond interests us because it enters into the tragic finale of the scene enacted above. Against Micaiah's advice the king sallied forth to battle, disguised as a common soldier; and a stray arrow found its way through his armor.

"Therefore he said to his charioteer: 'Wheel about and take me out of the fight; for I am badly wounded.'

"Now the battle grew fiercer that day, while the king held himself upright in his chariot facing the Syrians until evening, and the blood from the wound ran out into the bottom of the chariot. But at evening he died; and about sunset the cry passed through the army: 'Each to his city and each to his land, for the king is dead!'

"So they came to Samaria and buried the king in Samaria; and when they washed off the chariot by the pool of Samaria, the dogs licked up his blood, and the harlots washed in it according to the word which the Lord had spoken."

After examining the few items in the excavation which are still obvious and clear-cut, we took a look at the unchanging features of the site, the geographical layout of the hillside. The city is perched on an isolated hill in the midst of a wide valley. To the east and the north lie mountains. The Assyrian army probably came through those mountain passes to attack the city. Omri had been shrewd enough to choose a strategic hill which could withstand attack for a long time.

The power of the Assyrian empire grew steadily. The great emperor Tiglath-pileser III used a clever technique to add new provinces to his empire. He would conquer a small kingdom, deport the inhabitants, and send in Assyrian colonists. The king of Samaria decided to fight this powerful emperor. He made an alliance with the king of Syria and tried to persuade the kingdom of Judah to join them. In that way, a long strip of land near the sea would be able to contain the Assyrian advance. Judah refused to join and was attacked by the coalition forces. The king of Judah, after hearing Isaiah's prophecy, asked Assyria to intervene against Damascus. The Assyrian army attacked from the north, destroyed the Syrian kingdom of Damascus, and pushed deep into the territory of the Northern Kingdom.

The Destruction of the Two Kingdoms

Some years later the Assyrians attacked the remaining sections of the Northern Kingdom, and laid siege to Samaria in 725 B.C. The capital city put up a stout resistance. The Assyrian commander Shalmaneser died during the siege and Sargon took his place. After almost three years of fighting he managed to take the fortress. And with its fall the Northern Kingdom ceased to exist forever. Only Judah, the Southern Kingdom was left. Sennacherib set out to take it, but he was forced to withdraw. God wanted to give his wayward people one more century in which to repent. But they kept on sinning; and a new power, the Babylonian Empire, was given the task of fulfilling the Lord's decree.

Samaria lasted for two hundred years. But the only aspect of her history which we have been allowed to see is the destruction foretold by the prophet Amos.

"So now I will deal with you in my own way, O Israel! And since I will deal thus with you, prepare to meet your God, O Israel: him who formed the mountains, and created the wind, and declares to man his thoughts; who made the dawn and the darkness, and strides upon the heights of the earth: the Lord, the God of hosts by name" (Am 4:12–13).

"I abhor the pride of Jacob, I hate his castles, and I give over the city with everything in it; should there remain ten men in a single house, these shall die. Only a few shall be left to carry the dead out of the houses; if one says to a man inside a house: 'Is anyone with you?' and he answers: 'No one.' then he shall say, 'Silence!' for no one must mention the name of the Lord. Indeed, the Lord has given the command to shatter the great house to bits and reduce the small house to rubble. . . . Beware, I am raising up against you, O house of Israel . . . a nation that shall oppress you" (Am 6:8–14).

"Yes, days are coming, says the Lord God, when I will send famine upon the land: Not a famine of bread, or thirst for water, but for hearing the word of the Lord. Then shall they wander from sea to sea and rove from the north to the east in search of the word of the Lord, but they shall not find it. On that day, fair virgins and young men shall faint from thirst; those who swear by the shameful idol of Samaria . . . shall fall, never to rise again" (Am 8:11–14).

"I saw the Lord standing beside the altar, and he said: 'Strike the bases, so that the doorjambs totter till you break them off on the heads of them all! Those who are left I will slay with the sword; not one shall flee, no survivor shall escape. Though they break through to the nether world, even from there my hand shall bring them out; though they climb to the heavens, I will bring them down; though they hide on the summit of Carmel, there too I will hunt them out and take them away; though they hide from my gaze in the bottom of the sea, I will command the serpent there to bite them; though they are led into capitivity by their enemies, there will I command the sword to slay them. I will fix my gaze upon them for evil, and not for good, I, the Lord God of hosts' " (Am 9:1–5).

"The eyes of the Lord God are on this sinful kingdom: I will destroy it from off the face of the earth. But I will not destroy the house of Jacob completely, says the Lord" (Am 9:8–9).

52. THE SAMARITANS

To go from Jerusalem to Nazareth today, you must make a wide detour along the coast because the mountainous territory in between belongs to the Arabs. In the time of Christ the traveler made a detour along the right bank of the Jordan to avoid contact with the Samaritans; not because they were a warlike people, but because they were schismatics, heretics. Contact with them tarnished Jewish ritual purity. Jesus Christ did not hesitate to visit them in an attempt to convert them. So we have no scruples about visiting them for scholarly purposes.

The Samaritans in Nablus are looking forward to our visit, just as they look forward to welcoming all tourists. They have dressed up some of the young people in their best clothes and formed a welcoming committee; and they have put postcards on display. They realize their value as a tourist attraction and depend on it for much of their livelihood. Like people in other parts of the world, they try to delight the tourist with exhibitions of their peculiar local customs and mores.

There are about two hundred living representatives of this famous group. I guess, if there were even a few real Hittites still living, we would go to see them. They would be billed as the last survivors of an interesting race.

The Samaritans practice strict endogamy to preserve the purity of their race. So the surviving members are Samaritans through and through. But this practice has its disadvantages also; witness the European dynasties which had to get canonical dispensations for their matrimonial alliances.

But endogamy or no, the children ten years old or younger are cute looking in their bright smocks and sash, their red fez with its black tassel. At the age of twelve they begin to wear that strange hairdo which is deceiving at first glance. I had to take

[304]

a good look at one child before I was sure that he was a boy. And the external features themselves do not give too much of a clue. The boys also wear plaited braids. They are clean-shaven and have oval features; but they are tall and well built. They eagerly offer us ancient coins and other curious objects, but we prefer our modern currency and refuse to trade. Our conduct is a little shameful because we would readily exchange our coins for an ice-cream cone or a bunch of grapes.

There are no women in the reception committee; it is probably another Samaritan custom. I myself would have liked to see what their women looked like and how they dressed. Perhaps we saw one or two on the street or near the spring, but failed to recognize them.

Our hosts are very courteous. Even though there is a guide who has a good voice, speaks English, and can handle the tour, the different individuals offer us their services, their postcards, and their scraps of information. We are forced to disregard the spontaneous chatter somewhat discourteously, and devote our attention to the guide's commentary.

Their synagogue is a medium-sized building, whitewashed but not very bright. There are no decorations except for some cloths. Our guide proceeds to show us the most precious object in the synagogue and the entire village: a roll of parchment. It is a Samaritan copy of the Pentateuch transcribed by a copyist around A.D. 1100, an 850-year-old document containing a revered and ancient version of the Pentateuch.

The guide explains the value of this roll. "One of Aaron's nephews wrote it thirteen years after the Israelites arrived in Shechem. . . . The Israelites did not cross the Jordan around Jericho but around Shechem or Samaria; and on that mountain behind the house they proclaimed the blessings of the law. . . ." There is nothing more to say, no questions to ask.

I had understood that the Spanish ambassador persuaded them to let us photograph the whole roll. But they would not grant us such a favor. For five piasters (ten cents) each camera enthusiast was allowed to photograph the guide holding the parchment in his hand. The nonphotographers had only to drop a contribution into a plate at the rear.

The Destruction of the Two Kingdoms

So here we have a people believing in the one God, sacrificing the paschal lamb once a year, and recognizing only the first five books of the Bible (the Pentateuch). They are a peaceable group causing no trouble except to make a little profit on tourists. Why do they go on living sheltered in the custom of endogamy? Why do tourists keep coming to visit the manuscript? The second question is easier to answer. Tourists keep coming out of obedience to the first commandment of tourism: "Thou shalt look at every object worth seeing, like any good tourist should." For the answer to the first question we must go back into their past history.

HOSTILE LIONS

After a couple of centuries of independent existence, the Northern Kingdom was conquered by Assyria. Shalmaneser besieged the capital for two years. It was finally conquered by his successor Sargon in the third year. He deported 27,000 Israelites and brought foreign colonists into the area.

"Moreover the king of Assyria brought people from Babylon, Cuthah, Avva, Hamath, and Sepharvaim and settled them in the cities of Samaria in place of the Israelites. So they took possession of Samaria and dwelt in its cities. Now at the beginning of their settling there, they did not fear the Lord. Therefore the Lord sent lions among them which were constantly killing some of them. So they told the king of Assyria, saying: 'The nations which you have carried away and settled in the cities of Samaria do not know the custom of the god of the land; therefore he has sent lions among them and behold, they are constantly killing them, because they are not acquainted with the custom of the god of the land.' Then the king of Assyria gave command, saying: 'Send one of the priests whom I carried away from there; and let him go and dwell there, and let him teach them the custom of the god of the land.'

"So one of the priests . . . came and dwelt in Bethel and taught them how they should fear the Lord. But each of the nations had made gods of their own and had placed them in the temples of the high places which the Samaritans had made, each people in their cities in which they dwelt. . . . But when they came to

[306]

fear the Lord they made for themselves from their own number priests of the high places, who acted for them in the temples of the high places. Thus they came to fear the Lord, but they also continued to serve their own gods, according to the custom of the nations from which they had been carried away. To this day they continue to do according to the earlier custom" (2 Kgs 17: 24–34).

The result was the creation of a new race, a mixture of the new colonists and the remaining native inhabitants. Religious syncretism spread quickly. Yahweh was the god of this particular territory, but other regions had their gods who were just as good. The best thing to do was to pay reverence to all of them so that they all might render their special kind of help. The inspired author, who wrote up this account in Judah perhaps a century later (unless it is a later gloss), concludes: "So while these peoples came to fear the Lord, they were also serving their carved images; moreover their children and their children's children — as their fathers did, so do they continue to do to this day."

These words do not apply to the present-day Samaritans. They are strict monotheists and do not allow representations of animals or humans in cultic or ornamental objects.

VOLUNTEER WORKERS

We meet the Samaritans again when the exiles from Judah are allowed to return home by Cyrus' decree. By this time the Samaritans have been living here for almost two hundred years. The repatriated Israelites soon begin to rebuild the temple at Jerusalem. When the Samaritans hear about the project, they offer to help. Apparently they had no evil plan in mind. It was a gesture prompted by their tendencies toward religious syncretism, nothing more. Yahweh was one of the gods they venerated. "Let us build with you; for we seek your God, as you do, and we have been sacrificing to him since the days of Esarhaddon, king of Assyria, who brought us up here" (Ezr 4:2).

But the repatriates distrusted this syncretist spirit and feared contamination. So they replied: "You have nothing in common with us in building a house to our God; but we ourselves will

[307]

together build to the Lord, the God of Israel, as King Cyrus, the king of Persia, has commanded us" (Ezr 4:3).

"Then the people of the land continued to weaken the hands of the people of Judah, and terrorize them out of building, and hire counselors against them to frustrate their counsel, all the days of Cyrus, king of Persia, even until the reign of Darius" (Ezr 4:4-5).

These were the Samaritans which the Jews took such pains to avoid in the time of Christ. The Israelites who had remained in the country during the exile, had intermarried with the foreign colonists and diluted their faith. By contrast the exiles returned with a purified faith. They had overcome their polytheistic tendencies once and for all, and had not intermarried with the foreign peoples.

Today the situation is reversed. Two hundred and fifty Samaritans are living in isolation here and have preserved their faith intact. By contrast there are 2,200,000 Jews in Palestine and 14,-000,000 scattered all over the world despite persecutions, pogroms, and the terrible liquidations of World War II.

In the streets of Jerusalem, Tel Aviv, and Haifa we saw Jews of many different nationalities: Germans, Slavs, Anglo-Saxons, Arabs, etc. Their blood has intermingled with the blood of other races and it has been enriched. The Jewish people have not been exterminated by the persecutions, nor tarnished by their foreign contacts. As for their religion, we cannot make a general statement about 14,000,000 people.

Indeed the contrast in numbers between 250 Samaritans and 14,000,000 Jews gives food for thought.

53. *A TYPICAL CITY*

Up to now we have been visiting the historic places of Palestine. We have examined sites located in some beautiful or strategic spot and sporting more or less illustrious ruins. All of them have evoked important biblical memories.

For this very reason we may have overlooked the normal course of life in the days of old, life as it was lived from day to day in Palestine. So before we review the destruction of the Southern Kingdom, we will pay a visit to a city of no historical importance, a city mentioned only cursorily in the Bible. To erase the significance of even these few biblical references, we will choose a city which has not been identified definitively. Thus only the city itself and its ruins will stand as a witness to the past. The Bible will not fill in any gaps for us.

SCRIBE TOWN

The official account of an archaeological excavation is usually hard to digest. A brief readable introduction is followed by a series of dry chapters and long lists of the objects unearthed which the archaeologist regards as noteworthy. And to an archaeologist noteworthy objects include amulets, small statues of idols, layers of ash, potsherds, skulls and bones, baked or adobe bricks, etc.

Now and then an archaeologist comes along who can write up an excavation and its results in a charming style. He is invited to gives lectures and write books. And soon he has aroused the interest of the general reader. In the earlier generation of archaeologists Macalister was the best writer; today Albright is tops.

The best (and most enjoyable) thing we can do on this trip is let Albright tell us some facts and stories about the excavation (*The Archeology of Palestine and the Bible,* Chap. 2).

First a site had to be chosen, so a tour of inspection was made. The most likely prospect is some *tell,* a hill formed by successive layers of sediment. Its very texture suggests the ruins of one or more ancient towns and seems promising to the archaeologist. Albright was especially intrigued by a hill called Tell Beit Mirsim. It was of ample size and in a fine location. The revetment of the ancient walls was still exposed in part. On the surface of the hill lay many shards dating from the pre-exilic period. This would indicate that the town was not rebuilt afterwards. On the basis of historical evidence and the location of the site Albright tentatively identified it as the biblical city of Debir, formerly the Canaanite city of Kiriath-sepher (scribe town). All this took place in April, 1924.

The next two years were spent organizing the expedition. The most difficult problem was to raise the necessary funds. An archaeological expedition involves many expenses and seldom produces a financial profit. Equipment must be bought, workers must be paid, and the hill's landlords must be paid for excavation rights. The statues, potsherds, bricks, and inscriptions uncovered will scarcely pay for all this. An expedition can be financed in one of two ways — by a rich financier who can see the scientific value of the project, or by a university in good financial straits. Sometimes both sources are tapped.

Next you have to recruit your scientific personnel. The size of the staff may vary but it should include an architect, a good draftsman, a pottery expert, a doctor, laboratory technicians, and a good photographer. There is always some bright student or young professor who wants to join the staff to get practical experience. This group will live in well-installed tents. If the excavation work goes on for a fairly long period, houses may be built with ample space for laboratory facilities. If the expedition is backed by a stout wall of dollars, they may go as far as to build a tennis court. But this happened only once, at Megiddo.

Once on the site workers must be recruited. Usually they are Arab peasants over whom a trustworthy native foreman is placed. Dealing with the Arabs requires practical skill and patience. Their business practices would be quite strange to an American and they could even teach a few tricks to a loan shark. Albright spent many profitable hours chatting with them and listening to their traditions. Their ancestors had migrated to this region in the seventeenth century. Not long afterward an Arab girl was raped. At a banquet the tribe took its revenge and slew the townsmen. Their tales had all the ingredients of an epic. In the first campaign about fifty Arab laborers were employed. In the third campaign there were twice that many.

PROGRESS OF THE EXCAVATION

The day-to-day work in an excavation is terribly monotonous. The laborers gradually learn how to dig carefully, remove obstacles, and collect fragments. But they never fully appreciate the purpose of it all; so the staff must keep an eye on the finds, record zones and levels exactly, and give a tentative interpretation to the data. Sometimes they themselves become involved in the work of digging, and whole days may be spent at some particularly interesting or difficult spot.

But now and then the monotony of routine is broken by some event. It may be a particularly interesting find, like the ostraca at Lachish or the ivory works at Samaria. Or it may be the possibility of an imminent find. Some worker or overseer sounds the alarm. The secret dreams of the archaeologist well up to the surface, clouding his better judgment and his scientific training for the moment. An air of excitement sweeps the camp.

One day at Tell Beit Mirsim the picks struck a hollow. A hole appeared in the rock and gradually widened into a tunnel. Could it be the entrance to an ancient necropolis dating from the days of the patriarchs and containing precious historical data? Alas, at the end of the tunnel they found only cisterns. The Israelites, in digging a cistern, had broken into the Canaanite sepulchres, cleared and plastered them, and then used them as cisterns.

On another day the excitement was even greater. The workers found a cleft in the rock and were told to widen it. When the opening was big enough, the staff went inside accompanied by a group of excited Arabs. As they crawled through the labyrinthine passages, dimly lighted by tallow candles, the Arabs grew more intoxicated with the hope of finding buried treasure. One of them,

[311]

thinking that none of the experts understood Arabic, outlined his plan. When they discovered the gold, they would cut the foreigners' throats and run off with the treasure. Only Albright understood the muttered threat, but he was not at all disturbed. His archaeological instincts told him that they would find only a storage place for grain, straw, oil, and such things. The Arabs were let down miserably and slunk out muttering: "Poor people, they were peasants like us." The mastermind disappeared for a couple of weeks. When he returned to work, Albright made sure that he was not allowed to forget the episode.

SOME INTERESTING FINDS

One of Albright's disappointments in the first campaign was not finding jar handles stamped with the seal of a proprietor or tax collector. He had to be satisfied with the outer wall, a tower, some pillars belonging to two-story houses, and a dye plant. In the second campaign they found a stele of Astarte — the goddess of fertility, a well-preserved seal, and a few brief inscriptions on potsherds. The fertility goddess with her symbolic serpent is well known to the archaeologists. She was one of the principal deities in the Canaanite religion and crops up in many other places as well. The stele is flat in front and curved in the back. Undoubtedly it stood in some niche on the top floor of the house, where it was venerated by the family.

One find was of little interest to the student of comparative religion but may prick the curiosity of the modern reader. It was a set of game pieces; five little blue cones, five little three-cornered pyramids, and a die. The die is not a cube like our dice but a truncated pyramid. On each of its four sides are round holes, from one to four in number. The die is made of ivory and the other pieces are made of porcelain. However, no game board was found. To fill in the set we would have to borrow one of the game boards found in Egypt, or the magnificent one found at Megiddo with its rectangular sections on which the pieces were moved.

The set from Tell Beit Mirsim dates from the period of Egyptian influence. Few such game pieces have been found in Palestine. Apparently the earlier inhabitants of Palestine were not addicted to armchair games. The children preferred to romp in the open air and the adults chose music or conversation. They did not even have the foresight to leave us a book of instructions along with the pieces. So we can't explain the details of the game.

Other finds were less pleasant: traces of a violent battle and a devastating fire, bits of household furniture, chests and drawers — some of them inlaid. The strongest testimony with the different skeletons: adults and children, young men lying face down — slain in battle. There were also daggers, stone and bronze maces, and lance tips.

The artistic pieces found do not testify to a state of splendor and luxury. There are no ivory pieces to match those of Samaria and Megiddo. In the city of scribes we find the lion motif. Of course many pieces may have been destroyed in the devastating fire; but we can't be certain one way or the other. All we know is that the pieces uncovered are few in number and of second-rate quality. One piece is a stone lion rather crudely done, as are most works of that era. The only striking feature is the gracefully curved tail. The excavators also found a round offering table with three lions in relief around its rim. Apparently both finds were used for religious purposes. The lion was one of the favorite pets of the contemporary deities. The gods are pictured standing on the back of a lion or sitting on a throne supported by lions. Along with the serpent and the lion the workers also found representations of the dove. These items date from a later period, the era of Philistine domination. The goddess presses a dove with spread wings against her breast. One bizarre piece is a dragon painted on a large pot-sherd. The dragon has an elongated body, the legs and feet of a fowl, and a bird's head. The head is turned back over its shoulder, and a peculiar crest protrudes from the back of the head.

LIFE IN THE CITY

Albright took special care to study the structure of the houses and the layout of the successive cities. In the time of the Hebrew monarchy — three centuries of peace and prosperity — the houses were of ample size. They had a long courtyard and a second story supported by four thick stone columns. These columns are five to six feet high and weigh from 700 to 1400 pounds. You can imagine the work involved in hewing these huge monoliths at the quarry, dragging them up the hill, and setting them in place. The ceilings and roof are made of wood. The townspeople lived in the second floor of the house and housed their flocks in stables outside the city. The streets were rather narrow, about six feet wide; some were paved. Water was stored in cisterns and there were a few drainage channels running underground. Public affairs were conducted at the city gate, as we know from repeated statements in the Bible. Disputes between merchants cropped up frequently, so the magistrates had great need of standard weights. Several such weights have been found, including a beautiful eight mina weight of polished limestone in perfect condition.

The big industry of the city was the textile industry — the spinning, weaving, and dyeing of woolen stuffs. Many loom parts have been found along with dye plants. The latter are of fairly standard size, ten by twenty feet; each contains a couple of shallow cement basins at one end. The vats were constructed in a fashion quite strange to us but quite reasonable for the ancient townspeople. The liquid dye, you must remember, was a precious commodity in their eyes. A leaky vat which would allow some of the precious dye to escape could not be tolerated. So the vats were hewn out of single rocks about three feet high and three feet in diameter. The interior was hollowed out into a spherical basin about a foot and a half across, with a narrow mouth seldom over six inches across. Around the upper rim ran a deep circular channel with a hole in its bottom leading to the interior of the vat. This channel would catch any dye spilled on the rim and return it to the vat. Inside the dye plant they also stored jars of lime, an indispensable ingredient in the dyeing process.

The women of the town were not content with brightly dyed dresses. They also used their own brand of mineral cosmetics. Albright found several palettes on which the cosmetics were prepared: powdered turquoise to paint the lower eyelids green, powdered red clay to touch up the lips, and powdered *kuhl* to blacken eyebrows and eyelashes.

A Typical City

SCRIBES OR NO?

The city's name would lead one to expect some sort of publishing industry in it. A present-day periodical dealing with bibliographical questions is called *Kiriath Sepher;* but it refers to another place.

In spite of diligent investigation on the part of the excavators, only five meager inscriptions have been found — on potsherds. They merely indicate the owner of the jar or its capacity. Nothing more, in a city with such a promising name. If the city's name had any real meaning, we would presume that it had a well-organized profession of scribes and up-to-date writing equipment — stores of papyrus and parchment. One would not expect them to resort to outdated techniques such as writing on potsherds and tablets. Perhaps it really was a scribe town and up-to-date techniques were used; this may be the very reason why no traces of their work have survived. Papyrus and parchment cannot resist time and dampness; stone tablets and potsherds can. So we have learned much about antiquity from the countless tablets of the ancient empires, while the work of the scribes has been lost forever.

The city's name may be the only living witness to the work of the scribes; or else it may have been prompted by some other factors entirely unconnected with the writing profession.

Albright was able to tell us some other interesting facts about Tell Beit Mirsim. From the date of its definitive destruction (approximately 588 B.C.) until the start of excavation work in 1924, life ceased on Tell Beit Mirsim. Under the surface of the hill lay the ruins of successive ancient cities — a Hebrew city, a Philistine city, a Canaanite city, several Egyptian cities, a Hyksos city, and a city built by its earliest inhabitants.

Tell Beit Mirsim stands as a model excavation performed on a judicious scale, unlike Megiddo which was an economic and scientific *tour de force.* But discretion often produces more fruit than does audacity. And William F. Albright is generally recognized as the top Palestinian archaeologist of our day.

54. THE TUNNEL OF HEZEKIAH

But Juda remained, a tiny people, with its rulers from the house of David. Some of these did what was right, but others were extremely sinful.

Ezekias fortified his city and had water brought into it; with iron tools he cut through the rock and he built reservoirs for water. During his reign Sennacherib led an invasion, and sent his adjutant; he shook his fist at Sion and blasphemed God in his pride. The people's hearts melted within them, and they were in anguish like that of childbirth. But they called upon the Most High God and lifted up their hands to him; he heard the prayer they uttered, and saved them through Isaias. God struck the camp of the Assyrians, and routed them with a plague. For Ezekias did what was right and held fast to the paths of David, as ordered by the illustrious prophet Isaias, who saw the truth in visions. In his lifetime he turned back the sun and prolonged the life of the king."

(Sirach 48)

The Tunnel of Hezekiah

THIS afternoon we took one of the most interesting tours of the whole journey. It was an offbeat adventure underground, a trip through the 1700-foot tunnel of Hezekiah.

It is a hot summer afternoon. We walk along, hemmed in by the brook of Kidron. On our right is the Mount of Olives; on our left, the hill called Ophel, and behind it, the city of Jerusalem. When we reach the northern extremity of Ophel, our guide directs us toward a fountain (dedicated to the Blessed Virgin) where the tunnel begins.

At the top of the stairs leading down to the tunnel we prepare for the descent. We tie our shoes together and sling them over our shoulders. Our socks go into our pockets, and our cassocks are tucked up at the waist. Our strange appearance amuses the young Arab girls at the fountain — no wonder! Picture twelve stately gentlemen walking along barefooted and bare-kneed, wearing shorts or bathing suits under their tucked-up cassocks and helmets on their heads. The girls stare at us unabashed, giggle, and chatter in Arabic. Two women stare at the strange sight but manage to contain themselves. A man loaded down with tin cans full of water asks them to make way and restores an air of dignity to the proceedings.

When all the water carriers have cleared the entrance, we start down. I take the lead because of my height and my powerful lantern. If I do not crack my skull on the ceiling, the others won't either. Farther down they begin to run into problems. If the water reaches midway up my thigh, it means that the others are in deeper than they expected to be. At first contact the water seems cold in contrast with the warm environment. We are standing knee-deep in cool water in a cool, damp tunel. But this initial sensation wears off as we start through the tunnel. We move slowly along the walls, passing pockets of light seeping in from the roof and peering into niches, crevices, and archways. Now and then a warning or comment is passed along from one to another: "Watch your head, low bridge!" — "Watch your feet, stony bottom!" — "On the right, an interesting niche!" — "Look out, left curve!" — "Straight ahead, a grating with a hole in the middle."

The tunnel is really tricky. For about one hundred feet it follows a crooked line and has a ceiling about eight or ten feet high. The walls are smooth and polished. Then the tunnel straightens out, only to cut sharply to the left soon after. Watch your head! The ceiling is only five feet high and my helmet scrapes it now and then. Another left turn and the tunnel straightens out again. For the next two hundred feet we walk straight ahead, head bent to watch the water below and to avoid bumps. But suddenly we find a rough vault over our head. A natural concavity in the earth became a part of the tunnel roof. It is a perfect spot to stop and look around, raising the lanterns high above our heads. Then we move on, letting the lanterns light up the sandy floor ahead. The tunnel cuts right, then straightens out. And now we are at the point of no return. The tunnel twists and turns sharply every thirty or forty feet. Along the walls we find pickax markings showing the engineers' attempts to correct their calculations and link up smoothly with the workers who began at the opposite end. We move along the winding walls, noting how the bed of the stream was straightened out by the builders. Suddenly the roof of the tunnel rises about a foot. Obviously the workers at this end made the tunnel higher. We stop to look around once again, while the water, unconcerned, flows under our feet. For centuries it has followed its underground course, reflecting neither sky, nor tree, nor grazing herd on its surface.

Then we start through the second half of the tunnel. We note three side routes leading nowhere and then continue straight ahead. Again we come upon a vaulted roof, a man-made one about fifteen feet high. It once opened out on a well above, but was later plugged up. The tunnel room continues to get higher and higher, probably because the engineer made an error in his calculations. At one point he realized that the tunnel was too high up, considering the water level. So to correct his mistake he had the workers lower the floor of the tunnel. That is why the height of the tunnel is so great here as compared with its narrow width. You have to walk in single file.

Daylight gleams up ahead. Our trek is almost over. We stop for the last time to look at a marking on the wall. And once again we are disappointed that the archaeologists did not leave their finds in their original setting. At the end of the nineteenth century they found a stone here bearing an inscription which described the construction of the tunnel. The legible part read: "here the workers broke through to each other. When there was still . . . the pickax of one against that of another. When there was still three feet separating them, one worker shouted to his companion that he was off to the right. . . . And the day came when the pickaxes and workers broke through to each other. And the waters from the spring spurted toward the pool twelve hundred feet away. And the rock above the miners was one hundred feet thick."

We come out at the pool of Siloam. Our offbeat visit is over and we are back in the heat and dust of the open air. We can only marvel at the skill of the engineers and the awesome labor of the miners who built the tunnel. Working in a narrow area with nothing but iron pickaxes, they hollowed the tunnel out of sheer virgin rock. If the tunnel had run in a straight line it would have been only 1000 feet long. If it had been built in the form of a Z with a vertical entrance it would have been just over 1400 feet long. Actually it is over 1600 feet long.

When and why was this gigantic piece of construction undertaken? It is not an easy question to answer. The archaeologists are united in their admiration but divided in their interpretation. So we shall just cite a few verses from the Bible.

The Northern Kingdom and its capital, Samaria, had just fallen to the Assyrian invaders. Sennacherib turned his armies toward Egypt, intending to conquer Judah along the way. Hearing of the enemy's approach, the pious king of Judah, Hezekiah, made ready his defenses. "When Hezekiah saw that Sennacherib had come determined to attack Jerusalem, he decided in council with his princes and his leading men to stop the water of the fountains that were outside the city, and they helped him. Indeed a great crowd of people collected and stopped up all the fountains and the torrent that coursed through the midst of the land" (2 Chr 32:2–4). Thus the invader would not find himself with a plentiful supply of water. "It was Hezekiah who stopped the upper springs of Gihon and directed the waters straight down on the west side of the city of David" (2 Chr 32:30). Thus the city and its defenders would have plenty of water. The stopped-up fountains lay out in the open below the Mount of Olives, while the pool at the other end was inaccessible to the invaders.

These texts seem to provide the best explanation of the tunnel we have visited today. There are other factors involved, but we will not bother to discuss them. In Chapter 35 we explained the general problems connected with a city's water supply and its defense.

55. THE FORTRESS OF LACHISH

MORE than twenty-five centuries ago Lachish was an important military fortress. Today history is repeating itself and the environs of Lachish once again sport military trappings. The highway runs quite close to the Jordan frontier. At a key point along the road we contact a military post and ask permission to enter a side road.

While walking to visit some famous tombs we come across more signs of military activity. We find ourselves climbing over bullet shells and grenade pins. Once upon a time a real battle was fought here; later this area was turned into a boot camp.

There is a pleasant contrast here between the pockmarked earth and the signs of animal life. A couple of rabbits come scampering over the slope of that hill. At the sound of our motor a couple of wild doves take flight and a partridge breaks off his glide. But the best is yet to come. Our bus switches onto a dusty road. On our right lies a field of reeds, thin needles of greenery piercing the arid countryside. Amid the reeds a gazelle turns to stare at us out of curiosity. When she has had a good look, she trots off gracefully, scarcely grazing the reeds with her slender legs. As we start to climb the hill, a dove swoops up on our left. She has made her nest in a deep stone well. When we drop pebbles into it, we hear no splash, only the flapping of wings.

These cameos of animal life were unexpected, hence difficult to forget. Someone suggested that we do a little hunting, but the idea struck me as being almost blasphemous in these peaceful surroundings. But climbing over the bullet shells on the hillside I got a more sobering thought. These were not the silent witnesses to an animal hunt but rather to a manhunt. This area was a battleground six short years ago, even as it was twenty-five centuries ago.

THE HILL

The hill had the characteristic shape of any *tell*. After examining it closely I began to reconstruct the ancient setup. It was an easy task because the excavators have published a fine reconstruction based on their archaeological findings.

At the top of the hill stood the palace fortress surrounded by the houses of the villagers. This section was surrounded by an inner rampart wall. Farther down the hill stood a stout defense wall. Between the two ramparts ran one broad access road defended by towers and other fortification works. An invader would have to come up along a winding road to attack the fortress; thus he would be exposed to the firepower of the outer wall at every point. At one point the road is boxed in between this outer wall and a defense turret outside. It then turns at a right angle, cuts through the gate, and runs up between a double row of ramparts guarding the access to the inner wall. Once the invader got this far, he still would have to contend with the stout gates and turrets of this inner wall. An enemy probably would not choose such a perilous route to attack the city. Sennacherib conquered the city about 700 B.C. and set up his headquarters in it. Around 500 B.C. it was conquered and leveled by Nebuchadnezzer's commander, Nebuzaradan.

THE GREAT FIND

The excavations were directed by the young archaeologist J. L. Starkey. They took place in the winter, and in the summer the finds were put on display in London. They served to provide data for the scholars and to arouse public interest in this strange science of excavation. Craftsmen examined the pottery objects; artists delighted in the clean lines of the marble figurines (of animals) ; and women admired the multicolored necklaces.

Other finds could not be transported from the excavation site (walls, column pedestals, flooring, etc.) but they were of great interest to archaeologists. But what were they, compared with the great find of one particular day?

It is January 29, 1935. Near the entrance of the outer wall are the charred remains of plant life. Lying on the cement flagstones amid the ashes are broken pieces of pottery blackened by the fire. While he is examining these fragments, the director discovers traces of writing on them. A thrill of excitement, which we uninitiate can hardly appreciate, runs through him; and he quickly orders the workers to collect every pottery fragment and bring it to his headquarters. The technical experts spend the afternoon washing the fragments in finely filtered water, so as not to streak them. They scrape them gingerly with their fingers to remove any mud or dust which might be lodged in the crevices. When this work is finished, it is easy to see that some of the fragments have writing on them. No one knows as yet what the writing is. It may only be some kind of inventory marking such as the ones found in the royal archives at Samaria. But this uncertainty allows room for daydreaming and fantasy. With typical British restraint Starkey refers to "that memorable afternoon." And he leaves the outbursts of enthusiasm to an excited Dane.

THEY'RE LETTERS!

As yet the exact nature of the inscriptions was not known. Despite his calm outward behavior Starkey is impatient to show his find to a specialist. Before leaving the site he orders the workers to sift every inch of sand removed so far. After sifting about three truckloads of sand, the workers come up with two more inscribed fragments.

Starkey heads for Jerusalem with his precious fragments, suspecting that they probably are not very important. Once in Jerusalem he goes to see a Dominican priest who is recognized as an authority in Semitic philology and Palestinian archaeology. It is the noted Father Vincent, a professor at the famous Biblical Institute of St. Stephen.

After a cursory examination of the potsherds Father Vincent is able to decipher a few opening lines; they are greetings. The inscriptions are letters of some sort.

That night Starkey goes to bed with a feeling of great satisfaction. It is hard to say whether Father Vincent retired, or spent the night trying to decipher the rest of the treasure. At any rate the next morning he is able to give Starkey a complete list of the names found in one fragment, the name of the addressee in another, and the title "commander in chief" in a third.

The Destruction of the Two Kingdoms

The "letters" now became the center of attention. During the first week of February three specialists examined them at the excavation site. The following week, Harry Torczyner, a Jewish professor at the University of Jerusalem, agreed to take charge of them. Several more months of hard work led to quite satisfactory results.

Meanwhile Starkey would not rest until he had utilized every scientific tool at his disposal. Some of the letters were burnt beyond recognition. So he had them photographed with the most refined equipment, and examined under infrared and ultraviolet rays. Others examined the ink and vainly tried to magnify the illegible scratchings.

STRANGE MESSAGES

These letters were soon regarded as one of the most important archaeological finds in the field of biblical study. (This was twelve years before the discovery of the Dead Sea Scrolls.) Now what about the contents of these letters? Here are a few items. The letters are written by a man named Hosaiah to "my lord Joash." He begins the letters with the usual courteous formulas: "God grant you good news"; "Who am I, your slave, a dog, that you should send me a letter?" He makes protestations about his honesty as a public functionary: "I swear that I did not say a word." And he passes on enigmatic pieces of news. "They told me that the commander-in-chief has fled to Egypt and ordered the capture of Hodaiah and his people. I send you Tobia's letter which I got from the prophet, and which advises vigilance." "Semaiah has captured Semakaiah and carried him off to Jerusalem; write to find out where he is to be found." "We are following your signals now, because we no longer see any from Azekah." "The letter from the king and his officials says that the prophet's words are inopportune because they are undermining the people's morale."

What is so sensational about these random comments? What can we piece together from them? People coming and going, an army commander in Egypt who intends to carry others there, a prophet undermining morale, a city which no longer sends signals, a royal letter cautioning vigilance, top-secret letters coming from Jerusalem

[324]

which must be passed on without being read. Is this all there is to the great treasure of Lachish?

You must realize that the contents of these letters, like the pottery pieces themselves, are scattered fragments of an historical situation. With the help of the biblical data, we can fit these letters into their proper historical setting.

INTERPRETING THE PASSAGE (2 KINGS 24–25)

It is the beginning of the sixth century B.C., more than a century after the destruction of the Northern Kingdom by Assyria. The same fate is about to befall Judah at the hands of the Babylonian empire. Jerusalem has already undergone two sieges. In 605 B.C. Nebuchadnezzar, still only a prince, conquered the city and made it a vassal state. The Israelite king had to take an oath of fealty and pay tribute. In the eyes of Nebuchadnezzar, Judah was a key stronghold in Babylon's struggle against Egypt. So instead of deporting the king of Judah, he made him his vassal; it would put him in a more advantageous position should Egypt try to rebuild her crumbling empire.

That same year Nebuchadnezzar's father, King Nabopolassar, died. His son rushed back to the capital to head off any *coup d'etat* which might be in the works. When the king of Judah died, Nebuchadnezzar laid siege to Jerusalem once again and carried off the new king and his family. He also deported anyone with political influence or technical skill: army officers, craftsmen, blacksmiths, etc. And he put a young king, twenty-one years old, on the throne, thinking that he would be quite manageable. But the new king, Zedekiah, could also be molded by the new court officials in Judah; and gradually two factions arose in the country. One faction was pro-Egypt, and proposed to rebel against Babylon with the help of Egypt; the other faction was pro-Babylon, favoring the status quo and a revitalization of the country's religious life. The leader of this faction was the outspoken prophet Jeremiah. But the other faction gradually won over the young king, and Jeremiah was imprisoned and condemned to death. Zedekiah secretly pardoned him and Jeremiah went on preaching submission to the Babylonian empire.

The Destruction of the Two Kingdoms

The spirit of rebellion continued to spread and led to the inevitable disaster. Nebuzaradan entered Judah at the head of a great army. The different cities fell one after another, and soon only three fortresses were left: Azekah, Lachish, and Jerusalem.

The Lachish letters fit right into this turbulent period. Judah is making a last-ditch stand against the invader. A petty official in some intermediate fortress is transmitting the messages between Jerusalem and Lachish. At one point there is no papyrus left. So he grabs a pottery jar, breaks it, and inks a nervous message about the need for vigilance, some trips to Egypt (their ally in the rebellion), inquiries in Jerusalem, and the demoralizing effects of a prophet's words. This official receives messages from bonfires on other fortresses; but as the enemy troops advance, communication becomes more difficult. One of the neighboring fortresses, Azekah, falls and sends no more messages. The petty official can only look to Lachish now. But eventually the enemy is able to sack and burn Lachish too. Buried in the earth these broken shards with their brief, anxious messages are the only witnesses to the tragedy. There they waited for their appointment with history. In 1935 the time had come, and Starkey was the lucky one to discover them.

A TRAGIC ENDING

Was there a sinister curse linked to this find? Three years later Starkey was still directing the excavations at Lachish, basking in the glow of his famous discovery and his own personal charm. But political uprisings do not take such things into account. Starkey himself was on good terms with the Arabs and the Jews. However, in some way he represented the British Empire and its mandate in Palestine. On the afternoon of January 10, 1938, he set out for Hebron, the sacred city of Abraham which was now a bastion of Moslem nationalism. A band of Arabs attacked and killed him, mutilating his corpse.

The great excavator of Lachish, scarcely forty-two years old, met a tragic death after giving the world one of the most important archaeological finds connected with the Bible.

Today the famous letters can be seen in the museum at Jerusalem.

The Fortress of Lachish

The kingdom of Judah came to an end with the conquest and destruction of Jerusalem.

Standing on the terrace of the Biblical Institute on an August night I watched the bloodstained moon rise slowly over the Mount of Olives. It cast its glow on a nearby house and slowly climbed up over the tower of the Russian monastery. Then it cast its gaze on the city below and poured its sinister light over the countryside. Finally it came to rest in the night sky, now a glowing ball of pure, serene light.

That is how I picture the enemy invader. Streaking out of the East he made his way through the Mount of Olives and peered down on his hapless prey. Then he charged forward, drenching the city in fire and blood. When victory was secure, he climbed the mount once more to gloat over his conquest.

For all practical purposes it is impossible to excavate for the ruins of the ancient city. The archaeologists have just about managed to pinpoint some rows of wall and some subterranean constructions.

In Samaria we saw the ruins which testify to the great disaster. In Jerusalem this is impossible. So the fortress of Lachish, leveled by the invader just before Jerusalem was, will serve to close this story and conclude our travelogue.

> . . . Zedekiah was twenty-one years old when he became king, and he reigned eleven years in Jerusalem. He did that which was evil in the sight of the Lord his God, and did not humble himself before Jeremiah the prophet at the word of the Lord. He also rebelled against King Nebuchadnezzer, who had made him swear by God. But he became obstinate and stubbornly refused to turn to the Lord, the God of Israel. Also all the chiefs of the priests and the people proved utterly faithless, in accordance with all the abominations of the nations, and they polluted the house of the Lord which he had sanctified in Jerusalem. Still the Lord, the God of their fathers, eagerly sent

[327]

to them by his messengers, because he had compassion on his people and on his dwellingplace, but they mocked God's messengers and despised his words and derided his prophets, until the wrath of the Lord rose against his people till there was no remedy. So he brought up against them the king of the Chaldeans who slew their young men with the sword in the house of their sanctuary, and spared neither youths nor maidens, neither the aged nor the decrepit. He delivered them all into his hand. Also all the utensils of the house of God both large and small, together with the treasures of the house of the Lord and the treasures of the king and his princes — all these he brought to Babylon. Moreover they burned the house of God, and broke down the wall of Jerusalem, and all its palaces they burned with fire, and all its choice vessels were given to destruction. Those who escaped the sword he carried captive to Babylon, where they became slaves to him and to his sons until the dominance of the kingdom of Persia. . . .

(2 Chronicles 36)

SOURCES CONSULTED

APART from the books cited in A Select Bibliography, I have utilized the following materials:

1. Specialized periodicals which report or discuss recent finds:
   Biblica
   Revue Biblique: its section on archaeology is an excellent source of information
   Zeitschrift des deutschen Palästina-Vereins (ZDPV)
   American School of Orient Research (ASOR) and its bulletin (BASOR)
   American Journal of Archeology (AJA) discusses general archaeology
   Journal of Near Eastern Studies (JNES)
   Journal of the Palestine Oriental Society (JPOS)
   Palestine Exploration Quarterly (PEQ)
   Biblical Archeologist
   Journal of the American Oriental Society (JAOS)
   Revue d'Assyriologie et Archéologie Orientale (RA)
   Zeitschrift für die alttestamentliche Wissenschaft (ZAW)
   And some other less specialized ones

2. The official publications from each excavation. They are usually very technical and contain many pencil sketches, drawings, and photographs. All the finds are carefully cataloged according to type of material, level at which found, exact zone within the level. An introduction outlines the excavation process. Then each theme is treated in detail. Finally the general conclusions are presented. There may be several appendices devoted to specialized details.

3. General studies. In particular the pertinent articles in the *Dictionnaire de la Bible (Supplément)* begun under the direction of Vigouroux and continued under the direction of Pirot-Robert.

4. The main guidebooks: Baedecker, Nagel, Guide Bleu, Meistermann.

5. Finally, to find a pertinent article or book on some topic, I have consulted the survey notes of our professor and guide:
   R. NORTH: *Historia excavationis biblicae* (Rome, 1951)
        Descriptio terrae biblicae (Rome, 1952)
        Stratigraphiae Palestinae (Rome, 1954)
        Geographia exegetica (Rome, 1955)

A SELECT BIBLIOGRAPHY

AFTER finishing this book the reader may become interested in the topic and wish to do further reading. So I have included a list of books which are highly readable and also accurate in their information.

Albright, W. F., *Archeology of Palestine* (Penguin, 1949; Pelican, 1951). The author is considered to be one of the foremost authorities in this field. In less than 300 pages he has managed to outline the most important techniques of excavation work and the results obtained in Palestine. The book has been widely read in the English-speaking world. The *Penguin* pocket edition has many illustrations, and its low price is a further recommendation.

—— *Archeology of Palestine and the Bible* (New York, 1935). Some of the material is contained in the previous work. But it is mainly devoted to one particular excavation, the one at Tell Beit-Mirsim, and is told in a popular style. It is good to meet a scientific expert who is also a humanist, interested in the human aspects of the subject and willing to include anecdotes and interesting sidelights.

Baikie, J., *Amarna Age* (London, 1926). Packed with information and pleasantly written.

—— *Glamour of Near East Excavation* (London, 1927).

Barrois, A., *Manuel d'Archéologie Biblique* (Paris, 1939, 1953). These two volumes present a well-organized synthesis edited by a fine specialist in the field. Barrois has had firsthand experience in excavation work although he has not distinguished himself in this particular area. The book's chief merit lies in the fact that it is an admirable systematic summary of the work done in this field. The presentation is clear and balanced in the best French tradition. It does not purport to be easy reading, and is not meant to be read straight through. By reading chapters at random one can learn a great deal about various aspects of life in ancient times. The many sketches and pictures clarify the text and help to enlighten the reader.

Fernandez, A., *Geografía Bíblica* (Barcelona, 1951). The author has

[330]

lived in Palestine for more than twenty years and has covered almost every square foot of land on his own. This book is meant to be a reference work to aid scholars. It can help the reader to collate his information. (His more extensive work, *Problemas de Topografía Palestinense* [Barcelona, 1936], is very technical.)

Finegan, J., *Light From the Ancient Past* (Princeton, 1946). This book surveys the entire ancient Middle East and its various cultures. It is a fine, well-written synthesis, particularly useful to the reader who wishes to see the bible story in the framework of ancient cultures.

Garstang, J., *Story of Jericho*, 2ª (London, 1948). The author directed several excavation campaigns at Jericho. It is a lively, enthusiastic account and makes fine reading. However, he is sometimes too zealous in defending his own theories which are falling into disfavor more and more.

Glueck, Nelson, *The River Jordan* (London, 1946) and *Rivers in the Desert. A History of Negev, Being an Illustrated Account of Discoveries in a Frontierland of Civilization* (New York, 1959).

Grollenberg, Luc. H., *Atlas of the Bible* (New York: Nelson, 1956), 165 pages, 408 photographs, 35 maps in color. This is a splendid book, not only because of the exceptional quality of the photographs, but also because of the way they are mounted. In one or two pages various aspects of a biblical situation are summarized. The reader gets a general picture of the time and its setting, and can readily understand the accompanying commentary. This atlas is, for all practical purposes, a succinct and interesting history of the Bible.

Harding, G. Lancaster, *The Antiquities of Jordan* (London, 1959).

Jack, J. W., *Samaria in Ahab's Time* (Edinburgh, 1929). Scientifically, the book is untrustworthy. But it contains a series of reconstructions which tickle the reader's curiosity. Unfortunately, the reconstructions lack any solid foundation.

Kenyon, Kathleen M., *Digging Up Jericho* (London, 1951) and *Archaeology in the Holy Land* (London, 1950).

Kyle, Melvin G., *Explorations at Jordan* (London, 1926).

Laming, A., *La découverte du passé. Progres récents et techniques nouvelles en préhistoire* (Paris, 1952). The book is of a technical nature. It presents a clear treatment of some interesting questions being discussed today.

Lemaire, Paulin, and Donato, Baldi, *Atlante storico della Bibbia* (Marietti, Rome), 330 pages, 400 photographs, 56 maps in the text and 12 maps in color. The work is technical, scholarly, and precise. It is packed with up-to-date information and discusses geographical and historical problems. It is rather deep for the layman or the beginner, but excellent for the scholar, for institutions and libraries.

Macalister, R. C., *A Century of Excavation in Palestine* (London, 1925). The book is, of course, somewhat out of date. But no one has given a better description of the earlier excavations and findings. Macalister was one of the major figures in Palestinian archaeology. And he also was one of those fine British scholars with a solid background in the Humanities, who knew how to write with scholarly restraint and with a touch of good humor.

—— *The Philistines. Their History and Civilization* (London, 1911). In the same delightful style the author gives us a favorable view of this Indo-European tribe which gave Palestine its name.

MacCown, C., *Ladder of Progress in Palestine* (New York, 1943). The author himself has not played a distinguished role in excavatory work. But for many years he was the director of the American School of Oriental Research in Palestine. His book is a delightful synthesis arranged chronologically. Instead of commenting briefly on many topics, he chooses a significant point from each epoch and discusses it in detail. The reader is not detained by fine points, but he does get a rather vivid and accurate overall picture. The illustrations are good.

Parrot, A., *Découverte des mondes ensevelis* (Neuchatel-Paris, 1952). The methods and findings of archaeology told in a popular style.

Poidebard-Lauffray, *Sidon, aménagements antiques du port* (Beirut, 1951). The book is very technical. It will be of interest to an engineer who would like to know the ancient techniques for constructing ports. The aerial photographs are excellent.

Pritchard, James B., *Gideon, Where the Sun Stood Still, Discovery of the Biblical City* (Princeton, 1962) and *Archaeology and the Old Testament* (Princeton, 1958).

Scharff and Moortgat, *Aegypten und Vorderasien im Altertum* (Munich, 1950). The second part, written by Moortgat, a specialist in Accadian culture, presents a clear synthesis of the historical data. This section will be of particular interest to the non-specialist, and no one could have done it as well as Moortgat.

Smith, George Adam, *Historical Geography of the Land* (London: 1894, 1935[26]) . I have alluded to this book several times. Although the last edition is more than twenty-five years old, a great deal of the data are still valid. But the great merit of this book is the author's unique flair in presenting geographical data. For him geography is not a dry descriptive science but a humanistic subject. Man experiences geography through his encounter with the natural landscape of a given place and its history. The book is a pure delight. And I must confess that it has been my greatest help during the journey itself and during the preparation of this book.

Tellier, R. P., *Atlas historique de l'Ancien Testament.* A set of stylized maps which explains the whole history of Israel. It also contains all the pertinent biblical references. It is not something to be read through, but rather a fine tool for the scholar.

Vincent-Abel (besides their many collaborative efforts in *Revue Biblique*), *Jérusalem, recherches d'archéologie, de topographie et d'histoire* (Paris, 1912). A book of great scholarly value. Father Vincent is a delightful writer when he is not discussing a strictly technical subject.

Vincent-Mackay, *Hebron* (Paris, 1923). In an interesting introduction they discuss previous investigations and the circumstances surrounding this one. Then comes a technical discussion and a detailed treatment of special problems. The most interesting parts are the introduction and the medieval narrative cited in Chapter 4 of this book.

Woolley, L., *Ur of the Chaldees* (London: Penguin, 1952). Quite delightful, but some of his points are outlandish. In particular, his theory on the flood is no longer accepted. *Spadework in Archaeology* (New York, 1953).

Wright, G., and Filson, F., *Westminster Historical Atlas to the Bible* (Philadelphia, 1945). The maps are drawn in such a way that the ground configurations stand out. On any given map only a few sites are marked out, those which are pertinent to a given point. The synthesis of Israelite history and of the surrounding cultures is magnificent.

INDEX AND GLOSSARY OF NAMES

Aaron (in Hebrew *'Aharon,* meaning unknown), brother of Moses, 57
Abana, river of Damascus; probably the modern *Barada,* 271
Abdia, *see* Obadiah
Abias, *see* Abijah
Abiathar, high priest during time of David, 219
Abijah ("Yahweh is Father"), son of Jeroboam who died in infancy, 246
Abimelech ("father is king"), name of several persons: (1) a king of Gerar during time of Abraham, 24, 26; (2) a son of Gideon who became king at Shechem, 51 f
Abinoam, father of Barak, 172
Abinoem, *see* Abinoam
Abiram ("father is exalted"), an Israelite who revolted against Moses, 59
Abraham (popularly meaning "father of a multitude," cf. Gn 17:5), the ancient patriarch and father of the Chosen People, who at God's call left his homeland in Iraq and migrated to the land of promise, *passim,* but especially pp. 11–32
Abram, Abraham's name before the birth of Isaac
Absalom ("father is peace"), rebellious son of David, 216 f
Accad, city in northern Babylonia, 11
Accaron, *see* Ekron
Achab, *see* Ahab
Adama, *see* Admah
Admah, one of the five cities (*see* Pentapolis) forming a confederation along the Dead Sea during the time of Abraham, 6, 18
Adonias, *see* Adonijah
Adonijah ("Yahweh is lord"), David's son and pretender to the throne, assassinated by Solomon, 218
Afula, modern communications center in the valley of Esdraelon, 171, 173, 198

Agar, *see* Hagar
Ahab ("brother of father"), name of the seventh king of Israel, the northern kingdom, circa 874–853 B.C.; son of Omri and husband of Jezebel, 263 ff, 267 ff, 277 ff, 301
Ahaz ("Yahweh has taken possession"), name of the twelfth king of Judah, the southern kingdom, c. 736–716 B.C. When attacked by a coalition of Syrian and Israelite forces, he sought support from Tiglath-pileser III of Assyria, 280
Ahaziah ("Yahweh has seized"), name of two kings: (1) the eighth king of Israel, c. 853–852 B.C., who opposed the prophet Elijah, 269; (2) the sixth king of Judah, c. 841 B.C., who was killed by soldiers of Jehu of Israel, 280, 293 f
Ai ("the ruin"), a Canaanite city destroyed by Joshua, 151 ff
'Ain ("fountain"), found as "En–" in compound words; widely used in combinations as a place name, 25
'Ain Feshkah, a spring of bitter waters near the Dead Sea, 285, 287
Ain Sultan, a spring near the ruins of Jericho, whose waters were supposedly made drinkable by Elisha, 288 ff
Akhenaton ("he who is beneficial to Aton"), originally named Amenophis IV. The eighth Pharaoh of the New Kingdom in Egypt (c. 1377–1360 B.C.), who attempted to introduce monotheism into Egypt, 69 ff
Akhetaton, capital of Egypt under Akhenaton, built in honor of Aton, 69; *see also* El Amarna
Aknaton, *see* Akhenaton
Alexander the Great (337–323 B.C.), king of Macedon, 61 ff
Alexandria, important city on the

Nile delta and cultural center, 61 ff

Amalekite, a nomadic people often mentioned as enemies of Israel, 206

Amasias, *see* Amaziah

Amaziah ("Yahweh is strong"), the ninth king of Judah, 162

Amenhotep, *see* Amenophis

Amenophis III, Pharaoh of Egypt, c. 1382–1377 B.C., father of Akhenaton, 69

Amenophis IV, *see* Akhenaton

'Amman, present-day capital of Jordan (in biblical times, the region of the Ammonites), 91

Amon, the god of Thebes in Egypt, 69

Amos ("[God] has taken charge"), a prophet in the northern kingdom of Israel at the time of Jeroboam II (783–743 B.C.), who lashed out against the greed and infidelities of the people, 298

Amraphel, one of the four kings mentioned in Gn 14 who were aligned against the five kings of the Pentapolis, *see* Pentapolis

Anath, a personage mentioned in the Song of Deborah, 171

Anath-Reseph, a twin deity worshiped at Beth-shan, 171

Antigonus, the last of the Hasmonean rulers (named after the father of one of the Maccabees) who reigned from 40–37 B.C. over Palestine, 261

Anti-Lebanon, a nonbiblical name for a mountain range parallel to the Lebanon, with Mt. Hermon at its south end, 181

Antiochus, name of ten Syrian kings. The most noted was Antiochus IV Epiphanes (175–164 B.C.), whose persecution of the Jews led to the revolt under the Maccabees, 79

'Aqaba, Gulf of, the eastern arm of the Red Sea, 104, 223

Arad, a Canaanite royal city, 258

Aran, *see* Haran

Arioch, name of one of the four allied kings in Gn 14:6, *see* Pentapolis

Armaggeddon ("the mountain of Megiddo"), this city where Josiah was defeated and killed, is the symbol of disaster, 240; *see also* Megiddo

Arnon River, a torrent on the east

bank of the Dead Sea, 130

Aroer ("junipers"), name of several cities. One, north of the Arnon River, was situated in highlands assigned as one of the boundaries of the Israelites, 130

Asa, the third king of Judah (911–820 B.C.), 162, 280

Asarhadon, *see* Esarhaddon

Ascalon, *see* Ashkelon

Aser, *see* Asher

Ashdod, one of the five Philistine cities in the Pentapolis, 192; *see also* Pentapolis (2)

Ashkelon, one of the five Philistine cities in the Pentapolis, 126, 192; *see also* Pentapolis (2)

Asher, one of the twelve sons of Jacob, and the name of one of the twelve tribes of Israel, 46, 168

Ashur, city on the Tigris, the oldest and northernmost part of the Assyrian empire, 258

Ashurbanipal, *see* Assurbanipal

Assur, *see* Ashur

Assurbanipal, grandson of Sennacherib, ruler of the Assyrian Empire (669–626 B.C.), with his capital at Nineveh, 7

Assyria, 7 ff, 214

Aswan, a city on the Nile, site of a dam, 120

Aton, sun-god of Egypt worshiped by Akhenaton, 69

Augustus, Roman emperor (31 B.C.– A.D. 14), 297

Avaris, later Greek *Tanis,* capital of the Hyksos in Egypt; identical with Zoan; probably identical with modern San El-Hagar, 79 ff

Aven, a city in Lower Egypt also called On; identical with Heliopolis, 163

Avva, a place mentioned in 2 Kgs 17, 306

Azaria, *see* Azariah

Azariah ("Yahweh helps"), a common Hebrew name; most important person by this name was the tenth king of Judah (781–740 B.C.), 162

Azarias, *see* Azariah

Azekah, a city of Judah fortified by Rehoboam and besieged by Nebuchadnezzar and mentioned in the Lachish Letters, 326

Index and Glossary of Names

Byblos, Greek name of the city of Gebal, site of Hiram's sarcophagus, 250 ff

Cairo, important Egyptian city on the Nile, whose splendid museum houses many significant archaeological finds, 69, 78 f

Canaan ("land of purple?"), north of the coastal territory of Palestine and Phoenicia. In the Bible the word is sometimes used for the Promised Land, sometimes for Phoenicia proper, sometimes for the Philistine coast. The land is named after a "son" of Ham. It is the territory conquered by the Israelites under Joshua and the Judges and ruled over by the kings, *passim*

Cariath-arbe, *see* Kiriath-arba

Carmel, Mount, a mountain on the boundary of the territory allotted to the tribe of Asher and associated with the work of Elijah and Elisha, 157, 266

Cedron, *see* Kidron

Chaldeans, Aramaean tribe who settled in southern Babylonia, and founded an empire toward the beginning of the second millennium B.C.

Chanaan, *see* Canaan

Chedor-lahomer ("servant of [the goddess] Lagamer"), name of a king of Elam pursued by Abraham, 6

Chelmad (Chilmad), a region cited as trading with Tyre, 258

Chene (Canneh), a city mentioned as an important trading center, 258

Chetthim, biblical name for part or all of the island of Cyprus, 258

Chodorlahomor, *see* Chedor-lahomor

Cison, *see* Kishon

Cuthah, city in Mesopotamia whose inhabitants were sent to repopulate Samaria, 306

Cyrus the Great (c. 559–525 B.C.), founder of the Persian empire, who allowed Israelites to return to their land from their captivity in Babylon, 307

Dagon, Mesopotamian weather god, also worshiped by the Philistines, 194

Damascus, ancient city at foot of Mount Hermon and the Anti-Lebanon, an important trading center and frequently mentioned in the Books of Kings and prophets; also city in which St. Paul was baptized, 181 ff, 276 ff

Dan: (1) name of the son of Jacob and Bilhah, and hence name of one of the tribes of Israel, 46; (2) city formerly called Laish (q.v.), and the most northerly city in Israel (cf. "From Dan to Beer-sheba"), 179 ff

Darius, name of three Persian kings, of whom the first is the most important for it was under him that the temple in Jerusalem was reconstructed, 307

Dathan, a son of Eliab, who rebelled against Moses with his brother Abiram and was punished, 59

David, second king of Israel (c. 1010–970 B.C.) and real organizer of the united kingdom, 43, 165, 220 ff

Dead Sea, also called Salt Sea, Sea of Arabah, Asphalt Lake, Sea of the Plain, Eastern Sea. A body of water well below sea level, approximately 53 miles long, 10 miles wide at its widest point, *passim*

Debbora, *see* Deborah

Debir, a Canaanite royal city, formerly called Kiriath-sepher, 310

Deborah, a prophetess during the period of the judges who urged Barak to fight against Jabin, 169 ff

Dedan, district of Edom, mentioned as a trading center, 258

Deuteronomy, the "second law" and fifth book of the Pentateuch, 215

Dibon, place in Transjordan mentioned on the Moabite Stone, 134

Dina, *see* Dinah

Dinah, name of daughter of Jacob ravished by Shechem, 46 ff

Dothan, city north of Samaria, where Joseph was sold, 53 ff

Ebal, Mount, a mountain north of Shechem facing Mt. Gerizim, 155 ff

Edom, Edomites, name of a people who settled south of the Dead Sea; from the time of David frequently at war with Israel

name of one of the twelve tribes, 46

Galaad, *see* Gilead

Gath ("wine press"), one of the five Philistine cities (*see* Pentapolis [2]), where the Ark was sent, 194

Gaza, most southerly of the five Philistine cities (*see* Pentapolis [2]), mentioned frequently in Scripture, 126

Gebel Musa, a mountain in the Sinai peninsula, 99

Gehazi, Elisha's servant, figuring in the episode with Naaman, 281

Genneseret, Lake, another name for the Sea of Galilee, *passim*

Gennesereth, *see* Genneseret

Gerizim, Mount, near Shechem, south of Mt. Ebal, *passim*

Gesen, *see* Goshen

Gezer, Canaanite royal city west of Jerusalem, 211

Ghassul, *see* Teleilat Ghassul

Gideon, one of the great judges famous for his struggles against the Madianites, 122, 173 ff

Giezi, *see* Gehazi

Gihon, spring east of Jerusalem where Solomon was anointed king; it figures in Hezekiah's well, 218 ff

Gilboa, mountain chain in the territory of Issacher where Saul and Jonathan died, 173

Gilead, originally the name of a region of the Jabbok in Transjordan, then for all of Transjordan from the Arnon to the Yarmuk, 157

Gilgameš, hero of the Babylonian epic on the flood, 12

Giza, modern El Gizeh, city in Egypt near the pyramids, 61 ff

Goliath, the Philistine giant conquered by Samson, 185

Gomorra, *see* Gomorrah

Gomorrah, city of the Pentapolis of the Dead Sea (q.v.) destroyed with Sodom, 17 ff

Gosen, *see* Goshen

Goshen, region in Egypt where the Israelites settled, 81

Gozan, region devastated by the Assyrians, on the banks of the Habor, a site to which people of the northern kingdom of Israel were deported, 295

Gur, 294

Habacuc, *see* Habakkuk

Habakkuk, a prophet who lived toward the end of the seventh century, 84

Hagar, Sarah's maidservant and mother of Ishmael, 24 ff

Haggith, a concubine of David and mother of Adonijah, 218

Haifa, modern port on the Mediterranean at the foot of Mt. Carmel, 224

Halah, region of Assyria to which Israelites were deported, 295

Ham, youngest son of Noah, cursed for his misconduct, 57

Hamath, city in Syria on the Orontes River, mentioned as a terminus of the dwelling place of the Hittites, 168, 306

Hammurabi, sixth king of the first dynasty of Babylon (c. 1700 B.C.?), famous for his law code, 28

Hamor, name of a Hurrian king at Shechem during the time of Abraham, 47 ff

Haran: (1) name of several people, among them a brother of Abraham, 10 ff; (2) trading center in northern Mesopotamia, modern Harran, 120, 258

Harosheth, home of Sisera and scene of his defeat by Barak, 168

Harran, *see* Haran (2)

Hatsepsut, queen of Egypt, c. 1502–1480; daughter of Thothmes I, 102, 133

Hatshepsut, *see* Hatsepsut

Hattusa, *see* Hattushash

Hattushash, capital of the Hittite Empire; the ruins are near the modern city of Ankara, 236

Hazael ("God has seen"), the assassin and successor of Ben-Hadad II of Damascus, 279

Hebal, Mount, *see* Ebal, Mount

Hebron, also called Kiriath-arba, a Canaanite city visited by Abraham who bought a grave there; David's first capital; an important city of the Israelites, 19, 31 ff, 40, 53

Helbon, city which traded wine to Tyre, 258

Heli, *see* Eli

Heliodorus, chief minister of Seleucus IV, 240

Index and Glossary of Names

who composed a treatise on the care of horses, 236

Kiriath-arba, ancient name for Hebron, mentioned in particular in narratives dealing with the patriarchs, 31, 40, 46

Kiriath-sepher (Debir), 310; *see also* Tell Beit Mirsim

Kishon, name of a torrent in the plain of Esdraelon, 170, 269

Kuë, *see* Qewe

Laban, the wily father of Rachel and Leah, 42 ff

Lachish, city of Judah, an important military post, and famous for the letters discovered in 1935, 321 ff

Laish, city in the northern tip of Israelite territory, captured by the tribe of Dan and renamed Dan, 180

Latrun, 214

Leah ("cow"), elder daughter of Laban and first wife of Jacob, 34 ff

Lebanon, range of mountains north of Palestine and running parallel to the coast, famous for its cedars, 76, 253 ff

Leddan, a stream near modern Tell-el-Qadi, the ancient city of Dan, 181

Levi, the third son of Jacob and Leah and hence the name of one of the twelve tribes of Israel, the tribe entrusted with priestly work, 46

Leviathan, a mythological monster symbolizing the chaos vanquished by Yahweh in the creation, 76

Lia, *see* Leah

Lot, Abraham's nephew, 6 ff

Lud, name of a people at times associated with the Egyptians, 258

Luxor, small town in Egypt, situated with Karnak on the site of the ancient and famous city of Thebes, 69, 78 ff

Luz ("almond"), ancient name for Bethel, 44

Maccabees, a famous Jewish family who led the revolt against the Seleucid kings of Syria c. 168 B.C., 238

Machabees, *see* Maccabees

Machpelah, name of the field containing a cave which Abraham bought to bury Sarah; Abraham also buried there and after him Isaac, Rebekah, Leah, and Jacob. Hence a spot quite sacred for the Jews and to the Moslems who regard Abraham as their father, 32 ff

Machphela, *see* Machpelah

Madaba, a site in Transjordan famous for the map discovered there (called Medaba in the Bible), 124 ff

Madianites, a nomadic group that came in frequent contact, usually hostile, with the Hebrews, 56, 174, *passim*

Mageddo, *see* Megiddo

Mambre, *see* Mamre

Mamre, a site associated with Abraham ("he pitched his tent beneath the oaks or terebinths of Mamre"), close to Machpelah, 6, 33 ff

Manasseh ("making to forget"), eldest son of Joseph, progenitor of the tribe of Manasseh, 163

Manasses, *see* Manasseh

Manoah, Samson's father, 178

Medes, Media, a country northeast of Babylonia, the Medes later became part of the Persian empire, 295

Megiddo, a Canaanite royal city, the site of Solomon's famous stables, locus of important archaeological finds, 211, 238 ff

Memphis, ancient capital of Lower Egypt, 69

Menzaleh, Lake, nonbiblical name of a lake in northern Egypt, near the capital established by the Hyksos, 79

Meriba, *see* Meribah

Meribah, name of a spring near Kadesh, 117

Merom, waters of, site of a battle between Joshua and Jabin, 237

Mesha, a king of Moab, whose reign is described in part on the famous stele (the Moabite stone) found at Dibon, 139

Mesopotamia, the name given to the region "between the rivers," i.e., the Tigris and Euphrates, 68

Micah, a minor prophet and contemporary of Isaiah, 182

Micaiah, 300

Micheas, *see* Micah

Mitanni, a kingdom formed by a

Index and Glossary of Names

union of Horite principalities during the fifteenth century, B.C., 8, 77, 236

Moab, Moabites, a region east of the Dead Sea whose inhabitants were related to the Hebrews, a people consequently figuring prominently in the history of the Chosen People, 130 ff

Moses (according to a popular etymology given in Exodus 2:10 means "drawn out of water"), the great leader of the Hebrews who successfully led them in their exodus from Egypt and to whom the Commandments were given on Mount Sinai, 94 ff

Naaman, the Syrian general of Benhadad, who was healed of his leprosy by Elisha, 272 ff

Nablus, a city in the center of Palestine, near Shechem, 155

Nabonido, an ancient Babylonian ruler of Ur, 13

Nabopolasser, Nebuchadnezzar's father, 325

Naboth, owner of a vineyard which he refused to sell to Ahab, 264 ff

Nabuchodonnosor, *see* Nebuchadnezzar

Nabuzardan, *see* Nebuzaradan

Nachor, *see* Nahor

Nadab, second king of Israel (910–909 B.C.), son of Jeroboam, assassinated by Baasha, 246

Nahor, a brother of Abraham, 10

Nahr el-Kelb ("river of the dog"), a river in Lebanon near Byblos, 250

Naim, a village situated halfway up Mount Hermon, 198

Naphtali ("I have wrestled with my sister"), son of Jacob and Bilhah; hence the name of one of the twelve tribes, 168

Nathan ("He has given"), a prophet in the time of David who rebuked the king for his adultery and promoted Solomon as successor, 185, 219

Nazareth, small city in Galilee, 28, 53, 198, 201

Nebo, Mount, a mountain slightly east of the mouth of the Jordan; mount on which Moses died, 132

Nebuchadnezzar (Hebrew form of a Babylonian word meaning "Nabu

protect the son"), called Nebuchadrezzar in the Books of Jeremiah and Ezekiel, builder of the new Babylonian empire (605–562 B.C.), who leveled Jerusalem in 587 and deported the people to Babylon, 65, 164, 325

Nebuzaradan (Hebrew form of a Babylonian word meaning "Nabu has given offspring"), captain of Nebuchadnezzar's bodyguard, 164, 322

Necho, a pharaoh (609–594 B.C.) who defeated Josiah at Megiddo and was himself later conquered by Nebuchadnezzar, 240

Nefertiti, wife of Akhenaton, 72

Negeb ("dry land"), originally a name designating the area between Hebron and Kadesh in southern Judah, later extended to include the entire south, 17, 28

Nephthali, *see* Naphtali

Nile, one of the longest rivers in the world, rising in the region around Lake Tanganyika and running northward to the Mediterranean; the river whose annual innundations made possible the civilization of ancient Egypt, 49, 78 f, *passim*

Nineve, *see* Nineveh

Nineveh, city on the east bank of the Tigris; capital of Sennacherib, 7, 13

Noah, the hero of the story of the flood, 12

Obadiah ("servant of Yahweh"), name of several persons, among them a person who hid the prophets from Jezebel, 263

Olivet, Mount, a hill east of Jerusalem, separated from the city by the Brook Kidron, 131, 218

Omayades, Mohammedan rules of Damascus, 279

Omri, name of several persons including the sixth king of Israel (885–874 B.C.), founder of Samaria as capital of the northern kingdom, 247

On, a city in Lower Egypt closely associated with the sun cult; identical with Heliopolis, 163

Ophel ("swelling"), a fortified height near Jerusalem, David's official residence, 218

Index and Glossary of Names

Osee, *see* Hosea *and* Hoshea
Osiris, a popular Egyptian god, 69

Palestine, not a biblical name, but a term derived from the Greek and Latin word to designate the country of the Philistines and customarily applied to the Holy Land
Pasht, the cat goddess worshiped in particular at Bubastis, 79
Paul, name of the great Apostle, 281 ff
Pelusium, an ancient Egyptian city whose ruins are about 20 miles from Port Said, 83
Pentapolis (region of the "five cities"): (1) a name applied to the five cities of Sodom, Gomorrah, Admah, Zeboiim, and Bela (Zoar), 20, 22; (2) the name given to the five Philistine cities of Gaza, Ashdod, Ashkelon, Gath, and Ekron
Persia, originally applied to a small region east of the Persian gulf whose principal cities were Pasargadae and Persepolis; after the founding of the empire by Cyrus the Great the term was applied to the entire Iranian plateau.
Pharpar, one of the two rivers of Damascus, 272
Phasga (Pisgah), **Mount,** a height west of the plain of Moab with a good view of Palestine, 128
Philistines, a non-Semitic group who entered the region south of the coastal plain of Palestine about 1200 B.C. Principal foes of the Hebrews during the period of the Judges, 168 ff, 192 ff

Qadicha, a valley formed by a gorge near Byblos, 253 ff
Qewe, ancient ruins of Cilicia, 237

Rachel, daughter of Laban and wife of Jacob, 43 ff
Raguel, Moses' father-in-law, also called Jethro, 97
Rahab, the harlot of Jericho who helped Joshua, 147 f
Ramath-Gan, site of magnificent gardens, 215
Rameses II, pharaoh of Egypt c. 1290–1224 B.C., a great builder and ruler who waged many campaigns against the Hittites; the

Pharaoh, most probably, of the persecution of the Israelites, 77, 82 ff
Rameses III, Egyptian Pharaoh (c. 1145–1141 B.C.), who campaigned against the "Peoples of the Sea," 102
Rameses V (c. 115 B.C.), 102
Ramoth-gilead, a city in Transjordan and city of refuge, 288
Rasin, *see* Rezin
Ras Safsafa, a mountain in the Sinai peninsula, 109
Rebecca, *see* Rebekah
Rebekah, wife of Isaac and mother of Esau and Jacob, 34, 40 ff
Rechab, father of Jonadab, the companion of Jehu, 294
Red Sea, 58, 84 ff
Regna (Raamah), a trading center, 258
Rehoboam ("the people has spread"), a son of Solomon and first king of Judah (c. 931–913 B.C.), 162, 243
Reseph, the thundering storm god of the Canaanites, 207
Reuben, eldest son of Jacob and Leah, 46
Rezin, the last king of Damascus, conquered by Tiglath-pileser III, 280
Ribla, city on the Orontes, 163
Roboam, *see* Rehoboam
Rogel, a fountain near the confluence of the Kidron and Hinnon torrents, 218
Ruben, *see* Reuben
Rubin River, a river cutting through the valley of Soreq and coming close to Jerusalem, 255

Saba, *see* Sheba
Sahra ed-Dimas, a six-mile plateau near Damascus, 274
Samaria, the name of the capital built by Omri for the northern kingdom of Israel, later extended to include the whole region, 297 ff
Samasumukin, brother of Assurbanipal and appointed by the latter as ruler of Babylon, 7
Samgar, *see* Shamgar
Samson, the last of the Judges and popular hero, 176 ff
Samuel ("name of God"), judge and prophet during the time of Samson and Saul, 3, 43

Index and Glossary of Names

its ruins lie near the modern San El-Hagar, 79 f

Tarablus, a crusaders' city, 256

Tel Aviv, modern capital of Israel, 21, *passim*

Tel Basta, 79; *see also* Bubastis

Teleilat Ghassul, an important site for archaeology, particularly for the culture of the Pentapolis, 20 ff

Tell el-Yehudiye, 79

Tell Beit Mirsim, hillock possibly covering the biblical city of Debir, formerly the Canaanite city of Kiriath-sepher (scribe town), and site of important archaeological findings, 309 ff

Tell el-Far'ah, probably covers the ruins of Tirzah, 245

Tell el-Qadi ("hill of judgment"), probably covers the biblical city of Dan, the ancient Canaanite city of Laish, 181

Tell el-Sultan, a hillock covering the ancient city of Jericho(?), 148

Tell Qasila, a mound near the mouth of the Yarkon River, 255

Teshup, a Horite storm god, 207

Thaanach, *see* Taanach

Thabor, Mount, *see* Tabor, Mount

Thadal, *see* Tidal

Thare (Terah), Abraham's father, 10

Thebes, ancient capital of Upper Egypt, 69, 78

Thothmes III, Egyptian pharaoh (1490–1436), 69

Tidal, the king of Goiim, one of the four kings allied against the five kings of the Pentapolis, 6

Tiglath-pileser III, king of Assyria c. 745–726 B.C., called Pul in the Bible, 301 ff

Tigris, one of the two great rivers of Mesopotamia, 101

Timsah, Lake, 84

Tirzah, Canaanite royal city, later the capital of the kings of the northern kingdom of Israel from the time of Jeroboam to Omri; probably the modern Tell el-Far'ah, 246 ff

Tishbe, a village in Gilead, the home of Elisha, 267

Tobia, a name mentioned in the Lachish Letters, 324

Transjordan ("across the Jordan"), the land to the east of the Jordan, *passim*

Tutankhamon, an ephemeral successor of Akhenaton, 70

Tutankhamun, *see* Tutankhamon

Tuthmosis III, *see* Thothmes III

Tyre, commercial city of the Phoenicians, built on an island, 257 ff

Tyropoeon, valley separating the city of David and the temple from the upper city, 209

Ur, city from which Terah and Abraham set out for Canaan; site of extensive and important archaeological diggings, 10 ff

Uriah, husband of Bathsheba put into front lines by David, 218 f

Ur-Nammu, and the ziggurat at Ur, 13

Usdum, Mount, 21

Utnapistim, a Babylonian mythic hero, 12

Uzal, land mentioned as trading with Tyre, 258

Yahweh, Hebrew name for God, given in Ex 3:14, usually rendered "I am who am" but its exact meaning is uncertain

Yarkon River, 255

Yarmuk River, a tributary flowing into the Jordan from the east, 205

Zabulon, *see* Zebulun

Zacharia, *see* Zechariah

Zacharias, *see* Zechariah

Zadok, high priest who remained faithful to David and anointed Solomon, 219

Zarephath, city in Phoenicia where Elisha worked miracles, 258

Zeboiim, city of the Pentapolis, 6, 18

Zebulun, the sixth son of Jacob and Leah, name of one of the twelve tribes, 168

Zechariah, name of very many Old Testament figures; of the most importance are the following: (1) the son of Jehoiada, a prophet stoned to death by command of Joash; (2) the minor prophet, 240

Zedekiah, the name of several persons, among them the last king of Judah (598–586 B.C.), 299

Zion, originally the name of the Jebusite fortress captured by David, 164 ff

Zoan, city in Egypt; *see* Tanis; Avaris; San El-Hagar

Zoar, a city of the Pentapolis, 6, 18